Executions in America

EXECUTIONS IN AMERICA

Over Three Hundred Years of Crime and Capital Punishment in America

by Frederick Drimmer

Skyhorse Publishing

Skyhorse Publishing books may be purchased in bulk at special discounts for sales promotion, corporate gifts, fund-raising, or educational purposes. Special editions can also be created to specifications. For details, contact the Special Sales Department, Skyhorse Publishing, 307 West 36th Street, 11th Floor, New York, NY 10018 or info@skyhorsepublishing.com.

Skyhorse® and Skyhorse Publishing® are registered trademarks of Skyhorse Publishing, Inc.®, a Delaware corporation.

Visit our website at www.skyhorsepublishing.com.

10 9 8 7 6 5 4 3 2 1

Library of Congress Cataloging-in-Publication Data is available on file.

Cover design by Rain Saukas
Cover photo credit AP Images

ISBN: 978-1-62914-217-3

Printed in the United States of America

Dedicated
to the memory of
two great wardens
LEWIS E. LAWES
of Sing Sing
and
CLINTON T. DUFFY
of San Quentin

ACKNOWLEDGMENTS

For aid and comfort while this book was in the making, I owe a debt of gratitude to many good, generous people and organizations.

Without the assistance and encouragement of Allan J. Wilson, editor of Citadel Press, this book would not have been possible.

Corrections officials and police officers in many parts of the United States kindly provided essential information and illustrations. I am especially obliged to: Inspector Robert B. Davenport, Federal Bureau of Investigation, Washington, D.C.; Daryl F. Gates, chief of police, and Officer Paul A. Hord, Bureau of Special Investigation, Los Angeles Police Department; James G. Malson, director, Kansas Bureau of Investigation; Lieutenant Roy E. Kindrick, Portland Bureau of Police; James A. Lynaugh, commissioner, and Charles L. Brown, Texas Department of Corrections; Thomas A. Coughlin III, commissioner, New York Department of Correctional Services; Robert W. MacMaster, Florida Department of Corrections; David W. Guth, North Carolina Department of Corrections; Michael Van Winkle, California Department of Corrections; Michael Francke, Oregon Department of Corrections; Chase Riveland, secretary, State of Washington Department of Corrections, and Larry Kincheloe, director, Washington Division of Prisons; Richard E. Bauer of Washington State Penitentiary; and Mary Coffey, Nevada Department of Prisons.

L. Kay Gillespie, Ph.D., professor of sociology and criminology at Weber State College, Ogden, Utah, helped substantially by allowing me to read his work in progress about Utah's executed men. Jesse H. Meredith, M.D., professor of surgery, Bowman Gray School of Medicine, Wake Forest University, Winston-Salem, North Carolina, corresponded and provided information about organ transplantation he performed in connection with a North Carolina execution. Phillip I. Earl of the Nevada State Historical Society kindly sent me some of his writings about historic Nevada executions and furnished other materials.

Senator Christopher J. Dodd of Connecticut and Marge Broadman and Evelyn B. Elam of his office, as well as Edmund S. Muskie, former United States Senator from Maine and now of Washington, D.C., also provided valuable help, as did the NAACP Legal Defense and Educational Fund, Inc., of New York City.

Generous in the guidance they furnished were Isidore Ziferstein, M.D., Ph.D., of Los Angeles; Leigh Dingerson, director, National Coalition to Abolish the Death Penalty, Washington, D.C., and Gaby Monet, filmmaker, of Concepts Unlimited, New York.

viii ACKNOWLEDGEMENTS

For information about military executions I am indebted to John J. Slonaker, chief, Historical Reference Branch, United States Army Military History Institute, Carlisle Barracks, Pennsylvania, and Edward J. Drea, United States Army Center of Military History, Washington, D.C.

Others that offered a helping hand were the Library of Congress and the libraries of the New York Academy of Medicine, the John Jay College of Law, and the Research Division of the Public Library of New York City; J. Gary Nichols, Maine State Library; Sue Hill, Utah State Library; Suzanne Kuhne and Frank Ferro, Norwalk Public Library; David Ostergren, Wilton Library; Barbara Bojonell, Perrot Library of Old Greenwich; and other libraries in Connecticut.

For encouragement along the way I am also grateful to Andrew, Amelia, and John Iaderosa; John Drimmer, Anatole Konstantin, and Bernard Laderman, Michelle Manisoff, and Barbara Osborn. My daughter, Jean, devotedly undertook the demanding task of typing and retyping the manuscript and offered helpful comments.

To my wife, Evelyn, reference librarian at the Perrot Library of Old Greenwich, Connecticut, I owe much for keeping a stream of information and books flowing to me from libraries and organizations all over the United States. Although last on the list, she knows she is always first with me.

Contents

The sentence of the court is that a current of electricity be passed through your body until you are dead—and may God have mercy on your soul.

—Death sentence formula

Whoso sheddeth man's blood, by man shall his blood be shed: for in the image of God made he man.

—Genesis 9:6

And thine eye shall not pity; but life shall go for life, eye for eye, tooth for tooth, hand for hand, foot for foot.

—Deuteronomy 19:21

I have always maintained that the punishment should fit the crime. Too often when the death penalty is invoked critics have looked only to the guilty party and have failed to perceive the sorrow and loss inflicted upon the aggrieved victim and his loved ones. . . . Where there is no shadow of doubt concerning the guilt of the defendant, the public interest demands capital punishment be invoked where the law so provides.

—J. Edgar Hoover

Can it happen? Can an innocent person be executed? *Can it happen?* It has happened!

—Judge Michael Musmanno

Executions in America

ONE

███████████

Kemmler

August 6, 1890.

At 4:00 A.M., people were already spilling out into the shadowy streets of Auburn, New York. You might have thought that was because they'd found the night too warm for sleeping. But really there were too many of them for that.

By twos and by threes, bearded gentlemen—some carried canes and most had the look of professional men to them—slipped out of the Osborne Hotel and hurried toward the vine-covered old state prison. At the gate, they showed their passes to the guard on duty. He touched his fingers to his cap respectfully and the gate creaked open to admit them.

Within an hour, the thoroughfare in front of the prison was almost full of expectant people. Men and women, old and young—it looked as if everyone who could get himself up and out of bed was there. The tops of the houses around the prison were crawling with excited people. You could see young men who'd shinnied up tree trunks or perched themselves high on telegraph poles, looking over the prison wall, watching.

Across the street from the prison, the railroad platform had its contingent of curiosity seekers, stretching their necks for a better view. In the freight station, where the Western Union Telegraph Company had set up a temporary office, reporters busily scribbled their stories in their notebooks. They had to leave the stories unfinished, but what they'd written they transmitted to their papers. Then they waited for the rest to happen.

A prison guard, one of the night shift coming off duty, pointed out the illuminated window of the cell that was Kemmler's. Soon everyone who was close enough had his or her face pressed against the bars of the gate, eyes fixed on the pale oblong of light in the cell block.

They'd been waiting for it to happen for months, but time and again they'd been cheated out of it. Now, finally, in an hour or two (no one knew exactly when), it would actually come to pass—an event so remarkable it had drawn the attention of people all over the world to the small city in upstate New York.

Before long, the street in front of the prison was so jammed¹ it was impossible to make your way through the crowd.

Inside the prison walls, a bell clanged loudly. Some of the young men in the trees and on the telegraph poles began to wave handkerchiefs furiously, signals to the reporters in the telegraph office.

"He's killed! He's killed!" voices shouted from the crowd.

But he wasn't. Not yet. The bell was just the summons for the civilians who worked with the convicts in the prison shops to fall in line and enter. Grudgingly the people in the street made way for them.

Kemmler, it seemed, still had a little time left to live.

The Buffalo murderer, a short, thickset, black-bearded man of thirty, sat in his narrow cage, waiting for that little time to pass. As he waited, he listened to the muffled sound of the preparations in the death chamber on the other side of the wall. He was very close to the end now, but he didn't appear as upset as you might have expected. Not after fifteen months of waiting in prison. Fifteen months, during which his case had been tried and retried and he'd been sentenced and resentenced to death.

The day before, another condemned man, Fish, the Canandaigua murderer, had attempted to comfort him, as the men on death row always comfort the one who is closest to the end.

"I guess I'll behave all right," Kemmler had said. "It can't come too soon for me. Being so near the end is as bad as the actual going." And he had cheerily whistled, sung and danced to the accompaniment of Fish's banjo.

In the last days the newspapers had been talking about him endlessly. A sordid, miserable wretch, they called him—a creature devoid of all natural feeling. He felt they'd gone too far and he intended to straighten them out. In his mind he was rehearsing a little speech he would make in the death chamber.

"I'm going to die like a man," he'd told a visitor.

Only the day before, Kemmler had looked at Warden Durston's face, worn by worry and lack of sleep. It was to be the warden's first execution and the prospect haunted him as much as it did the condemned man.

"I'm not afraid, Warden." Kemmler had almost patted Durston on the shoulder. "I won't break down if you don't."

The crime for which Kemmler had been sentenced to death was a brutal drunken murder, not very different from the thousands that are committed each year.

Kemmler, a boozer, had deserted his wife and child in Pennsylvania and run off with a married woman named Tillie Ziegler. They'd settled in a Buffalo slum, where Tillie passed as his wife. Between bouts of drunkenness Kemmler worked as a peddler. Late on the night of March 28, 1889, he'd come home drunk and in a nasty mood. Tillie was just as drunk. Soon they were pounding each other with their fists. Kemmler realized the quarrel had ended only when, through a rift in the alcoholic fog surrounding him, he saw Tillie lying at his feet. His hand was grasping the haft of a bloody hatchet. She was barely alive, and she died soon after the police arrived.

"She deserved it." That was all he would tell the police by way of explanation.

Kemmler had been caught red-handed and his trial was brief. His eyes rested unwavering on the judge as he heard himself sentenced to death. Kemmler's face, as the newshawks like to note on such occasions, displayed no emotion. Doubtless he must have felt some.

In the last months, Kemmler had been showing signs of remorse. Maybe it was because he'd been off the booze so long or maybe it was because of the solitary confinement to which he'd been condemned. Like many others in his desperate situation he'd found comfort in religion. Almost illiterate, he pored over the Bible, puzzling over the difficult words and absorbed in the grim illustrations. He'd accepted baptism as a Methodist. Only the day previous, Kemmler had asked for a final communion. The two ministers who prayed with him hadn't come prepared and the concerned warden had rushed off to his own kitchen to fetch the wine and the bread for the ritual.

So far Kemmler's story had much in common with countless others.

What was about to set him apart from the rest—from, in fact, every one of the thousands and thousands and thousands of men, women and children who'd ever been sentenced to suffer the brutal, wrenching violence of death at the hand of the state—was the singular method chosen for him to suffer it.

William Kemmler was about to become the first man to die in the electric chair.

While the people of Auburn waited and wondered outside the walls of the state prison early that August morning, Warden Durston was approaching Kemmler's cell. The condemned man was sitting on the edge of his bunk. By the dim light of the gas jet, he saw three men with familiar faces accompanying the warden. They were Chaplain Yates, the Reverend Dr. Houghton, and Deputy Sheriff J. C. Veiling. Veiling had been the prisoner's keeper when he was locked up in Buffalo, and the two men had hit it off well. Kemmler greeted his callers warmly.

From his pocket, Durston drew a paper and began to read it to Kemmler in a trembling voice. It was the death warrant. After he had finished, Kemmler said, "All right, I'm ready to go."

The condemned man insisted the deputy sheriff should have breakfast with him. The warden nodded his approval and left.

Now the two clergymen and Kemmler got down on their knees and prayed together, while Veiling watched solemnly. Kemmler bowed his head penitently as he made his responses. Then they rose and shook hands. Kemmler joked, perhaps to ease the tension, and the clergymen left.

Breakfast arrived. Veiling pecked at the hearty meal. Kemmler ate his dishes clean. When they had finished, the deputy sheriff produced a pair of shears.

Would Kemmler mind if he cut his hair, he asked.[2]

Kemmler wouldn't. The warden had told him it would be necessary to remove the hair on the crown of his head to obtain good contact with the electrode, and he was pleased Veiling had volunteered for the job.

The deputy clipped away nervously, brushing shorn locks of hair off the top of Kemmler's head.

"They say I'm afraid to die," Kemmler said thoughtfully, "but they will find that I ain't . . ."

Veiling continued to crop away.

"I want you to stay right by me, Joe, and see me through this thing, and I'll promise you that I won't make any trouble. . . . Don't let them experiment on me more than they ought to.''

Veiling stopped clipping and woefully surveyed his handiwork. The bare area he had cut in the black bush on Kemmler's crown looked like an enormous scar.

Another unpleasant job still lay ahead. He asked Kemmler to stand up and turn around. With the shears, he made a cut in the back of the condemned man's trousers, over the spine, where the second electrode would be placed.

The warden's drawn face appeared outside the cage. The door swung open and he beckoned. "Come, William."

Kemmler shook hands with his friend and said goodbye to his troubled-looking keepers. He glanced back at the cell that had been home to him for so long, and walked with the warden to the death chamber. He was wearing a fine new outfit the state had provided for the occasion—trousers with a mixed yellow pattern, a sack jacket of dark gray and matching waistcoat, a white linen shirt, a bow tie, and brightly polished black shoes. As he entered the chamber, self-consciously he straightened his tie.

The electric chair, stark and ungainly, dominated the chamber. Fastened to the floor, with its feet insulated, it had broad arms and a high back with braces across it and a headrest. Thick leather straps dangled from it. Two stout wires ran to it, culminating in the lethal electrodes, which were attached to the chair by springs.

The instant Kemmler and the warden appeared in the doorway a hush fell over the witnesses. Most were seated in a semicircle, facing the chair. There were twenty-five of them: prison officials, the judge and the district attorney who had tried Kemmler, reporters, clergymen, and fourteen distinguished medical men. One was Dr. A. P. Southwick, known as the father of the electrical execution law. Another was Dr. George E. Fell. Fell had invented a patent resuscitator with which he had revived three apparently dead people. He was hoping to try it on Kemmler.

Very few of the witnesses had ever seen anyone put to death. Still, looking at the two people who'd just entered the chamber, not a man of them would have chosen Kemmler as the one who was about to be executed.[3]

Warden Durston licked dry lips. "Gentlemen, this is William Kemmler."

Kemmler bowed gravely. He was given a place to sit next to the chair of death. The clock on the wall said 6:34 A.M. Durston asked him if he had any last words.

"Gentlemen," said Kemmler in a bold tone, speaking as if it were a piece he had memorized, "I wish you all good luck. I believe I'm going to a good place, and I'm ready to go. A great deal has been said about me that's untrue. I'm bad enough. It's cruel to make me out worse." He gave a knowing nod to the deputy sheriff and bowed again.

At a sign from the warden, Kemmler rose, moved to the death chair and seated himself naturally and easily, like someone who'd been out on a long, long walk and was eager to rest. The morning light from the window splashed over his pale face. To one spectator it seemed to wear a quizzical, half-amused look.

In the rush of last-minute preparations, something had been forgotten, and now Durston remembered it. He asked Kemmler to get up again.

For this first experimental electrocution, it had been decided to apply one electrode to the condemned man's head, another to the base of his spine. Each electrode consisted of a hollow rubber hemis -phere containing a metal disk faced with a wet sponge, at the end of the wire that would carry the fatal current. Kemmler's trousers had been cut in the rear to allow a clean contact, but now it was seen his shirt hadn't.

With a pocketknife Durston carefully cut away some cloth to assure direct contact between the electrode and the skin.

Kemmler sat down on the edge of the chair. Taking off his jacket, he gave it to Durston. The two clergymen stood on either side, praying. Durston began to adjust the back electrode. He'd rehearsed the procedure just the day before with Dr. Fell sitting in for Kemmler; they'd even given Fell a slight, harmless dose of electricity. But now, in the excitement of the moment, Durston fumbled.

"Take your time, Warden, and do it right." Kemmler sounded as cool as a man giving instructions to his barber. "There's no rush. I don't want to take any chances on this thing, you know."

"All right, William."

Holding a watering can with a long spout, Fell moistened the electrodes. Durston fitted the headpiece in position. Leather bands held it in place, running over the doomed man's chin and forehead, partly concealing his face.

Kemmler shook his head, like someone trying on a new hat. "Warden, make that a little tighter. We want everything all right, you know."

The warden, with Deputy Sheriff Veiling assisting, began to buckle Kemmler in. There were straps to restrain the condemned man's torso, his arms, his legs. As the two men pulled each strap tight, Kemmler put pressure on it, making sure it would hold.

"All right," he said when they had finished. His hands rested peacefully on the arms of the chair.

Two medical experts had taken positions in front of the chair. One was Edward Spitzka, a celebrated anatomist. Next to him stood Dr. Carlos MacDonald, head of the Auburn Asylum for Insane Criminals. A third man held a stopwatch in his hand.

The warden took a last look at the straps. "This is all right."

Spitzka nodded. "All right." He bent over. "God bless you, Kemmler."

"Thank you." The little man was quiet and composed.

"Ready?" The warden was looking at Spitzka and MacDonald.

"Ready," they replied.

The warden had moved close to the door leading to the next room. Inside it, the electrician, Edwin F. Davis, was standing by the switchboard that controlled the voltage.

"Goodbye, William," Durston said.

Kemmler made no reply. He lifted his eyes as if to catch a last glimpse of the window and the blue sky beyond.

The warden rapped twice on the door. In the next room, a lever clicked.

A dynamo hummed to life somewhere. The witnesses heard an eerie whistling sound.

Kemmler's shoulders shot up. Every muscle in his body went rigid. The leather thongs creaked as he strained against them, driven by a power far greater than his own. If he hadn't been strapped in the chair, the first surge of the current might have hurled him clear across the chamber.

The seconds ticked by. Kemmler's face and hands had turned an intense red. Now an ashen pallor took its place. He seemed to stare at the witnesses, but his eyes were glazed, the pupils dilated, unseeing. One of the fingers of his right hand had clenched so tight the nail had bitten into the flesh; blood was trickling down the arm of the chair.

Spots appeared on his face, intensely red spots, like the mark of some terrible disease.

Seventeen seconds had passed since the current had been turned on.

Spitzka was leaning forward, close to Kemmler but not touching him. "He's dead."

MacDonald, by his side, nodded.

The warden signaled Davis to shut off the electricity.

The witnesses had been sitting hunched forward, breathless, on the edges of their seats. Now, almost like one man, they exhaled in an audible sigh. One of them tumbled from his seat and fell heavily to the floor in a faint. Another, the district attorney who'd prosecuted Kemmler, ran gasping from the chamber.

Kemmler's body, released by the current, sagged like a rag doll. It was held upright in the chair only by the leather thongs.

The warden loosened the strap on the convict's face, preparing to take off the headpiece.

Then the thing happened that no man in that chamber would forget as long as he lived.

As the warden bent over the slumped form in the chair Kemmler's chest heaved.

The hoarse, unnatural breathing of the man who had just been pronounced dead filled the room.

Durston stopped, paralyzed.

Foam bubbled out of Kemmler's mouth. From his throat came a gurgling sound.

The witnesses had jumped from their seats, sleepers startled out of a nightmare only to find it was real.

"He's alive!" one of them shouted.

"He's breathing!" screamed another.

"For God's sake," cried a third, "kill him and be done with it!"

"Quick, turn on the current!" Spitzka ordered.

The warden pulled the headpiece strap taut. Almost immediately he signaled the electrician.

In the bowels of the prison the dynamo began to hum again.

The rag doll in the chair sat up taut. Impelled by the fiery power of the current, it thrust itself forcefully against the straps restraining it.

A wisp of smoke rose from the top of Kemmler's head and hovered in the air above him.

It had taken a long time to come, that triumph of modern civilization, the first electrocution, which took place in Auburn State Prison on August 6, 1890.

Until that day, America had been disposing of persons convicted of serious felonies in more primitive ways. It had shot them, it had burned them, and occasionally it had drawn and quartered them.

But mostly it had hanged them.

Toward the end of the nineteenth century, with the growth of humanitarian movements, hanging was falling into increasing disfavor in the United States. Executions were usually the responsibility of the local sheriffs, who as a rule weren't notably proficient as hangmen. The result was that the poor devil who'd been sentenced to hang by the neck until dead might do just that. Instead of having his neck vertebrae neatly snapped the instant he fell through the trap, he might twist and turn at the end of the rope for twenty or thirty minutes as life was painfully choked out of him.

Or, if he didn't strangle to death, he might suffer the other extreme: the force of the fall might rip off his head, and the witnesses might feel his warm blood spattering over them like rain.

Even under the best of circumstances, an execution by hanging was a grisly sight for people of any sensitivity.

In 1885, New York's new governor, David B. Hill, gave voice to the rising tide of objections. "The present mode of executing criminals by hanging," said he, "has come down to us from the Dark Ages." The science of the day, continued Governor Hill, might well be able to provide a less barbarous means for the lawful taking of a life, and he asked the state legislature to find one.

The following year a legislative committee buckled down to the task. It was popularly known as the Death Commission and its chairman was Elbridge T. Gerry, politician and philanthropist, who had organized the Society for the Prevention of Cruelty to Children. The commission studied more than forty methods of putting criminals to death but decided only four could come up to the standards of humanity—the garrotte, the guillotine, the hypodermic injection of deadly poison, and the application of an electrical current.

A questionnaire was sent out to a group of judges, medical men and scientists, asking them to express their preference. Two hundred replies came back. Eighty said they were satisfied with hanging; they wanted no change in the method of execution. Eighty-seven were in favor of electricity (one of these was Thomas Alva Edison). The remainder preferred the other three methods.

The Death Commission voted against the garrotte because it was slow and sometimes there were problems with it. Besides, it was practiced in Spain, a country with which the United States wasn't on the best of terms.

The guillotine did its work in a flash, but blood was shed in the process and the commission felt that "did not accord with the temperament of the American people."

Gerry himself favored the hypodermic injection of morphine. But what if the condemned man was an addict? Then it would be most difficult to use it to do away with him. Besides, morphine was widely employed by physicians as a painkiller and they were afraid its use in executions could persuade the public it was unsafe.

So the commission voted for electricity, which, according to the best scientific opinion, would render a victim instantly unconscious and simultaneously extinguish all signs of life.

No one knew then, or knows now, exactly what electricity is. In that day, however, two different kinds of electric current had been developed, alternating current (the familiar AC of today) and direct current (DC). Each kind had its advocates, and each group fought the other tooth and nail, determined to drive it out of the marketplace.

Today we know how the struggle ended: alternating current was victorious. Only a small fraction of modern electrical power is supplied by direct current. But in the 1880s, direct current appeared to hold the winning hand. Its chief backer and proponent was the reigning genius of American invention, Thomas Alva Edison, who had developed the first electric power system in 1882. Convinced the future belonged to his low-tension direct current, he'd sunk a fortune into its development and promotion.

Pitted against Edison was another industrial Goliath, George Westinghouse, Jr. Westinghouse current (as alternating current was often called) had some striking advantages: high voltages could be transmitted over great distances and at extremely low costs. Direct current, by contrast, could be sent only over short distances and at low voltages. It was distinctly the less economical of the two.

But direct current is much safer! cried Edison. Alternating current, with its powerful voltages, could easily produce a fatal shock. It was too dangerous for electric lights and other everyday purposes. By the same token, he suggested insidiously, it was superbly adapted for use in electrical executions. When anyone touched an exposed live wire powered by alternating current he died as instantly as if he'd been struck by lightning. Westinghouse retorted that Edison was mistaken; alternating current was much safer than direct.

It was called "the war of the currents," and Edison fought to win it with every trick he knew. He worked hard to persuade local legislators around the country to pass laws banning electric systems powered by alternating generators. As part of his campaign, he put on demonstrations at his Menlo Park laboratory in West Orange, New Jersey. He paid the children of the neighborhood twenty-five cents for each stray cat and dog they could bring him. Then the barking, mewing procession was forced onto a sheet of tin charged with a high voltage from an alternating generator and instantly executed. These demonstrations resulted in at least one of his employees receiving such a shock that forever after he had "the awful memory of body and soul being wrenched asunder."

Harold P. Brown, an electrical engineer, played a key role in persuading the New York State legislature to make electricity—and specifically the kind produced by a Westinghouse alternating generator—the official method of execution. Brown (it can hardly be a coincidence) had once worked for Edison. He traveled up and down the state delivering public lectures in which he asserted that "with a pressure of 1,500 volts there cannot be the slightest doubt of instantaneous death." To show how instantaneous, Brown put animals to death in demonstrations reminiscent of Edison's. Infuriated, Westinghouse waged a tireless campaign of counterpropaganda.

In 1888, the legislators at Albany, convinced by the Death Commission's report as well as Brown's and Edison's demonstrations, passed the act that abolished hanging and substituted death by electricity.[4] "This is a step forward in the cause of humanity," proclaimed *The New York Times*. A handful of other state legislatures introduced similar statutes.

A short while later, electrical equipment manufacturers held their annual convention in Chicago. They went on record against supplying any of their products for "such ignoble purposes" as executions.

Brown, by now something of a public figure, signed a contract with the state to produce the killing apparatus. His first need was for the powerful alternating generators. When he applied to the Westinghouse Electrical and Manufacturing Company to buy them, he was turned down. Resourcefully, he arranged to have a man in Rio de Janeiro order three used generators. These were reshipped to Brown, who sold them to the state for $8,000. The machines were installed in the Auburn, Sing Sing and Clinton state prisons.

George Westinghouse had lost the first battle. He condemned Brown's underhanded tactic. Westinghouse generators were so safe and harmless, he repeated, that a vast amount of work would have to be done to make them capable of killing a man. Then he cast about for a new strategy to carry on the war.

In March 1889, members of the Death Commission, with Harold Brown and Dr. Carlos MacDonald, took a ride out to Menlo Park. The state had to determine the parts of the body to which the electricity should be applied to produce death with a minimum of struggle and pain, and Edison had graciously placed his staff and facilities at their disposal. He also provided them with four dogs, four calves and a horse for their experiments.

The investigators executed these creatures one after another, using 500 volts for the smallest, 1,000 for the biggest. The animals died at the first shock, without convulsions, to the considerable satisfaction of the commission.

With the help of Edwin F. Davis, who would become the world's first electrical executioner (we shall meet him again and again plying his craft in later pages), Brown proceeded to design and build an electric chair. In its final form, it would be constructed under Davis's supervision by convict labor at Auburn.

Kemmler had gone on trial for murder on May 6, 1889, and been found guilty just four days later. It took more than a year for all the appeals made in his behalf to be heard.

Standard-bearer of the struggle to save Kemmler from the chair was W. Bourke Cockran, prominent attorney and political luminary. How could a penniless, dissolute killer like Kemmler afford such fancy legal assistance? Westinghouse, the newspapers hinted. Westinghouse denied it. Cockran denied it. He had simply become "interested" in the case. He was retained "by Philanthropy." The newspapers were far from convinced.

Execution by electricity, Cockran insisted in his brief, was cruel and unusual, and therefore a violation of the state constitution. To support his claim the attorney went to great trouble and expense to muster a massive array of witnesses. First to be called was Harold P. Brown. Under sharp questioning, the advocate of electrical execution conceded that the subject of such an execution could be tortured if the current was too weak. He also admitted no man-made generator could produce a current with the concentrated force of a bolt of lightning—yet people had been struck by lightning and not been killed.

To hammer home his point, Cockran presented a train of witnesses, all of whom had either been struck by lightning or severely shocked by electricity (including a dog named Dash), so that they were to all appearances dead—and then had been miraculously revived.

Another witness, Franklin Pope, a Westinghouse expert, declared the maximum power a Westinghouse generator could produce was only 1,050 volts, and that wasn't enough to kill a man.

To demolish the Westinghouse evidence, the state prosecutor called on his big gun. Thomas A. Edison. According to Edison, the Westinghouse generator could produce a much greater voltage than its rated capacity. Furthermore, two Westinghouse generators could be used in tandem, producing 2,000 volts at rated capacity, more than enough to kill a human being. He offered his facilities at Menlo Park for further experiments and the state accepted.

After weeks of hearings, the court decided the new method of execution was neither cruel nor unusual and Kemmler would have to face death by it. Electric company money apparently continued to work for him as other attempts, going as high as the United States Supreme Court, were made to prevent the electrocution. One even went so far as to sue for the return of the alternating generators Brown had bought.

When each of these cases was initiated, Kemmler, who was scheduled to be executed in a short while, was given a reprieve. He showed scant appreciation but simply went on pacing his cell.

What, after all, did he have to rejoice about? If the pleas made in his name had succeeded, the best he could hope for was to be resentenced to die at the end of a rope.

But, as it happened, all the pleas failed.

That was why, on the morning of August 6, 1890, William Kemmler sat strapped in the new electric chair at Auburn, seared by an invisible flame of electricity from a secondhand generator while he wheezed and foamed at the mouth.

The dynamo was wailing sharply, brokenly. Like a sick animal.

Kemmler, driven up against the straps, sat as rigid as a figure cast in bronze.

Under his skin the capillaries started to rupture. Drops of blood sparkled on his face.

An acrid, disturbing smell had begun to spread through the chamber. A mingled smell of singed hair, burned cloth, charred skin, urine, feces. There was a sizzling sound, as of meat frying in a pan.

The witnesses, their flesh crawling, squirmed in their places. To them it seemed they'd already beheld Kemmler die once and now they were watching him undergo the same excruciating death again. Only this one, the second execution, appeared to go on and on, endlessly.

Actually, little more than a minute had passed since the electricity had been turned on a second time when Spitzka, standing in front of the chair, signaled the warden to shut down. It was 6:51 A.M.

Durston removed the electrodes and loosened the straps. Head sagging, Kemmler's body sat motionless in the chair. No question now as to whether he was alive or dead.

The spectators, frozen in their seats, began to thaw. Dazed, dry-mouthed, sick to their stomachs, they pulled themselves to their feet and wobbled out into the stone corridor. A few were so ill that prison attendants had to assist them.

Guards brought up a dissecting table and set it in front of the chair. The New York law required an autopsy to make certain that the convict couldn't return to life. Kemmler's body was lifted out of the chair and placed on the table.

Bizarrely, the corpse retained the position it had in the chair. Rigor mortis had already set in.

Five medical experts were selected to perform a preliminary autopsy on the grotesquely contorted cadaver. Spitzka and MacDonald were among them. It was a textbook rule of medicine that a warm body wasn't a dead body. The temperature of Kemmler's corpse, at the points of contact with the electrodes, was higher than normal body temperature. Although the doctors had no doubt Kemmler was dead, they decided to wait a few hours before beginning the postmortem. No one was going to say that the convict had died under the scalpel.

While the doctors waited, they grumbled among themselves about the defective electrical equipment, the inexperienced electricians, the rattlebrained warden who'd changed the arrangements at the end; everything seemed to have conspired to make the first electrocution less than it should have been. If Kemmler hadn't been so manly, they agreed, the scene in the death chamber might have been even more gruesome.

When they went to work, they found that directly under the electrode of the headpiece the blood vessels had carbonized and the outer part of the brain hardened. On the back, the wet sponge covering the electrode had burned. So had the body beneath it, clear through to the spine. The flesh had the appearance of overdone beef. Kemmler's face, however, bore an expression of repose.

Reporters scurried about, interviewing everyone present at the execution who could be persuaded to talk.

Most of the witnesses expressed revulsion.

"I'd rather see ten hangings," said Dr. Jenkins, New York's deputy coroner. "It was fearful. No humane man could witness it without the keenest agony." He'd been among the first to dash out of the prison; although hours had gone by since then, his voice shook as he talked about the scene.

"I've seen hangings that were immeasurably more brutal, but I've never seen anything so awful," said Spitzka. "I believe this will be the first and last execution of the kind."

Dr. Shrady, editor of the *Medical Record,* had already written an editorial about the execution. "The death chair will yet be the pulpit from which the abolition of capital punishment will be preached," he said.

Another witness, Sheriff O. A. Jenkins of Buffalo, compared Kemmler's execution to hangings he'd attended and declared they were infinitely more humane. "Electrical executions will never do," he concluded. He was so upset he'd taken to his room at the Osborne Hotel.

Not surprisingly, Dr. Southwick, the so-called father of the new method of capital punishment, was completely satisfied with the execution. So was Warden Durston. No, he'd never seen a hanging, but, judging from what he'd been told by those who had, the electrical execution was vastly superior.

A newsman asked how much voltage had been used to kill Kemmler. Durston bristled. "I won't tell you."

The New York Times reported the next day that the second person to leave the prison had been one of the electricians handling the apparatus. The man had headed straight for the Western Union office across the street and dispatched a telegram. The *Times* reporter had succeeded in learning its contents.

The telegram was addressed to the Westinghouse Company. "Execution was an awful botch," it said. "Kemmler was literally roasted to death."

Had the Westinghouse interests been responsible? Spitzka refused to give a direct answer. But he did comment, "The dynamo and apparatus . . . didn't furnish sufficient power and it didn't furnish a steady current . . . Yes, there might have been corrupt reasons for this. The interests of the company who manufacture the dynamos would certainly be advanced by the defects of the machinery. They failed to kill electrical executions in the courts, but the last resort wasn't there. Their ends would be served quite as efficiently if this execution was a botch, as it largely was, and would consequently meet with public disapproval."

According to someone behind the scenes (possibly Edwin F. Davis, the executioner), the first charge had been 700 volts. That was much weaker than the 1,500 volts recommended by experts. Spitzka insisted that the first shock had rendered Kemmler instantly unconscious and in effect had killed him, since he couldn't have been revived. (The first contact, as we've seen, had lasted just seventeen seconds—about one eighth of the time that later became standard for the entire execution.)

What about the breathing and the foaming at the mouth when the current was first cut off?

That, Spitzka said, was simply the result of reflex action. However, since this was the first electrical execution, Spitzka hadn't wanted to take any chance he might be mistaken, so he'd requested the current to be turned on again. The second charge had gone no higher than 1,300 volts. Spitzka conceded he'd allowed the current to be kept on too long (hence the burning of Kemmler's body). Personally he preferred the guillotine.

"Far Worse Than Hanging," complained *The New York Times* in a front-page article the following day. "Kemmler's Death Proves an Awful Spectacle." In a long story that flowed over onto and took up much of page 2, the paper reported every detail of the grisly event. Kemmler, who the day before had been a "wretch," one "incapable of thinking and feeling as other men feel," had now become "a sacrifice" to the "whims and theories of a coterie of cranks and politicians." He had suffered "a death so fearful that people throughout the country will read of it with horror and disgust."

To the *New York World* the new method of execution was "very cruel and very shocking." It called for prompt repeal of the statute.

"Old-fashioned hanging is good enough, provided it is administered by trained and skillful hangmen." The *New York Herald* called the new method "torture."

Newspapers in other countries echoed these opinions. "We cannot believe," wrote the *London Standard,* "that Americans will allow the electrical execution act to stand." For the *Times* of London it was "impossible to imagine a more revolting exhibition." For the *Chronicle* the scene seemed worthy of the "darkest chambers of the Inquisition." Berlin and Vienna expressed equal dismay. Paris decided it would stay with the guillotine.

One who could take particular satisfaction in the bungling of Kemmler's execution was George Westinghouse, Jr. At first unwilling to talk to newsmen, he finally told them it was "a brutal affair." He added a few words. "They could have done better with an axe. My predictions have been verified. The public will lay the blame where it belongs and it will not be on us."

A. T. Howand, secretary of the Westinghouse Company, was less reserved. "I'm inclined to think Kemmler wasn't killed by electricity," he said with irony, "but that when the application of the 1,300 volts roasted and sizzled him, the electrocutioners completed the horrible work by hitting him on the head with a club . . .

"I am of the opinion this will be the first and last execution of the kind in this country."

TWO

██████████

Old Sparky

The voice of the great Thomas Edison crackled with ire.

"I've merely glanced over an account of Kemmler's death," he fumed. "It wasn't pleasant reading. One mistake was in leaving everything to the doctors.

"With their great knowledge of nerves and nerve centers they said that the cap should be placed on top of the head." He snorted. "Now, thirty or forty men have been killed by an electric current through their hands. Many of them died instantly. That manner was good enough, but the doctors thought differently."

But Edison wouldn't let it drop there. "Don't they know it's the water in the body that conducts the electricity? In the top of the head there is little water and the current of electricity strikes the hard skull. In the hand, there is a great deal of water and the flesh is soft. Hence it's the best possible place to receive the shock. The better way is to place the hands in jars of water in which there is a little potash to eliminate all grease from the hand, and let the current be turned on there . . .

"Undoubtedly all those present were greatly excited. In that excitement, there may have been some bungling. When the next man is placed in the chair to suffer the death penalty, that death will be accomplished instantly—and without the scene at Auburn."

The Wizard of Menlo Park had spoken. But if he wasn't satisfied with the way Kemmler's execution had been carried out, he was at least content with the result. So was the State of New York. Kemmler had been killed in less than a minute and a half of exposure to the lethal current, a record it would have been hard to match in the annals of hanging.

A year passed before another electrical execution occurred. On July 7, 1891, four murderers paid the extreme penalty. They were the first men to die in the new chair at Sing Sing.

The New York law carried a provision that no details of electrical executions beyond a brief statement of fact could be reported in the press. After the lurid accounts that followed Kemmler's execution the state decided to enforce this requirement. New York papers that had reveled in the grisly details of Kemmler's death were indicted, and no members of the press were permitted to witness the next executions. On the day the four murderers were to die, Warden Brown of Sing Sing posted guards armed with rifles in front of the prison. Reportedly they had orders to shoot anyone trying to cross the "deadline" he'd established.

Still, the warden showed some consideration for the hundred eager reporters waiting outside. As each of the men was killed a different colored flag—white, blue, black and red—was run up over the prison. One of the men was a black, and for him the warden chose the black flag. Newsmen were also informed this convict had been given a stiffer dose of electricity than the other three. He had, it was said, a thicker skull.

Because of his fear the execution would be a failure, the warden had pledged the witnesses to secrecy. They were willing to tell reporters the executions had been "successful"—that and very little more. Rumors were soon circulating that the group execution had been another botch.

For the next execution—"Governor Hill's Sixth Victim" was the way one paper headlined its account—armed guards were again posted to make reporters keep their distance. Witnesses were as reluctant to talk about this execution as they'd been about the previous four.

Details leaked out. A horrifying picture emerged of a murderer, Martin D. Loppy, who was in a state of collapse and had to be half-carried to the chair. He was given four shocks. During the second, his left eyeball popped and the aqueous humor ran down his cheek. Dr. MacDonald, who'd supervised all of the executions so far (he called them "experiments"), explained that the current was shut off periodically so he could moisten the electrodes to keep them from overheating. In his opinion, the execution had been a "perfect success." Other witnesses disagreed, mentioning the "frightful stench" as the sponges burned and the overpowering smell of roasting flesh that day in December 1891 at Sing Sing.

Were the witnesses exaggerating? Probably not. Otherwise, why would the state have tried an entirely different procedure for the next execution? By now, the New York law had been amended, and newsmen were permitted to be present. The execution took place in February 1892, at Sing Sing. The condemned man was Charles E. McElvaine, who'd murdered a grocer.

New York had finally decided to hearken to the wisdom of Thomas Edison. For McElvaine's execution, the arms of the chair were altered. They were placed high, fitting close under the convict's armpits, and slanting downward to the front, ending below the seat of the chair. Under the end of each arm was a two-quart jar filled with saltwater. A wire carried electricity to each jar.

McElvaine, who entered the death chamber holding a brass crucifix at eye level in front of him, looked terrified. He was strapped in the chair, a leather visor was fastened over his face, and his hands were inserted in the jars.

With the first half of the preparations completed, the second half began. A metal headpiece containing an electrode was put into place; another electrode was attached to the calf of his leg after the trouser had been rolled up. Rubber sacks were set up to feed saltwater to these electrodes and keep them moist. Similar electrodes had been used in the latest executions, but with McElvaine they were to serve merely as standbys—in case some unexpected difficulty cropped up with the hands-in-water method.

It was, all in all, a wise precaution.

McElvaine may have run out of prayers or more likely the elaborate preparations unnerved him. "Let 'er go!" he cried at last in an agonized voice.

The warden, finally ready, dropped a handkerchief, a signal to the executioner, Davis, to throw the switch.

Lights flashed in the control panel. The current flowed into the jars. For fifty seconds, McElvaine tugged against the straps. When the electricity was turned off, a deep groan came from his lips. His chest collapsed. Sputum poured out of his mouth.

He was still alive. It was the Kemmler execution all over again. "Switch the current to the head and leg electrodes!" Dr. Mac-Donald called sharply.

McElvaine went rigid. Water from the rubber sacks began to run down over his clothing, drenching it. The electrodes steamed. The witnesses squirmed as the smell of burning flesh and hair spread through the chamber.

After thirty-six seconds, the power was shut off. McElvaine was dead now, but little thanks was due to Thomas Edison. The electrical genius, it seemed, had miscalculated the electrical resistance by half. His method would never be tried again.

A few months later, wife-killer Joseph L. Tice sat down in the chair at Auburn and was executed with the now-standard head and calf electrodes. Four successive charges burned through him for a total of fifty seconds. No one observed any revolting details or signs of suffering—or so it was reported.

By now, the men in charge of executions had learned their trade. Electrical execution was no longer an experiment but was becoming a tested and reliable method of killing, the first major step forward in the fine art of putting men to death since the invention of the guillotine.

The new method of killing needed a new name. At first it had been called electrical execution or electrothanasia. Edison, who'd been so close to it since the beginning, hoped he might be able to name it. How about "electromort," "dynamort," or "ampermort"? he asked. A New York attorney proposed "electricide," but then suggested Westinghouse deserved a bow for his alternating generator—why not say a person who was executed by electricity was "Westinghoused"? The word "electrocution" (in quotation marks) began to appear in the year of Kemmler's death and soon edged all rivals out.

Over the years other states began to follow New York's lead, substituting electrocution for hanging. Ohio was first, in 1896; Massachusetts second, in 1898; New Jersey third, in 1906. But the states moved slowly in adopting the new method, in part because it was more expensive and in part, perhaps, because they believed a prisoner's death should be painful if it was to serve as a deterrent to crime.

Not all the electrocutions after Tice's went smoothly. One of the most horrifying took place on July 27, 1893. William G. Taylor, a convict, had killed another prisoner and was sentenced to die in the electric chair at Auburn. When the current hit him, his legs stiffened and shot out so hard they pulled out with them the front of the chair, to which they were strapped. The electricity was instantly shut off. A box was hurriedly found and shoved under the chair to keep it from collapsing. The execution was resumed.

But more trouble lay ahead. When the current was shut off, the prison physician noticed Taylor's chest was moving up and down. The executioner was ordered to turn on the current again. After he threw the switch, Taylor remained slumped in the chair. No electricity was flowing. A quick check with the dynamo room revealed the generator had failed.

Postponing the execution of the half-dead man was unthinkable. The electricians ran with wires to make a tie-in with the power lines outside the prison. Meanwhile, poor Taylor was removed to a cot and given drugs to kill any pain he might be feeling.

During the hour or so it took to complete the electrical connection, Taylor died. Still, to make certain his sentence had been carried out to the letter of the law, his body was strapped in the chair and a powerful current shot into it for thirty seconds.

Mechanical failures have been responsible again and again for bizarre spectacles in the death chamber. In 1931, shortly before two men were to be executed in Sing Sing, the motor generator burned out. As in Taylor's case, wires were strung up to connect with the city power lines. The current in these lines was stronger than that used in the prison: the witnesses in the death chamber were treated to a frightening display, complete with sparks flashing around the men in the chair, smoke, and the stench of burning flesh. On other occasions the equipment has jammed, making it impossible to reduce the current, with the result that the bodies were severely burned.

Sometimes mechanical failure has raised the possibility of a legal complication. In 1946 in Louisiana, a fifteen-year-old black named Willie Francis was to be executed in the state's portable electric chair. When the current was turned on, the doomed youth strained against the straps, then was heard to whisper, "Let me breathe." Obviously not enough current was reaching the electrodes. The power was turned off and on again. The boy's body arched spastically. "Take it off," he gasped. The warden ordered the dynamo shut down. Willie was unbuckled and he stood up from the chair unaided. He was given a week's reprieve so the mechanical defect could be corrected.

Willie's case had captured the public's attention. A lawsuit was started, declaring a second execution would be "cruel and unusual punishment'' under the Eighth Amendment. The United States Supreme Court decided against Willie and he went to the chair in 1947. This time it worked.

Electricity has its mysteries, which sometimes cause more than the condemned man to feel the current. On occasion, a doctor applying a stethoscope to the breast of an electrocuted convict has jumped back after receiving a strong shock. Or a guard touching the dead man has been severely burned.

Physical peculiarities not always observable before an execution have sometimes introduced a complication. In 1903, a strange one occurred during the electrocution of the Van Wormer brothers at Dannemora. The three young men had been convicted of the murder of their uncle, whom they hated because he'd foreclosed a mortgage on their stepmother's house.

The three brothers chose the order in which they would go to the chair. The executions went off without a hitch and the brothers were pronounced dead. Later, after they'd been laid out in the autopsy room, a guard saw one of them, Frederick Van Wormer, move a hand. Then an eye flickered. The prison doctor was immediately summoned. Putting a stethoscope to the ''dead'' man's heart, he discovered it was still beating. Van Wormer's heart (it was determined later) was bigger than that of anyone executed up to that date, so two charges of full current had failed to kill him. The convict was carried back to the chair and kept in it until he was dead beyond the shadow of a doubt.

In part because of accidents like these during the early decades of the electric chair, numbers of people weren't convinced it was as deadly as it was supposed to be. One of the doubters was Sheriff Julius Harburger of New York City. In 1912, Harburger declared that previously, as city coroner, he'd come across cases of suspended animation—people who'd been pronounced dead after an electric shock and had then revived. He said that, in common with many physicians, he believed convicts didn't die in the chair but under the knife in the autopsy room.

To prove his case, Sheriff Harburger attended an execution at Sing Sing. He personally wanted to make tests on the body of the electrocuted convict before it went under the scalpel, but his request was rejected. He was, however, permitted to witness the autopsy. The surgeon in charge demonstrated to him that the dead man's tempera-

ture was 128 degrees—far above the limit at which life can continue—
and Harburger went away satisfied.

Electricians and physicians worked constantly at improving the
apparatus and procedures used in electrocution. After Kemmler's
death, the switchboard and the man who operated it were moved into
the death chamber, to a cabinet or alcove in back of the chair. There
the executioner wasn't visible to the condemned man, but he could
keep an eye on the operation and respond instantly to any emergency.
By electric signals to the power plant, he could order the generator
turned on and off.

Special measures were taken to prevent reflex movements and
sounds from being made by the dead man. At Sing Sing, it became the
duty of the chief prison physician to give the signal to the executioner
to throw the switch. This was because, standing in front of the chair,
the physician could presumably judge exactly when the convict emptied his lungs. In Kemmler's case, there had been breath in his lungs
when the current was turned on. When it was shut off, his chest
collapsed, expelling the breath with a loud and frightening sound and
producing foam at the lips. But if the switch was thrown at the precise
moment the convict emptied his lungs, it was reasoned, the distressing
aftereffects could be avoided. (Unfortunately, it wasn't always possible to judge the exact moment of exhalation.)

Most people have an idea of what the electric chair looks like from
seeing it in motion pictures. Like other instruments of execution or
torture, it holds a special fascination for many, and visitors to peniten-
tiaries that have an electric chair often want to see and sit in it. The
chair has changed over the years and it varies somewhat in different
states. In Sing Sing (from which it was removed in 1971), it was bolted
to the floor and stood on a rubber mat. It was sturdy, with broad arms
and a high four-runged back tilted to the rear. It was varnished brown.
In back the chair had two legs, but in front it curved inward to form a
single broad leg. Two grips to hold the ankles were attached to this.

An adjustable flat headrest, padded with rubber, was attached to the
back. Rubber matting covered the seat, which had sufficient capacity
to accommodate the largest person who might have to sit in it.

Eight straps with buckles fastened the condemned person to the
chair. The straps were black and made of heavy harness leather. Two
of them secured the ankles in the grips; the others fastened both upper
and lower arms and the chest and waist.

To make the entire ceremony as speedy as possible and shorten the prisoner's anguish, a team of seven prison attendants was drilled in strapping him¹ into the chair. These men, working with split-second timing, could do the job in half a minute or less. Over his face they attached a mask of leather extending from the forehead to just above the mouth (or below it), with openings for the eyes and nostrils. The mask extended back to the chair and was fastened to it, holding the head immobile.

Over the decades executioners refined their technique of applying the current. When they first threw the switch, they kept it at a high voltage for a few seconds, then at a low voltage for a longer period, and then repeated the sequence. Why? Because at a high voltage the electrodes became overheated (sometimes they even melted) and sparks played around the chair. It may have been this phenomenon that earned the chair the nickname of ''Old Sparky,'' which it has in many prisons. If prolonged, the high voltage would burn the body at the points of contact, as we've seen.

Human bodies differ in their resistance to electricity. A current that may stun one person can kill another. Even the same person may differ at various times in the resistance he presents. The condition of his skin and blood has much to do with this. A prisoner who has been fasting and is dehydrated requires a stronger current than one on a normal diet. On a hot day, when a person perspires, he doesn't require as powerful a current as on a cool one. The strength (rate of flow) of the current, or the amperage, required in an electrocution depends on the resistance of the convict's body—which may even change during the execution. From seven to sixteen amperes are used, with an average of eleven.

Over the years, the voltage has gradually been increased. During the last electrocutions in New York State (in the 1960s), the executioner usually made his first contact at 2,000 volts. He maintained this voltage for three seconds, after which he reduced it to 500 volts, keeping it there for fifty-seven seconds. Then he raised it to two thousand for a few seconds and lowered it again. At the end of the second minute he brought it up to 2,000 volts, held it there for a few seconds, and shut off the current. Other states follow different practices. For the execution in 1981 of Stephen T. Judy, who brutally murdered a young mother and her three children in Michigan, a ten-second charge of 2,300 volts was applied, then a twenty-second charge of 500 volts. Automation has entered the death house. With the most modern equipment the sequence of charges can be programmed in advance.

After the current has been shut off, an attendant exposes the chest of the convict and wipes off the perspiration. The prison physician listens for a heartbeat and when he finds none pronounces the prisoner dead. If he hears heartbeats or observes a reflex of any kind—or just to be sure—he orders another shock. Ethel Rosenberg, the atomic spy executed in 1953, required two more shocks than her husband, Julius.

Motion pictures portraying executions at Sing Sing have shown the lights of the prison dimming when the current is turned on. Scenes like these may be very dramatic but they aren't accurate. The electric chair at Sing Sing had its own generator and circuit, so its use had no effect on prison power lines. The sound made by the apparatus is much like that of an X-ray machine—a kind of buzzing.

THREE

Electricians Extraordinary

And Some Notable Electrocutions

To execute someone in the electric chair, ideally a man should have a good knowledge of electricity. Most who practice the peculiar trade of electrocutioner have come to it because they are electricians, and highly qualified ones at that.[1] That they are not averse to increasing their incomes by the practice of legal homicide goes without saying.

In some states, throwing the switch is the warden's responsibility, although usually there will be an experienced electrician on hand to make sure all goes well. But what if the warden is unwilling? When the electric chair was introduced in Texas in 1924, five black men were awaiting execution in the Huntsville state prison. The warden inquired who was going to put them to death and he was informed that he was. Like some other wardens you'll meet later, he hadn't embraced the idea of capital punishment, especially when carried out by his own hand. He resigned. A short while later the new warden, a former sheriff, willingly pulled the switch.

Unlike hangmen, who often measure and truss up their victims, electrocutioners normally have no contact with them. What they need to know about their prospective clients' physical peculiarities they

27

usually find out from prison officials so they can make the necessary adjustments in their equipment or procedures. As a rule, they see their clients for the first (and last) time when they're seated in the chair. In some states, the electrocutioner wears a special outfit; in Florida, it's a black hood, just as in the Middle Ages.

Electrocutions have been decreasing in number for the past fifty years. Therefore, electrocutioners aren't as well known as hangmen were some generations ago, particularly in Great Britain. As a group, the men who throw the switch lack the colorful personalities of the old-time hangmen. Most have sought to conceal their identities as well as their private lives from the public, which, however, has had an insatiable curiosity about them. So has the press, with the result that some of these electricians extraordinary have achieved a remarkable degree of notoriety.

Edwin F. Davis, who became the world's first official electrocutioner when he pulled the switch on William Kemmler, was a short, wiry man with intense eyes and a drooping mustache. He came to his profession by sheer chance—and, one must add, by having a strong stomach. A professional electrician, he was employed by Harold P. Brown to help set up the apparatus for Kemmler's execution. As a result, he was appointed state electrician, the first man to hold that title in New York.

Davis practiced the profession of executioner for twenty-four years, until his resignation in 1914. In that long stretch of time he sent some 240 persons to their death, earning, it was said, $10,000. He was the official executioner not only for New York but for New Jersey and Massachusetts as well. It was a profitable sideline and he was highly jealous of his professional secrets, fearing that someone might learn them and steal his job.

Besides designing the original chair and apparatus, Davis improved them substantially in the years following Kemmler's death, with the help of Harry L. Taylor of Corning. Davis perfected the electrodes and owned patents on them.

He traveled from prison to prison in pursuit of his killing trade. On these occasions, he usually wore a black felt hat and a Prince Albert coat. Before an execution, he used to test the electrodes on a chunk of beef. He attached sponges to the beef, inserted the wires in the sponges, and turned on the current. As soon as the beef began to sizzle, he knew the apparatus was in working order.

Eventually, New York corrections officials became concerned about how they would carry out electrocutions if Davis should become ill or die. They asked him to train assistants who could take his place and to transfer his patents. His suspicions inflamed, he refused to do either. After prolonged negotiations, however, he trained two men and sold his patents to the state for $10,000.

Because of the nature of his work, Davis (like all those who followed him) received many threats against his life. He went to enormous lengths to avoid being recognized, even forbidding acquaintances to address him by name in public places. When he traveled to a prison where he was scheduled to perform an execution, he often took a time-consuming roundabout route to stay out of the way of possible troublemakers.

Davis kept bees as a hobby. A friendly, compassionate man, he was opposed to capital punishment. He told many stories about his trade, not all of them grim. One of his favorites concerned a murderer who, shortly before being put to death, asked if he could meet his executioner. It was an unusual request and Davis, curious, came to the man's cell.

"Well, how do I strike you?" he asked the convict.

The answer didn't take Davis entirely by surprise. "Man, you're the ugliest sonovabitch I ever seen."

Thirty minutes later, the man was brought into the death chamber. Looking at Davis, who was adjusting the head electrode, he said: "I still think you're the ugliest sonovabitch I ever seen."

Davis had the unenviable privilege, on March 20, 1899, of putting to death the first woman sentenced to the electric chair, Martha Garretson Place.

Martha Garretson had married William W. Place, a widower of Brooklyn, New York, after working as his housekeeper. By his first wife, Place had a child, Ida, to whom he was exceptionally devoted, and the second Mrs. Place grew insanely jealous of her. On February 7, 1898, she murdered the seventeen-year-old girl. First she threw acid in her eyes, then she hacked her with an axe, and finally she smothered her with pillows. Place came home later and his wife attacked him with the axe, fracturing his skull. The injured man managed to stagger out of the house and summon help. When the police arrived, they found Mrs. Place unconscious after attempting to take her life with gas.

At her trial, the murderess pleaded innocent by reason of insanity.

Alienists (physicians who treated mental diseases) questioned her and found her sane, however, and she was sentenced to die in the electric chair at Sing Sing.

A plea for clemency was made to Governor Theodore Roosevelt. Electrocuting a woman was a sensitive matter, and the governor decided to have Mrs. Place reexamined by physicians. Again they determined she was sane at the time of the murder and was still sane. Next, Roosevelt counseled with the judges who presided at her trial and appeals. All declared so depraved a person had to be put to death. The governor now felt obliged to order the "solemn and painful act of justice" to be done. But every effort, he emphasized, must be made to avoid sensationalism, and Mrs. Place was to be attended at her execution by members of her own sex.

The condemned woman was struck dumb by the governor's decision. So confident had she been she would be given a new trial, she'd even made herself a black gown to wear in court. Now she decided it would do just as well for her execution, but in her few remaining days her weight fell off so rapidly that she had to take a tuck in the waist. Reading the Bible with the warden's wife and with her spiritual adviser afforded her some consolation. She slept very little on the night before her execution, and that in her black gown.

During her trial, the press had described Mrs. Place as "the stone woman." Although she didn't wail or collapse on that last day, she was leaning heavily on the warden's arm as she entered the execution chamber, a small Bible clutched in her hand. "God help me!" she was heard to say as she sat down in the chair.

Davis, like many other executioners, had misgivings about putting a woman to death. For every person about to be electrocuted, the final haircut, to assure good contact with the head electrode, is a stark, agonizing reminder of what lies just ahead. It was a sign of Davis's delicacy of feeling that he had advised Mrs. Place's hair shouldn't be clipped until she was seated in the chair. Fortunately, she turned out to be more self-possessed than he'd expected. She was, he said later, "one of the coolest people I've ever executed."

The prison physician and a female assistant buckled Mrs. Place in the chair. She still clutched the little Bible in her hand. Her head was erect, her eyes were closed, her lips moved in prayer as the mask was strapped over her face.

Matrons pressed close in front of Mrs. Place, attempting to shield her from the witnesses' eyes. These, however, kept wandering from her to the woman physician in attendance at the governor's request. Dressed in a gray gown and a huge hat with pronounced crimson trimmings, she presented a striking figure.

The shock that flung Mrs. Place into eternity was 1,760 volts. As it struck her, her thin lips tightened and the little Bible slipped partly from her hand. Four seconds later, Davis cut the pressure to 200 volts and held it there for most of a minute. Then he gave her a third shock. From the warden's point of view, the execution was "entirely success-ful." The electrodes, he said, "scarcely" left a mark on her body.

So died Martha Garretson Place, the first woman in the electric chair. It would be ten years before another would find herself in one. That was Mrs. Mary H. Farmer, executed at Auburn after she had murdered another woman for her property.

On August 12, 1912, close to the end of his career, Davis executed the largest number of men put to death in a single day in the chair at Sing Sing—seven, one after another. Five of them, Italian immigrants, were executed for a single crime, the murder of Mrs. Mary Hall. It was an odd fact that not one of these men had wielded the death weapon, but by a quirk of the law all shared in the guilt.

Mrs. Hall had been stabbed to death during the commission of a robbery. Four of the condemned men had been involved in that robbery, but not one of them had even set eyes on the woman. The fifth, named Giusto, had held Mrs. Hall while the sixth, Zanz, plunged the knife into her. Zanz had been executed a month before his confed-erates.

Four of the five Italians couldn't understand why they had to die, since they hadn't taken part in the murder. They shrieked and screamed nightmarishly throughout the executions, insisting they were innocent, until the last of them was silenced by death. Later, their bodies were taken by relatives to Brooklyn, where they were exhibited for a fee (to raise funds for their funerals) until health officials inter-vened.

After Davis resigned in 1914, he directed a cider mill until his death in 1923. His successor was John Hurlbert, an electrician at Auburn Prison. Hurlbert, a short, stocky man and a native of Auburn, had assisted Davis in executions and been trained to succeed him.

As state executioner, Hurlbert was paid $50 for each person he put to death until 1919, when the fee was raised to $150. Besides New

York, he performed executions in Massachusetts, Kansas and other states. In 1925, it was reported he earned $2,100 for the execution of fourteen persons.

Hurlbert was credited with 140 executions. The public was intensely curious about him, and hundreds of photographers tried to take his picture, but not one ever succeeded. Considered somewhat withdrawn and unsociable by those who knew him in the prisons, he was dubbed by the newspapers "the man who walks alone."

In 1922, when Hurlbert was scheduled to execute a woman, the rumor spread that he had scruples of conscience against doing the job. A reporter managed to corner him and ask if there was any truth to the story. He denied it. Executing a woman, he said, was the same to him as executing a man. Before the reporter could ask him another question, Hurlbert had fled.

During his thirteen years as executioner, Hurlbert grew increasingly depressed and subject to outbursts of violent temper. Like Davis, he carried his own electrodes with him. Once, when he was getting the chair ready for an execution, he was told the warden wanted to use the prison electrodes in place of his own. Hurlbert replied that he intended to use his own and no others. Informed he had to obey the warden's orders, he burst into a rage and flung the prison electrodes as far as he could. That time at least he had his own way.

On another occasion, two men were scheduled to be put to death at Sing Sing. During his preparations, Hurlbert fainted. The prison physician, who was barely able to detect a pulse, diagnosed the condition as a nervous collapse. With the aid of stimulants, he succeeded in bringing Hurlbert around and the executions were carried out, albeit a half-hour late. The physician tried to persuade him to give up his stressful sideline but Hurlbert insisted he couldn't manage without the money it brought.

Some time afterward, in 1926, on the eve of another double execution at Sing Sing, Hurlbert abruptly resigned. The press reported that unless another executioner could be found quickly, Warden Lewis E. Lawes himself would have to pull the switch. It was a typical example of journalistic melodrama, since in modern times any report of an opening for the job of executioner has brought a flood of applications, as happened in this case.

Three years later, Hurlbert was found dead with two bullet wounds, in the basement of his Auburn home. Stories circulated that he'd been shot by a vengeful relative or friend of one of the many convicts he'd put to death. However, a .38 caliber revolver lying beside him was identified as one he'd carried when he was at work in Auburn Prison. The newspapers next suggested he'd been driven to suicide by horrifying memories of convicts he'd executed. This tale couldn't stand up against the reality that Hurlbert had been severely despondent over the recent death of his wife and his own continued ill health.

The man who took Hurlbert's place as New York's new executioner was Robert Greene Elliott. Born in rural New York in 1874, Elliott came of age with electricity. As a boy, he dreamed of being an electrician, and when he read of Kemmler's execution, he wondered how it might feel to throw the switch at an electrocution. Studying electricity at school, he eventually went to work as an electrician for the state at Clinton Prison in Dannemora. There he became acquainted with Davis, who trained him to assist in executions.

Later, Elliott left the state's employ and went into business as an electrical contractor. When Hurlbert resigned in 1926, Elliott's application was one of hundreds submitted to Warden Lawes. His experience as Davis's assistant helped him win the job.

Although for most of a year Elliott's identity as New York State's official executioner was kept from the public, before long the slight man with the white hair and the deeply lined face was to become the best known of American executioners. In time, he numbered five more states among his clients—New Jersey, Massachusetts, Pennsylvania, Vermont and Connecticut.

The peak period of executions in the United States came in the 1920s and 1930s. Elliott was often called upon to execute three or four men in succession. His busiest day came in 1927, when he put six men to death, three in New York and three in Massachusetts. Executing six seemed to affect him no more than executing one. His chief concern in group executions, he said, was to have enough electrodes on hand as well as the facilities to cool them off for prompt reuse.

In his thirteen years as official executioner, Elliott electrocuted 387 people, five of them women. At $150 a head, during his entire career he earned some $57,600—a handsome supplement to the income from his contracting business.

Elliott was a witness to the conclusion of some of the most celebrated criminal cases of the era. Among the convicts to whom he gave their quietus, none were better known than two who died in the chair of Boston's Charlestown prison a few minutes past midnight on August

23, 1927. Their trial and death probably caused a greater furor around the world than any others in the twentieth century. Books debating their guilt or innocence are still being written.

Bartolomeo Vanzetti was a fish peddler in Plymouth, Massachusetts. His friend Nicola Sacco was a shoe-factory worker in nearby Stoughton. Like many other Italian immigrants of the day, they were active in the anarchist movement.

In 1920, the two were picked up by the police on suspicion. They'd been seen with men who had a car resembling one used in a payroll robbery in South Braintree, Massachusetts, the previous April. In that crime, a paymaster and his guard had been shot to death and $15,000 stolen. Sacco and Vanzetti were charged with murder and robbery—and Vanzetti was additionally charged with an attempted robbery the previous year.

None of the stolen money was ever found. Identifications of the two suspects by witnesses of the crimes were highly contradictory. But the United States was in the grip of anti-Red, antiforeign hysteria. Sacco and Vanzetti were convicted and sentenced to die in the chair.

The pair languished in prison for years while their lawyers tried one appeal after another to save them. Sympathy for the condemned men spread around the globe and money poured in to support their defense. Labor organizations, liberal and radical groups, heads of foreign governments, prominent figures like Albert Einstein, H. G. Wells, Alfred Dreyfus and Felix Frankfurter questioned the fairness of the trial the two had received and called for a new one. Giant demonstrations and general strikes shook one country after another.

In 1925, Celestino Madeiros, a thug and a murderer under sentence of death, entered the case. Madeiros alleged he'd been involved in the South Braintree robbery and neither Sacco nor Vanzetti had any part in it. The court threw out his confession.

The storm of protest continued to mount. Finally, Governor Fuller of Massachusetts appointed a committee headed by President Lowell of Harvard University to investigate the case. On August 3, 1927, Fuller announced his committee had found no error in judicial procedure that would justify retrying the condemned men. They were to be executed promptly.

Fearful that violence would erupt on the night of the executions, the authorities took extraordinary precautions. Eight hundred policemen, many armed with rifles, were deployed around the prison. Troopers sat on their horses, canisters of tear gas ready. Firemen had hooked up hoses to water lines to fight off unruly mobs. People living within half a mile of the prison had been warned to stay indoors.

Elliott arrived at the prison hours early to avoid the expected crowds. He checked the current. Charlestown Prison had its own generator now, installed only recently when the Boston Edison Company had declined to provide power for executions. The switchboard was located behind a screen in back of the electric chair. Behind another screen three litters stood ready.

Madeiros, who'd tried to save the two men, was slated to die with them. He was brought in first. He'd taken full advantage of the condemned man's right to a final meal of his choice. His last words were apologetic: "I feel seeck. I eat too much." He walked slowly to the chair between his guards as if in a trance, shrugged, and sat down. He said nothing more. An epileptic who'd had a wretched childhood and a brief, violent career of crime, he docilely allowed himself to be strapped in. A few minutes later, he was lifted out of the chair dead. The nauseating smell of singed hair filled the chamber. He was twenty-five years old.

Sacco was next. He'd fasted for most of a month and he looked frail and weak but he walked to the chair unassisted. His eyes flashed as he was strapped in.

"Long live anarchy!" he shouted in Italian. And then, in broken English, "Farewell, my wife and child and all my friends." Suddenly, he seemed to take notice of the seven witnesses. "Good evening, gentlemen," he said politely. By now the electrodes were in place. "Farewell, *mia madre!*" he cried.

Somehow the death mask couldn't be found. A guard went off in frantic search of it. He found it behind the screen shielding the litters, snagged on Madeiros's clothing. Hurriedly he carried the mask back and it was fixed over Sacco's face.

Water and salt are basic electrical conductors and the little Italian had lost a good deal of both during his prolonged fast. To compensate, Elliott boosted the charge.

Eight minutes after Sacco had entered the room, he was a dead man. He was thirty-six years old. Six of those years he'd languished in prison waiting for this moment. It had been one of the longest stays on death row up to that time.

Six years of imprisonment hadn't cracked the courage of Sacco's fellow prisoner, Vanzetti, who entered the chamber a minute later. Of the pair, the scholarly, poetic fish peddler was the more controlled. He shook hands with Warden Hendry. "I want to thank you for everything you've done for me, Warden."

Hendry, deeply affected, was unable to reply.

Vanzetti seated himself in the chair. He addressed the small group in the chamber. "I wish to tell you I'm innocent. I never committed any crime . . . but sometimes some sin. I thank you for everything you've done for me. I'm innocent of all crime—not only of this one but of all. I'm an innocent man."

The mask had been fastened over his face. "I wish to forgive some people for what they are now doing to me." He spoke no more.

Six minutes after Vanzetti had entered the room, he was pronounced dead. He was thirty-nine years old.

A short while after, Elliott managed to slip from the prison unnoticed, although large numbers of excited people were still standing in the street. When the bodies were removed to a funeral home for cremation, thousands of sympathizers marched with the hearses. News of the executions was flashed around the world, setting off riots in major cities in the United States and foreign countries and attacks on American embassies.

The tragedy of Sacco and Vanzetti has been chronicled in paintings, film, drama, fiction, many books. Nothing left a deeper imprint on its time, however, than the words uttered by Vanzetti in his last speech to the court which condemned him and Nicola Sacco to the electric chair:

> If it had not been for these thing I might have live out my life talking at street corners to scorning men. I might have die, unmarked, unknown, a failure. Now we are not a failure. This is our career and our triumph. Never in our full life could we hope to do such work for tolerance, for justice, for man's understanding of man, as now we do by accident. Our words, our lives, our pains—nothing! The taking of our lives—lives of a good shoemaker and a poor fish peddler—all! That last moment belongs to us—that agony is our triumph.[2]

Ruth Snyder was the first and the most notorious of the five women Elliott put to death. She, with her lover Henry Judd Gray, had murdered her husband in Queens, New York, on March 20, 1927, for $95,000 in insurance she'd taken out on his life without his knowledge.

As a murderess, Mrs. Snyder was notable more for her persistence than her ability. She had already made seven attempts to kill her husband by herself, trying a variety of lethal substances: gas, carbon monoxide, narcotics (substituted for medicine), bichloride of mercury. Several of these she tried twice. Snyder, as durable as he was unobservant, survived each one.

Finally, Mrs. Snyder connived with Gray, a corset salesman, to murder her husband in a pretended burglary. Snyder was asleep in bed when she and Gray set upon him. He was clubbed and chloroformed and, when he still clung to life, strangled with picture wire. The pair hid some valuable objects to support the burglary story, then Gray tied up Mrs. Snyder and ran away.

When the police were called, they searched the Snyder home and quickly found the objects reported stolen. Their suspicions aroused, they questioned Mrs. Snyder, who obliged them by confessing and implicating her lover.

The three-week trial of Mrs. Snyder and Gray, with its morbidly appealing tale of blood and lust, became a national sensation. As an added attraction, the pair turned on each other, Mrs. Snyder declaring Gray had done the killing, and Gray that she had. The press and public sympathized strongly with Gray, viewing him as the obliging tool of the strong-willed Mrs. Snyder. She was described as "the marble woman," Gray as "the putty man." Both were found guilty and sentenced to die at Sing Sing. (After 1916, all executions in New York State were held there.)

The spotlight now turned on the executioner, Elliott, who became the target of hundreds of threatening letters, much more concerned with Ruth Snyder's fate than Gray's. When a rumor spread that Elliott might refuse to put a woman to death, many people offered to fill in for him, including one woman who wrote, "I could execute Ruth Snyder with a good heart and think I had done a good deed." (She suggested the state should have a female executioner for women.) Fifteen hundred people wrote Warden Lawes asking if they could be witnesses at the execution.

The pair were to die on the night of January 12, 1928. Ruth Snyder went to the chair first. (In a group execution, the person regarded as the most likely to break down is generally put to death first; when the group includes a woman, she is usually, though not always, accorded this favor.) Dressed in a khaki smock over a black skirt, she was accompanied by two tearful matrons and the Catholic chaplain. When she saw the chair, she almost collapsed. Sobbing loudly, she was led to it quickly and seated. The chaplain stood in front of her praying, holding a crucifix.

"Father, forgive them for they know not what they do," she moaned as she was buckled in.

Since it was to be a double execution, Elliott had brought his own electrodes. For the headpiece, he'd cut down a standard football helmet and lined it with sponge. He had advised the warden to spare Ruth Snyder the agony of the pre-execution haircut. Now he separated her thinning, graying hair at the back of the head to assure good contact. An attendant applied the leg electrode, for which her black cotton stocking had been rolled down in advance.

The silver-gilt radiators in the overheated room rattled and whined. The twenty-four witnesses sat motionless on the benches. Physicians and attendants lined the walls. The two matrons, weeping, withdrew.

The death mask covered Rush Snyder's tear-stained face. "Jesus, forgive me, for I have sinned." Her voice was shaken by sobs.

Elliott, at the instrument panel in his cubicle, threw the switch. The current crackled. Warden Lawes stood toward the back of the chamber, his eyes fastened on the floor. He was one of the country's most outspoken and tireless opponents of capital punishment. His job required him to be present, but he never watched.

After two minutes Elliott turned off the current. Three physicians pronounced the woman dead and her body was wheeled into the autopsy room.

In a few minutes, Gray, walking briskly, entered the chamber between two guards. Behind him came the Protestant chaplain. Clad in gray trousers and a white shirt open at the neck and wearing felt slippers, Gray stepped forward, repeating the Beatitudes in a strong voice after the chaplain.

The bright glare in the death chamber and the rows of witnesses seemed to take the condemned man by surprise. His pale face flushed. Then, hearing the chaplain's voice at his shoulder, he took courage. "Blessed are the pure of heart," he intoned after him, sitting down in the chair. His voice was loud and unnatural.

Strapped in the chair, Gray saw the attendant was having difficulty fitting on the black leather mask and he twisted his neck to make the job simpler. It was, witnesses felt, another example of the obligingness that had made him such an easy tool for the murderous Ruth Snyder. Through the death mask Gray recited the Lord's Prayer. The current surged through him for three minutes before the signal came to turn it off.

The following day New Yorkers looked with horror or fascination or both at the photograph that filled the entire front page of the New York *Daily News*. It showed Ruth Snyder in the electric chair with the deadly current flowing through her. Cameras were forbidden in the execution chamber, but a clever photographer had smuggled one in, a miniature, strapped to his ankle and concealed by his trouser leg. Seated in the front row with his legs crossed, he'd raised his trouser cuff and pressed a plunger in his pocket, snapping the picture.

A ruse like that could work only once. From that day forward, all witnesses of executions at Sing Sing were searched with elaborate care.

One person that publication of the picture didn't offend was executioner Elliott. To him it seemed that if enough such photographs were published, they might produce a groundswell of public protest that could lead to the abolition of capital punishment.

On April 3, 1936, at the state prison in Trenton, New Jersey, Elliott electrocuted Bruno Richard Hauptmann. Hauptmann's crime, the most sensational since the Gray-Snyder case, even outdid that one in the drama of his arrest, his trial, and his hairbreadth reprieves. Interest in Hauptmann's fate ran so high that one newspaper offered the executioner $10,000 if he would provide it with exclusive information about the criminal's death.

The shocking crime that cost Hauptmann his life was the kidnapping and killing of the infant son of Colonel Charles Augustus Lindbergh. Lindbergh had become an international hero in 1927 when he made a daring flight across the Atlantic to France in a little single-engine airplane. In March 1932, people everywhere were dismayed to learn that the Lindbergh baby had been stolen from his crib in his parents' Hopewell, New Jersey, home. Left behind on the windowsill of the child's second-story room was a ransom note demanding $50,000 ransom. Misspellings suggested the kidnapper was a German. On the grounds was found a broken handmade ladder, abandoned by the kidnapper in his flight.

After secret meetings with the kidnapper late at night in cemeteries the ransom money was turned over to him. But the promised happy conclusion didn't follow; Charles Jr. wasn't restored to his anxious parents. Instead, a month later someone stumbled on a shallow grave containing the baby's mangled body near his home.

Over the next few years, some of the ransom banknotes—the numbers had been recorded—began to turn up. Police traced one of the bills to Hauptmann. He insisted he'd had nothing to do with the crime, but part of the ransom money was found in his garage.

Hauptmann, who'd entered the United States illegally, had a criminal record in Germany. He was a carpenter by trade, and wood in the abandoned handmade ladder matched wood in his home. The evidence against him was largely circumstantial but it was abundant and far more persuasive than his clumsy attempts to explain it away. He was tried in 1935 and, protesting his innocence, sentenced to death for the murder of the child, who apparently had died after being dropped when the ladder broke during the kidnapper's escape.

Several times, Hauptmann's execution was put off at the last minute on the plea that sensational new evidence had been discovered. It hadn't. The next appeal was rejected and the execution was scheduled for 8:00 P.M. on April 13, 1936.

That night, at the Trenton State Prison, witnesses were admitted to the death chamber only after attendants had searched them repeatedly for weapons and cameras. To prevent any repetition of the Ruth Snyder photograph incident a length of canvas three feet high was strung across the room between the witnesses and the electric chair.

Because of the possibility of an eleventh-hour reprieve the execution was delayed forty minutes. At 8:40, when Hauptmann, head cropped close, was brought in, accompanied by two ministers reading from the Scriptures in German, his face was the color of the whitewashed wall. The delay had convinced him he would be spared again; apparently he still couldn't believe what was happening.

A ghost of a smile seemed to flicker across his face as he was buckled in the chair. In an instant, the black mask hid his features. Elliott placed the head electrode on him and retired to his post at the control wheel ten feet behind the chair.

At 8:44 P.M., the executioner turned the wheel. Hauptmann's hands, gripping the arms of the chair, turned red. Three and one-half minutes after he had sat down in the chair he was dead.

Later, the ministers read a last statement made by Hauptmann. In it he once more insisted he was completely innocent. If, however, his death served the purpose of abolishing capital punishment, he said, he would not have died in vain. "I am at peace with God," he concluded.[3]

Whenever Elliott was scheduled to execute a well-known criminal, every mail was sure to bring threats against him and his family. At these times, his home had a police guard. Presumably the letters were written by crackpots, for none of the threats ever materialized.

When real danger finally came, it came without warning. In 1928, in the middle of the night, he was awakened by a terrifying explosion. A bomb had gone off, damaging a substantial part of his home. Fortunately no one was injured. For a long time afterward, police manned a special booth in the house. Elliott was never troubled again.

If the executioner had his enemies, he had his admirers, too. He often received letters that praised him for his public services or asked for his autograph. If the radio or newspapers carried a report that he was ill, scores of "get well" cards came to him in the next mail.

A methodical, conscientious man, Elliott kept a detailed record of every person he executed, with the circumstances of his crime and of his death. He was convinced that capital punishment was futile as a deterrent. He often expressed his sympathy for those he executed—and much more strongly for their families. One of his greatest fears was that he might have to sit on a jury that brought in a verdict of guilty in a capital crime.

As for his own role as an executioner, Elliott insisted he was merely a technician, a servant of the people. He denied he killed those he put to death. "You have done it through the laws you've passed," he said. "Judges and juries, people who represented you, have done it. I have carried out your orders."

A churchgoer, the executioner was devoted to his family and his flower garden. He died in 1939. During his final illness, his place was taken by a substitute known only as "Mr. X." Mr. X wasn't the expert Elliott had been. When he executed two young men in Boston for a holdup slaying, it took him nearly forty minutes and he had to give one of them five separate shocks. He was severely criticized.

Warden Lawes of Sing Sing was deluged with applications from people who wanted to become New York's next executioner. Close to twenty percent of them were women. The man chosen was Joseph Francel of Cairo, New York. Francel, a native of Minnesota, had been severely gassed in World War I. Appointed executioner in 1939, he was to take the lives of some 134 men and three women in Sing Sing and more than one hundred in the prisons of other states. For each person he put to death he was paid the same fee as Elliott, $150. The best-known prisoners he executed were Julius and Ethel Rosenberg.

On June 19, 1953, the United States put to death at Sing Sing Julius and Ethel Rosenberg.[4] They were the only Americans ever executed in peacetime for espionage in this country.

The crime for which the Rosenbergs died was also a first. The atomic bomb had been invented only in the previous decade, and the couple were found guilty of transmitting top-secret information about it to the Russians. Since the trial and execution of Sacco and Vanzetti, no case had aroused so much controversy.

Until the moment the Rosenbergs sat down in the electric chair, their lawyers kept working desperately to save them. On that last day, the attorneys presented their fifth appeal to the Supreme Court. It was turned down. Less than an hour later, President Dwight D. Eisenhower for the second time that week refused to grant the pair executive clemency. In announcing his decision, he declared they had immeasurably increased the chances of atomic war.

Few people could have seemed less like dangerous atomic spies than the doomed couple. Julius Rosenberg was an earnest-looking, hardworking electrical engineer; his wife, Ethel, was a plump little New York housewife devoted to her children.

In 1944, during World War II, Rosenberg was a secret member of the Communist underground. He was disgruntled that the United States wasn't sharing the atomic bomb with its ally, the USSR. Learning that Ethel's brother, David Greenglass, a machinist in the Army, was working on the atomic bomb project in Los Alamos, New Mexico, the couple persuaded him to supply drawings and technical data about the project, and Ethel typed up the information. Then Rosenberg passed the material on to Russian agents. He continued this and other illegal work after the war ended.

In 1950, the government moved to crack down on the spy ring. Rosenberg was just getting ready to leave the country when he was arrested. A month later, his wife was taken into custody. The children were placed in the care of friends.

In the trial that followed, the machinist Greenglass was a major government witness. The Rosenbergs denied all the charges, maintaining they knew nothing about the atomic bomb. They insisted they were loyal American citizens and denied being members of the Communist party.

In March 1951, the Rosenbergs were found guilty and were sentenced to death. For more than two years, their lawyers fought the convictions through the courts. Around the globe, prominent people spoke out for the condemned, contending the sentence was too severe. (Their accomplice, Greenglass, received only a fifteen-year prison sentence.)

Early in the afternoon of their execution day, June 19, 1953, Julius and Ethel Rosenberg heard that the Supreme Court and President Eisenhower had turned down their latest appeals. With their end at hand, the warden gave them permission to spend their little remaining time together. Louis Nizer, in his book *The Implosion Conspiracy*, has described how they spent it.

A mesh screen was set up in front of her cell and she was permitted to leave the cell and sit on a chair facing Julius on the other side of the screen. The matrons and guards were instructed to stand back far enough so that they could converse privately.

At 7:20 P.M., the guard moved up behind Julius and put his hand on his shoulder. He knew that he had to be prepared for his death at eight. He put two fingers to his lips and pressed them toward her on the mesh screen. She did the same. They pressed so hard that the tips of their fingers bled as they touched through the mesh. This was their good-bye kiss.

The couple were returned to their cells, where they were prepared for execution. Even if they'd had the appetite, there was no time for a last meal.

Earlier that day, the Rosenbergs had written a final letter to their two sons, Robert, six, and Michael, ten. It closed with these words:

We wish we might have had the tremendous joy and gratification of living our lives out with you. Your Daddy, who is with me in these last momentous hours, sends his heart and all the love that is in it for his dearest boys. Always remember that we were innocent and could not wrong our conscience.

We press you close and kiss you with all our strength.

The two boys were staying with a friend of their parents. She had tried to keep knowledge of the impending execution from the children. But Michael, who'd visited his father and mother a few days earlier, had some inkling of what was happening. He was watching a game between the Detroit Tigers and the New York Yankees on television when it was interrupted with the announcement of the President's decision not to grant a reprieve.

"My mommy and daddy—that was their last chance," the boy said.

Later, there was a second interruption, announcing when the execution would take place.

"That's it, that's it," the boy sobbed. "Goodbye. Goodbye."

At 7:45 P.M.—fifteen minutes before the Rosenbergs were to go to the chair—their attorney made a final appeal. It was to the judge who'd sentenced them to death. The judge saw no reason to grant a reprieve.

But they still had one last chance. A week earlier, the Department of Justice had promised them a reprieve if they'd make a full confession of their part in the plot. Their answer had been the same as always: they were totally innocent, they had nothing to confess. Even as they were being made ready for execution, a federal marshal was keeping a telephone line in the prison open to Washington, D.C., just in case they changed their minds.

But they didn't change them.

Shortly after 8:00 P.M., Julius, contrary to the custom that the woman should go first, stepped into the glare of the bright lights in the execution chamber. Before him walked the chaplain, reciting, "The Lord is my shepherd, I shall not want." Witnesses noted he moved unsteadily as he approached the massive, dark-stained chair.

At 8:04, a heavy charge of electricity slammed into the condemned man and he was pronounced dead. His body was promptly placed on a gurney and removed.

Ethel, clad in a green dress with polka dots, now appeared, escorted by matrons. She stopped in front of the chair, shook hands with one of them, and kissed her on the cheek. The matron, breaking into sobs, rushed from the chamber. The other matron clasped Ethel's hand. The chaplain intoned a psalm.

Ethel was seated in the chair and the electrode was set on her head. At the touch of the cold metal, she seemed to draw back, then relaxed.

One of the witnesses said she looked very composed as the leather mask was lowered over her face.

At 8:11 P.M., the executioner, Francel, loosed the first blaze of electricity, then followed it with two more. Two doctors came up and placed their stethoscopes to Ethel's breast. They looked surprised. The woman's heart was still beating; it was too big. At a signal, Francel gave her two more shocks and she died.

Ethel Rosenberg thus became the second woman to be executed by federal authority. The first had been Mary E. Surratt, who died on the gallows in 1865. Surratt, implicated in the plot to assassinate Abraham Lincoln, also maintained her innocence to the end. Her story is told in a later chapter.

After the Rosenbergs' execution, many people argued their punishment was too severe.[5] It had been imposed, they said, in a climate of political hysteria resulting from the Cold War between the USSR and the United States. Another and more important Communist agent, it was pointed out, the British physicist Klaus Fuchs—he had helped develop the atomic bomb—had transmitted to the Russians information that was far more top secret. Tried in England, he'd received only a prison sentence, and after nine years had gone free.

A few months after the Rosenberg executions, Francel, aged fifty-seven, resigned. The papers said he was disturbed by threats against his life. It was also reported his resignation was due to dissatisfaction when the state refused to raise his fee. Certainly he had every reason to ask for an increase. Executions had been falling off year by year (in 1945 there wasn't a single execution in New York) and by 1953 they'd hit a twenty-three-year low nationally. Still, thirty-one men and one woman applied for the post he'd vacated.

Changes in the capital punishment law and its application continued to reduce the number of electrocutions. In 1965, New York abolished capital punishment except for the murder of police officers and prison guards. In 1971, the chair, with its electrical apparatus and old witnesses' pews, was moved from Sing Sing to the Green Haven Correctional Facility. Three men who had murdered police officers were sitting in the nine-by-five-foot cells there, waiting for the higher courts to decide their fate.

How many states have had statutes calling for capital punishment by electrocution? Only twenty-five, plus the District of Columbia. Until a few decades ago, a couple had electric chairs on trucks equipped with generators; the trucks would journey from county to county to put convicts to death. By 1989, the number of states using the electric chair had fallen to fourteen. In that year, Florida used it to settle accounts with one of the most sensational murderers of recent times.

"I don't want to die, I kid you not," the handsome serial killer said. Until lately, he had been self-assured, manipulative, arrogant. But now the facade had cracked: he was in tears. "I deserve, certainly, the most extreme punishment society has."

That was Ted Bundy, speaking in Florida's state penitentiary, with his execution date, January 24, 1989, just days away. Condemned for the brutal murders of two women college students and a girl, he was suspected of killing many more young women.

Still he tried to stave off his execution. In exchange for a reprieve, he offered to reveal the facts about others he had slain. "For him to be negotiating for his life over the bodies of victims," said Florida's governor, Bob Martinez, "is despicable." On January 18, he turned Bundy's offer down.

Law officers came from Colorado, Idaho, Utah and Washington State to persuade the former law student to tell them about the unsolved murders of young women in their states. On January 20, a police detective who'd spent years tracking Bundy questioned him on death row.

Bundy, the detective would say later, had been "totally obsessed with murder twenty-four hours a day. He was constantly searching for victims, planning his next murder, visiting the dump sites [where he hid their bodies]. He didn't have time to go to law school or hold a job."

As the end edged nearer, Bundy confessed to sixteen murders. Law officers thought he'd committed as many as fifty.

On January 23, the United States Supreme Court turned down three emergency petitions for a delay and Ted Bundy, age forty-two, realized that, after fighting off execution for a decade, what remained of his life could be measured in hours.

No one could have seemed less like a modern Jack the Ripper than Theodore Robert Bundy. Born in 1946 and reared in Tacoma, Washington, he was athletic, intelligent, attractive to women. He'd been a Boy Scout, studied Chinese, psychology, and law, and been active in Republican politics in Seattle, where he drew the favorable attention of the governor. Appointed assistant director of the Seattle Crime Prevention Advisory Committee, he wrote a pamphlet for women about rape prevention and was a trusted counselor in the city's Crisis Clinic.

Yet at the same time, this promising young man (people said he looked like "the boy next door") was committing a multitude of appalling crimes. He was shoplifting, purloining, burglarizing left and right, but that was the least of it. Driven by an irresistible urge, coolly and with premeditation he was raping and murdering one young woman after another, mutilating their bodies, and dumping them in remote places. For years he succeeded in eluding the police—"the most competent serial killer in the country," a federal judge called him; "a diabolical genius."[6]

For his victims, Bundy chose young women who were total strangers. He would approach them on a college campus, on the street, in a public place. He used a variety of ruses to get them to go off with him. He might flash a police badge and ask them to help him identify a car. Or he might appear with a crutch and a fake cast on his leg and pretend he needed help to carry his books to his VW. Or he might have his arm in a sling. "Excuse me," he'd say. "Could you help me put my sailboat on my car? I've got this broken arm." It was hard to refuse a policeman or a good-looking young man in need of assistance.

Picked up on suspicion in Utah in 1975, Bundy was convicted of kidnapping a young woman. In 1977, he was extradited to Aspen, Colorado, to face a charge of murdering a vacationing nurse. In the midst of his trial he vanished. (A woman later reported seeing someone jump from a second-story window of the courthouse.)

Six days later, Bundy was recaptured. Back in jail, he asked policemen in which state a murderer was most likely to be executed. Their answer was Florida. Incredibly, he escaped again.

When he reappeared it was in Florida.

In January 1978, at Florida State University in Tallahassee, somebody went on a murder rampage, smashing the skulls of two co-eds at the Chi Omega sorority house and severely beating three others. In February, Bundy was arrested.

More than two hundred reporters attended Bundy's trial in Miami in 1979, and the proceedings were televised. He denied all guilt. Brash and articulate, he conducted his own defense. One gruesome piece of evidence he couldn't talk away: his teeth marks in the buttock of one of the dead girls. Convicted of murder, assault and burglary, he received two death sentences.

In 1980, Bundy was on trial again, this time for the killing of a twelve-year-old Lake City girl in 1978. An unusual event interrupted the proceedings. In open court Bundy, taking advantage of a Florida law, married Carole Ann Boone, a longtime friend. Just hours later, he was convicted.

During the condemned man's long fight to escape from death row, the state spent six million dollars to keep him there. Interest in the charismatic killer continued at high pitch. Five books were written about him; millions saw him portrayed in a TV miniseries.

In the early morning of January 24, 1989, Bundy's struggle to save his life came to an abrupt stop.

Outside Raiford State Prison in Starke, Florida, the execution provided an occasion for high revel. A crowd of about three hundred, many of them students from the University of Florida close by, had gathered to celebrate. Cars were decorated with slogans like THANK GOD IT'S FRYDAY. People guzzled beer, waved sparklers, sang, and held up signs and banners saying ROAST IN PEACE; BURN, BUNDY, BURN; BUCKLE UP, BUNDY, IT'S THE LAW; and THIS BUZZ IS FOR YOU. One placard, in an allusion to the sorority of the two murdered co-eds, read: CHI-O, CHI-O, IT'S OFF TO HELL I GO! A hawker was peddling electric-chair pins. One young woman sported an electrocution head-piece made of tinfoil. A sophomore wore a T-shirt with a recipe for "fried Bundy."

Demonstrations by opponents of capital punishment, like those by its supporters, have become a regular feature at executions.[7] This night, however, the opponents were few in number, perhaps thirty, and unusually subdued.

The sky began to lighten. Inside the prison, a switch was thrown and for one minute two thousand volts of electricity coursed through the body of the man strapped in the electric chair. At 7:16 A.M., he was pronounced dead.[8]

A prison official relayed the information to the crowd outside. They lit firecrackers, cheered, jeered and whistled. After a while, a white hearse appeared and drove out of the prison yard. The crowd cheered again.

A while back we saw that physicians have declared electrocution produces death instantly and painlessly. It should be pointed out, however, that they've never offered any absolute proof their assertion is correct. That, in the final analysis, could only come from someone who has died in the chair.

One convict, about to be executed, promised Robert Elliott that he would wiggle his fingers if he felt any pain after the current was turned on. He died without stirring. Elliott found in that a confirmation of his belief that

the first terrific shock of 2,000 volts shatters the person's nervous system instantaneously and beyond recall, and paralyzes the brain before the nerves can register any pain. Medical experts declare that unconsciousness is produced in less than one two-hundred-fortieth of a second. This, then, is as humane as ordered death can be.

At the same time, Elliott seemed to contradict himself by recommending a change in the execution procedure that would make death "more instant." His suggestion was to place one of the two electrodes over the heart so the action of that organ would be arrested the moment the current struck the body. His recommendation was never taken up.

Dr. Amos O. Squire, Sing Sing physician who gave the signal for the deaths of 138 convicts, likened the sensation of receiving 2,000 volts of electricity in the body to getting a terrible blow on the head. "The current entering the body at the top of the head travels to the brain faster than the nerves can carry sensation . . . paralyzes the brain before it can feel anything. So it may be said that death by electrocution is painless."

How painless can a terrible blow on top of the head be?

Nicola Tesla, pioneer in the field of high-tension electricity and designer of the great power system of Niagara Falls, suggested an answer back in 1929. He pointed out the brain has four parts. "The current may touch only one of these parts; so that the individual retains consciousness and a keen sense of agony. For the sufferer, time stands still; and this excruciating torture seems to last for an eternity."

L. G. V. Rota, a noted French electrical scientist, shared Tesla's doubts about the method. "I do not believe that anyone killed by electrocution dies instantly . . . even though the point of contact of the electrode with the body shows distinct burns," he told a reporter for the *London Daily Mail* in 1928. "The condemned person may be alive and even conscious for several minutes without it being possible for a doctor to say whether the victim is dead or not. . . . This method of execution is a form of torture.''

These comments apply, of course, to ''normal'' executions. But what of the botched and bungled ones, where the equipment is defective or the executioner inexperienced? We looked at some of these earlier and the picture was not a pretty one.

Although the introduction of execution by electricity had been hailed as a great humanitarian advance, there were many who, like Tesla and Rota, weren't convinced it brought death on the instant and without suffering. Foreign countries, except for a few like the Philippines and Nationalist China, didn't adopt electrocution. Neither did half of the states—and a number of those that did gave it up later.

Some of the states, dissatisfied, kept looking for a better, more compassionate way.

In 1921, in Nevada, people thought they'd finally found it.

It was a kind of death that wouldn't strangle a man or stretch his neck like hanging—or sledgehammer him with electric charges and burn or roast him.

It was a kind of death that would steal upon the condemned man unawares and unannounced and take his life silently, painlessly, while he slept.

They called it lethal gas.

FOUR

The Big Sleep

Tom Quong Kee was an elderly Chinese laundryman who lived in a lonely cabin in Mina, Nevada, a small mining town. On the night of August 27, 1921, a loud pounding on his door awoke him from sleep.

Shuffling to the door, Kee opened up and recognized the boyish, familiar face of Hughie Sing, who had lived with him for two years. Standing behind Sing was another Chinese, a total stranger. He was holding a revolver aimed at the old man's chest.

The gun roared twice. Kee, shot through the heart, crumpled lifeless to the floor.

A couple of days later, the police picked up two suspects in Reno, some 175 miles away. They were Hughie Sing and Gee Jon, identified as a highbinder, or hatchetman, of the Hop Sing tong in San Francisco.

Both men protested they were innocent. In jail, however, Hughie, thinking he would be released if he told the truth, made a full confession.

Old Kee, it turned out, was a casualty in a tong war.[1] He had injured no one, but had been chosen for extermination simply because hostilities had broken out between his tong and the Hop Sings over a stolen slave girl, it was said. Gee Jon, sent from San Francisco to execute him, did not know the laundryman by sight and had brought young Hughie along to identify him.

51

A Reno attorney was hired (presumably by the Hop Sing tong) to defend the two Chinese. Hughie Sing promptly retracted his confession. But the evidence was too strong. Both men were found guilty of murder in the first degree and sentenced to death.

In the normal course of events, the convicted men would have enjoyed a speedy execution at the state penitentiary in Carson City and been forgotten in a week. But the normal course of events in Nevada's system of crime and punishment had just undergone a dramatic change, and the fate of at least one of the pair would be like that of no other condemned man before him.

From 1912 to 1921, Nevada granted its condemned criminals the privilege of choosing between two methods of execution, the gallows and the firing squad. Both methods were in the tradition of the brusque, crude justice of the Old West, and forward-looking Nevadans had leveled many complaints against them. Electrocution, to which more and more states were turning, was horrifying to behold. Wasn't there a method free of this objection—as well as of the frequently heard complaint that the condemned man suffered terrible pain?

There did seem to be one. It had been proposed by an Eastern toxicologist, Dr. Allen McLean Hamilton, and it was called lethal gas. According to authoritative studies, it would kill quickly and painlessly. Nevada's legislators were eager to demonstrate how advanced their state had become. In 1921, within a brief three weeks, a bill replacing the old methods with this new one was introduced, passed almost unanimously, and signed into law.

One reason lethal gas won out so readily was the unique, humane way it was to be applied. Death by lethal gas, according to the new law, would take the condemned prisoner unawares. He was to be lodged in a special airtight cell provided with two sets of valves. One set would admit the air he breathed. He was not even to be told the date set for his execution. Instead, one night, as he lay sleeping, the air valves would be shut and the other set of valves opened, admitting the gas. The prisoner would simply continue to slumber, until he awoke in a better world. It seemed a wonderful way to go.

The Eighth Amendment to the Constitution prohibits executions that are cruel and unusual. The new method, however, if not cruel, was certainly unusual. The attorney for Gee Jon and Hughie Sing insisted it was both, and over the next two years he conducted a lengthy series of legal maneuvers that took the case from the Nevada Supreme Court to the United States Supreme Court and back to the state again.

The execution of the first man in the electric chair, William Kemmler, on August 6, 1890, attracted almost as much attention in the press as a presidential election.

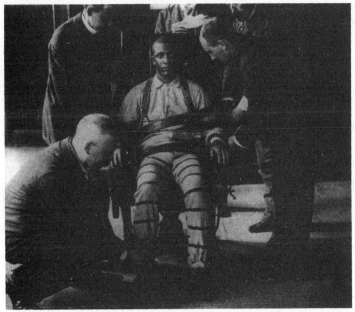

Prison officials strap an unidentified black man into the electric chair early in the century. (Library of Congress)

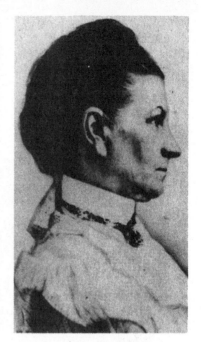

Martha Place

New York's electric chair at Green Haven. The state put 695 prisoners to death by electricity before executions ended in the 1960s. (New York Department of Correctional Services)

Martha Place leans on the warden's arm as she is led to her execution. She was the first woman to die in the electric chair.

Nicola Sacco and Bartolomeo Vanzetti, anarchists, were executed in 1927 for murder. Fifty years later their names were cleared in a special proclamation issued by the governor of Massachusetts.

Housewife gone wrong, murderess Ruth Snyder went to the electric chair with her lover, Judd Gray.

Bruno Richard Hauptmann, accused of the murder of Colonel Charles A. Lindbergh's baby son, being fingerprinted at the time of his arrest in 1934.

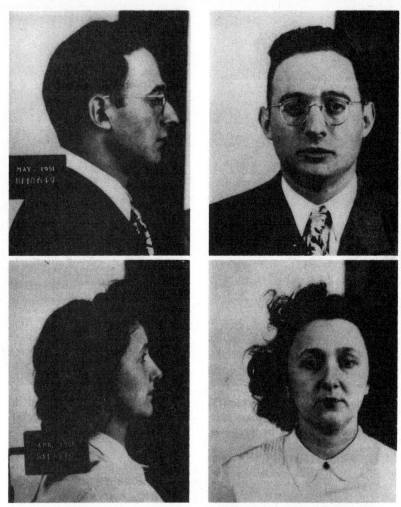

The atomic spies Julius and Ethel Rosenberg were put to death in 1953 at the height of cold-war tension between the United States and the Soviet Union. (Federal Bureau of Investigation)

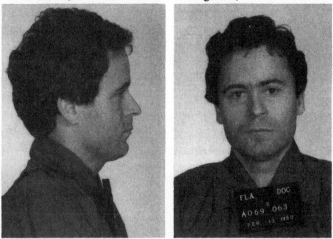

A serial killer, Ted Bundy specialized in the rape and murder of young women he had never seen before. (Florida Department of Corrections)

Gee Jon, executed in 1924 in Carson City, Nevada, was the first person put to death by lethal gas. (Nevada State Prison)

California's death chamber, in San Quentin prison, contains two chairs for a double execution. (California Department of Corrections)

Portrait of a man dying. Aaron Mitchell, condemned for the murder of a policeman, breathes lethal gas in San Quentin's death chamber. The drawing and notes were made by Howard Brodie, well-known sketch artist, who witnessed the execution.

May 2, 1960

Dear Dr. Ziferstein:

I have been busy most of last night and this early morning putting my affairs in order, writing last letters, discussing legal moves with the attorneys, etc. If the courts do not intervene, I do want to have this note ready so that you will know how deeply and truly grateful I am for your ceaseless efforts in my behalf. I am sure the fact my life finally was forfeited will spur your determination to see this ugly practice of capital punishment abolished. And that makes dying easier and gives my death an affirmative meaning it otherwise would be denied.

Kindly be sure and pass along my best regards to your family and those many, many compassionate people who have worked with you in trying to help me.

As always,
Caryl

Caryl Chessman, known as the. "red light bandit," fought off execution for twelve years. (Los Angeles Police Department)

Letter written by Chessman the day of his execution. (Dr. Isidore Ziferstein)

A cell on San Quentin's death row.

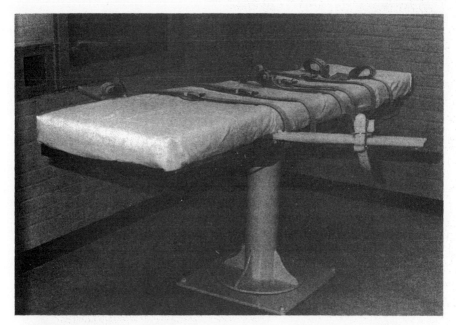

The death gurney in Huntsville prison, Texas. The two-way mirror at left enables the executioner to watch. The lethal tubes run out of the small square opening next to it. (All Texas photographs, Texas Department of Corrections)

Huntsville's holding cells, where condemned prisoners are made ready for execution.

Charlie Brooks, executed in 1982, was the first to die by lethal injection.

James D. Autry, who murdered a store clerk for a six-pack of beer, died on the gurney in 1984.

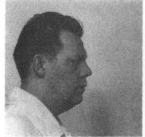

Known as the Candy Man because he poisoned his son with Halloween candy, Ronald Clark O'Bryan donated his eyes to an eye bank.

The prison ID card of Margie Velma Barfield, who murdered five, including her mother and husband. She was the first woman to die by the needle. (North Carolina Department of Corrections)

In 1924, scraping the bottom of the legal bucket, the attorney approached the State Board of Pardons. Pleading for a commutation of his clients' sentences, he emphasized their poor mental ability and the "inferiority" of their race. At the same time, petitions and letters poured in from sympathetic university students, the League of Women Voters, and citizens at large. The effort won a partial victory: Hughie Sing's sentence was commuted to life imprisonment because he had acted merely as an accomplice and was just nineteen at the time. Gee Jon's sentence remained unchanged.

On February 7, the day before Gee Jon was to die, his attorney made a last appeal to Governor Scrugham. So did the consul general of imperial China. Both appeals failed.

Gee Jon, a slight man in his early thirties, understood little English but he knew very well what lay in store for him. Frightened and depressed, he had not taken a mouthful of food for ten days and, as his end drew closer, was repeatedly racked by fits of shivering and weeping. In the words of his keepers, he was "a nervous wreck." Some of them seemed almost as disturbed as he did. Three were to be chosen by lot to form a death squad to operate the new equipment. Rather than risk winning that honor, a number of guards quit their jobs.

In the yard of the Carson City State Prison stood an old barber shop. This had been remodeled into a death house. The humanitarians' dream of gassing the condemned man as he slept in his cell had been abandoned because of technical difficulties. Instead, on February 8, Gee was to be brought to the death house and executed while in full possession of his senses.

Late in the afternoon of February 7, prison officials held a rehearsal. Two cats were carried into the airtight death cell and the door was shut on them. In an adjoining room, a tank containing hydrocyanic acid had been set up. At a signal, a member of the death squad began to work a tire pump connected to the tank. The action of the pump turned the acid into gas and sprayed it into the death cell.

For the new method of execution a new post had been created: gas adviser to the State of Nevada. The expert who bore this title and had charge of the operation was E. B. Walker. Walker's everyday job was secretary of the California Cyanide Company of Cudahy, California, which supplied the liquefied gas for wiping out infestations of scale insects in fruit orchards and rats and mice in warehouses and the holds of vessels. Since the law prohibited shipment of hydrocyanic acid by rail, a prison employee had trucked it from southern California to the prison in Carson City.

The hiss of the liquefied gas into the death cell could barely be heard, but officials, peering through the window, could make out the fine spray shooting in. After a few seconds, the two cats wobbled, then collapsed and lay still. Everyone was very satisfied the test had gone well.[2]

But how would it go with a much larger creature named Gee Jon?

The morning of February 8 was cold and cloudy. Gee Jon broke his fast to accept a last meal—ham and eggs, toast and coffee. At 9:30, the guards unlocked his cell door. He began to whimper.

"Well, Gee, ready?" asked Miller, the captain.

Gee nodded, trembling. His hands strapped to his thighs, he was marched out into the yard. All the prisoners had been locked in their cells. About thirty witnesses were clustered outside the remodeled barbershop. Gee hardly seemed to notice them as he was led into the death cell.

The only furniture in the room was a chair. Gee Jon was seated in it. As two guards nervously strapped him fast, tears streamed down his cheeks. One of the guards, finishing his job, was in such a hurry to leave that, forgetting his companion, he rushed out and shut the door behind him. The second man, unable to get out, pounded on the door until it was opened up for him.

It was 9:40 now. In the next room, the three members of the death squad were waiting expectantly. One of them had his hands on the pump; the others were standing by to relieve him.

The signal came. The guard at the pump began to work it vigorously. In an instant, gas would begin to rise from the vent behind Gee's chair.

Hydrocyanic acid requires a temperature of 75 degrees Fahrenheit to turn to gas. The morning was cold, so an electric heater had been provided to raise the temperature. But the heater was not doing its job well. A pool of liquid began to form on the floor in back of Gee's chair. Part of the four pounds of acid sprayed into the room did become gas, however. The witnesses pressed up close against the thick glass just a few feet from the doomed man.

Gee could hear the hiss of the gas behind him. His body was held fast by the straps, but he could still turn his head and now he strove to do so.

He never completed the movement. Witnesses observed his head suddenly sag backward, then forward. He appeared to lose consciousness. But for several minutes his head continued to bob, the movements growing weaker and weaker. His eyes remained open.

The execution plan had called for Gee to enter the chamber with the endpiece of a stethoscope attached to his chest. The instrument was to be connected to a rubber tube leading outside the room, where the prison physician would listen to Gee's heartbeats through the earpieces of the stethoscope. This plan had been abandoned, so Gee's condition had to be determined by eye. At 9:46, six minutes after the guard had begun pumping, the physician judged Gee was dead.

But he had to make sure. Gee's limp body was left in the gassaturated chamber for another half hour. The room was equipped with a blower to exhaust the gas, and after the witnesses had been told to leave the yard, the blower began to whine its monotonous tune. When it was turned off, the smell of the gas still lingered. It reminded one witness of the odor of "bitter almonds, crushed."

It was 12:20 before the door of the death chamber was unlocked. Guards moved in gingerly, unstrapped Gee's body and removed it to a nearby building, where four doctors examined it. No autopsy was performed.

One of the physicians was an observer for the military, Major Delos A. Turner of the United States Veterans Bureau. Major Turner had brought with him a supply of adrenalin and camphor. He wanted to perform an experiment on Gee Jon's body "in the interests of science."

"I think I could revive him," the major said, "with injections of camphor. This has proved successful in other cyanide deaths and I believe a man executed this way can be brought back to life."

Warden Denver S. Dickerson refused to permit the experiment. Turner, convinced the dead man could have been resuscitated, recommended in his report to the chief of the Chemical Warfare Service that convicts executed by lethal gas should be hanged or shot afterward to make certain they remained permanently dead.

As for the witnesses, most expressed satisfaction with what they had seen. Gee Jon had lost consciousness, they said, in a matter of seconds, and his death had seemed painless. It was pretty much like watching a man fall asleep in a chair.

Turner agreed with them. "The lethal gas method is the quickest and most humane method of putting a human to death. . . . There is no chance for pain or suffering.'' It was true that in Gee Jon's case the arrangements had been less than perfect. ''With proper equipment and a specially constructed glass-lined chamber, death could be made both instantaneous and painless.''

Not everybody was as pleased. The first execution by lethal gas brought howls of dismay from a number of major newspapers, which saw it almost as a replay of that horror of thirty-four years earlier, the first electrocution. Gee Jon, the Philadelphia *Public Ledger* brooded, had ''died shut away from men, as the stray dog dies in the pound-keeper's death-cage''; it found ''a terror in this thing that even Edgar Allan Poe could not equal,'' and concluded that Nevada had ''stumbled into new refinements and depths of cruelty.''

The Philadelphia *Record* pulled out all the stops; not since the Dark Ages, it declared, had the civilized world produced such a piece of official barbarity. To the editors of *The New York Times* gas was ''the most terrible of all known poisons,'' and they dwelled on the ''peculiar horror a man must feel as he meditates for days or weeks on such an ending for his life.'' They even scented racial prejudice: a white man had been condemned to die with Gee Jon, but his sentence had been commuted at the last moment, so that the new method was tested on a Chinese. ''That will need a good deal of explaining.'' (The reprieved man, as it happened, was a Mexican.)

No one was more upset by the new method than the man in charge of Gee Jon's execution, Warden Dickerson. Death by a firing squad would have been better, he opined; it was quicker and he was sure it was less painful.

Governor Scrugham, who had refused to spare Gee's life, also disapproved of the way it had been taken. In 1925, Scrugham and Dickerson joined in an attempt to persuade the state legislature to repeal the new execution law. They failed, and in 1926 a young Serbian immigrant, Stanko Jukich, became the second murderer to die in the gas chamber. More than two dozen slayers followed Jukich in the next four decades. Then, for an eighteen-year span, Nevada had no executions—until 1979, when Jesse W. Bishop broke the long hiatus. Even he might have been spared, but he insisted on dying, declaring he was guilty of eighteen murders.

Meanwhile, other states had gradually turned to lethal gas as a capital punishment. Arizona and Colorado introduced it in 1934 and North Carolina in 1936. By 1960, eleven states were killing with gas.

California adopted lethal gas in 1937. Until then, the state had executed its condemned criminals on the gallows. The warden of San Quentin, Jim Holohan, often complained of the gruesome sights and sounds he witnessed every time he officiated at a hanging. Death by electricity seemed to him almost as brutal. Attending an execution by lethal gas in neighboring Nevada, he came away an ardent convert to the new method. Later, as a member of the state legislature, Holohan conducted a successful one-man campaign for the adoption of lethal gas. Soon after, wondering longshoremen unloaded a massive object of riveted steel on the dock at San Quentin. It was to become California's first gas chamber.

Many advances in equipment and procedure have been introduced since the first execution by gas in the remodeled barbershop in Carson City in 1924. California's death cell has eight sides, with windows through which witnesses watch (they stand behind the prisoner, where he can't see them unless he turns his head). The room is equipped with two chairs, so a pair of convicts can be put to death simultaneously.

Adjoining the death cell is the mixing room. On the morning set for the execution, two pounds of cyanide are brought in by the executioner and poured into two one-pound bags. Then he mounts each bag under one of the two chairs in the death chamber. (This is done even if only one prisoner is to be executed.) Directly below each bag there is a well.

In the mixing room, there are two one-gallon jars. Shortly before the prisoner is to be put to death, the executioner fills each of these with a mixture of distilled water and sulfuric acid. A pipe runs from each jar to the well below each of the chairs in the death chamber. Next, the executioner checks that the death cell is airtight.

The prisoner has spent the night in a holding cell, under the watchful eyes of his guards. Now, with a stethoscope endpiece taped over his heart, he is brought by the guards down the short corridor that leads to the death chamber. They strap him securely into one of the chairs and connect the stethoscope to a tube that passes out of the chamber through an airtight opening; at the other end of the tube is the prison physician, ready to monitor the convict's heartbeats. (In Oregon, the tube also accommodated the wires of a cardiograph.)

After the door has been locked on the prisoner, the executioner turns on an exhaust fan, which draws some of the air from the chamber. Now the sulfuric acid mixture in the jars is released into the pipes and gurgles out into the wells beneath the chairs. The executioner is waiting for a signal from the warden. When it comes, he pulls a lever and the bag of cyanide pellets drops into the well. They dissolve instantly and the pale cyanide fumes begin to form.

How long does it take to extinguish a human life with cyanide gas? That depends very much on the physical condition of the prisoner. The warden of San Quentin once estimated that a prisoner lapsed into unconsciousness forty seconds after entering the gas chamber. Execution records vary, however.

Here is one as supplied by the prison physician:

Prisoner entered the chamber at 10:00 A.M.
Chamber door locked at 10:03
Sodium cyanide enters 10:04
Gas strikes prisoner's
face   10:05   Grimaces and breathes violently, throws weight
                against straps.
        10:05   Grimaces. Gasps. Feet and hands extended.
        10:06   Grimaces. 3 gasps.
        10:07   3 gasps.
        10:08   Gasps.
        10:09   2 gasps.

Finally, at 10:15 A.M., the heart stopped beating. That was eleven minutes after the cyanide became active. After the gas has been drawn from the chamber, the body may be sprayed with liquid ammonia to neutralize any gas lingering in the clothing.

The first men to die in the small green chamber at San Quentin were Robert Lee Cannon, twenty-four, and Albert Kessell, twenty-nine, executed on December 2, 1938. Both had been sentenced to death for the murder of the warden of Folsom Prison in a jailbreak the year before.

Cannon and Kessell passed their last night in the holding cells listening to hillbilly music on a battered phonograph and singing and yahooing to each other until dawn. The execution was set for 10:00 A.M. They had a hearty breakfast and at 9:50, as their time grew short, each asked for and received a drink of whiskey and a cigar. ("No sedatives, narcotics, nor drugs," said Warden Clinton T. Duffy, "are administered to prisoners who are executed. On rare occasions, a prisoner may be given one ounce of whiskey shortly prior to his scheduled execution time should he request it, which is administered under the supervision of a physician.'')

Barefoot, dressed in jeans and a white shirt, Cannon was led to the death cell, his hands fastened to his sides and a stethoscope attached to his chest. ''Hello, boys—so long,'' he called out flippantly to the thirty-nine witnesses. After strapping him in one of the chairs, the two guards went for Kessell and fastened him in the other. ''Quite a congregation here,'' quipped Kessell to his companion.

The stethoscopes were connected to the doctors' earpieces. The prison physician, Dr. Stanley, had invited Dr. Geiger, a San Francisco health officer, to assist. As a precaution, Geiger had brought a supply of methylene blue, which he had used successfully in the treatment of cyanide poison victims.

Both convicts joked grimly in the few seconds they had left to live. The witnesses watched silently. Grayish blue vapor appeared over the pots beneath the chairs. ''Nothing to it!'' cried Cannon while the fumes rose lazily. Warden Court Smith, who abhorred capital punishment, looked away.

Now the gas reached Cannon. ''There it is!'' he cried. He moved his lips as if to say more but his eyes glazed and he lost consciousness.

Kessell seemed to be holding his breath. As the gas hit him, his body went rigid, his hands clutched the arms of the chair. ''It's bad!'' he gasped. His head went back, then forward and down.

At 10:19, the two convicts were pronounced dead by the physicians listening through their stethoscopes and the witnesses filed out. It had taken twelve minutes for Cannon to die. Kessell's heart continued to beat three and one-half minutes longer.

For more than two hours, a suction device drained off the deadly fumes, which were carried up a tall chimney and discharged into the air high over the prison. It was nearly 1:00 P.M. before Warden Smith decided it was safe to remove the bodies.

The state was well pleased with its first executions by lethal gas. At a cost of just $1.80 for cyanide and sulfuric acid it had disposed of two convicted killers. As in Gee Jon's case, most of the witnesses were impressed by the speed and apparent painlessness of the operation.

But not all.

''It was brutal,'' said Melvin Belli, a well-known San Francisco attorney. ''Brutal to the men and to the spectators.'' Like Warden Smith, he had turned his eyes away from the scene taking place on the other side of the glass panels. He said he was determined to begin a fight against capital punishment at the next legislative assembly.

The man who was best qualified to judge, the prison physician, Dr. Stanley, was convinced the prisoners had died in terrible agony. "The idea that cyanide kills immediately is hooey. These men suffered as their lungs no longer absorbed oxygen and they struggled to breathe. They died of an internal suffocation against which they had to fight and from which they must have suffered."

Equally disturbed was the prison chaplain, Father George O'Meara, who had comforted the condemned men in their last moments. O'Meara had accompanied more than sixty convicts to the gallows. "I'd rather go through a dozen hangings than this thing again," he said. "Distinctly I saw Cannon's lips form the words 'It's terrible!' as the gas struck him. The muscles of his neck bulged and fought, his eyes bulged, his mouth opened! It was terrible indeed . . . Such things as happened at San Quentin today can't go on."[3]

But they did, and in very substantial numbers. Clinton T. Duffy, who succeeded Court Smith and served as warden of San Quentin for almost twelve years, was obliged to oversee the executions of eighty-eight men and two women. A bitter opponent of capital punishment, he did everything in his power to make the lot of the condemned easier. Visiting the inmates of the death house, Duffy observed that their curiosity about the gas chamber and what went on inside it sharpened noticeably as execution day approached. When an inmate first asked Duffy what death by gas was like, his reply was: "It's like going to sleep." Soon after, he found that they were calling it "the big sleep"—a name by which it came to be known throughout the prison.

Convicts who were about to enter the gas chamber were advised not to inhale the cyanide fumes as soon as they heard the pellets fall. Instead, they were told to hold their breath for a few seconds and then inhale deeply: the brief pause would allow the gas to concentrate sufficiently to make them lose consciousness promptly, without choking. Warden Duffy, who stood on the other side of the glass, where the prisoners could see him, used to give them a signal to breathe when the fumes were thick and high enough. Once, a convict who didn't wait caught a whiff of the gas and called out to him, "It smells just like rotten eggs!"

Because of the relative simplicity of the equipment, errors are much rarer with executions by lethal gas than by electricity or hanging.

However, there have been close calls. In Raleigh, North Carolina, in 1943, for example, John Redfern sat strapped in the chair waiting for the cyanide eggs to fall. The executioner tripped the mechanism. Nothing happened. He tripped it again. Still nothing. There was a hurried conference with the warden. The warden opened the door to the chamber and held it while the executioner stepped inside, released the cyanide sack by hand, and dashed out just as the fumes began to form.

Although lethal gas doesn't mutilate the victim, executions have occasionally been gory. On April 18, 1956, Robert O. Pierce was in the holding cell of San Quentin's death house, being comforted by the chaplain. Suddenly, Pierce's hand, holding a piece of glass, flashed upward and his throat began to spurt blood. The chaplain called for help. A doctor tried to staunch the flow but without success. Should Pierce be taken to the hospital and treated? The decision was against it. Kicking and screaming, Pierce was carried by five burly guards to the execution chamber. There, even with his neck slashed, he managed to live long enough to die by gas.

In another curious incident, a man named Henry McCracken endured a long stay on death row while his appeals were being heard. Finally, in 1954, he went out of his mind. A panel of psychiatrists agreed he was insane, which made it illegal to execute him. Electroshock therapy was prescribed, and with its help McCracken was brought back to sanity enough for him to be held legally competent. Before his condition could change again, he was hurried to the green chamber.

Readers will remember the army doctor, Turner, who asked permission to try to revive Gee Jon after his execution in 1924. A similar incident occurred in San Quentin in 1948. Dr. Robert Cornish of Berkeley had been making experiments in restoring life to "dead" animals[4] and had succeeded in reviving some dogs he had killed. Now he wanted to try his method on a human being put to death in the gas chamber. The doctor asked Thomas H. McMonigle, a condemned kidnap killer, to will him his body, a request that was willingly granted. Then Cornish applied to Warden Duffy.

It was imperative, the doctor said, that he get McMonigle's body immediately after he was pronounced dead. His method, Cornish explained, was to inject the body with antidotes and stimulants and then place it in a machine that would start the heart beating again. He had already tried the experiment with carbon monoxide victims but it had failed because he couldn't get the bodies early enough.

Duffy pointed out Cornish would run into the same trouble with McMonigle's body, since it would have to remain in the death chamber for an hour while the air was cleared.

That wouldn't do, insisted Cornish; he had to have McMonigle's body immediately; didn't Duffy realize a successful experiment could blaze the trail to saving hundreds of accident victims?

The warden stood firm, as the law obliged him to, and Cornish sued. To his disappointment (not to mention McMonigle's), the court rejected his suit.

The men who perform executions with lethal gas are unknown to the public at large. Unlike the hangman and the electrocutioner, they have no physical contact with the condemned person, playing only a technician's role in the proceedings.

In Nevada, an ingenious way was worked out to keep the executioner anonymous even to himself. Under the condemned man's chair were suspended not one but three sacks. Of these only one contained cyanide; the others held stones or other material of equal weight. The sacks were attached to strings extending through a pipe to the executioner's post. There the warden and two guards manipulated the strings, causing all three bags to drop into the acid below. No one knew which bag contained the fatal chemical or who had caused it to fall.

In some states the executioner was a prison guard, and he received extra pay for this special service. In California in the 1950s, the executioner was a guard, who received $125 and a week off. Caryl Chessman (more about him shortly) told in his book *Trial by Ordeal* about two condemned men who won a last-minute reprieve, causing the guard-executioner to fly into a fury because he felt he had been cheated out of his double fee and his holiday.

Of the hundreds who have died in California's gas chamber, few have attracted as much attention—and sympathy—as Barbara Graham. The third member of her sex to die in the little green room at San Quentin, she was only thirty-two and, some said, lovely enough to be a movie star. In fact, a few years after she was executed in 1955, her pathetic story was told in a motion picture, *I Want to Live!*, with the actress Susan Hayward playing her role. According to the film, Graham was innocent of the crime for which she paid with her life, and to this day many people believe she was unjustly executed.

Barbara Graham's unhappy life followed the classic pattern of the female criminal. Her mother had been sent to reform school at nineteen; Barbara, an illegitimate child, matriculated at the same alma mater when she was fourteen. Released two years later, she became a "seagull"—a follower of the fleet at San Diego. Later, she worked as a decoy, steering innocents into the hands of crooked gamblers. Convictions for prostitution, lewd conduct, perjury and vagrancy made her a familiar figure in the courts.

Graham spent seven years in prison. In between convictions, she married four times and bore three sons. Periodically she made efforts to go straight—she was an officeworker, waitress, store clerk, telegram delivery girl—but always she drifted over to the wrong side of the law.

In 1953, Graham was tried and convicted with Emmett Perkins and Jack Santo for the murder of Mrs. Mabel Monahan. Supposedly Mrs. Monahan had $100 thousand hidden in her house, but actually she didn't; according to a participant in the crime (who traded his testimony for immunity), Graham helped to beat her to death. The young woman swore she was innocent but she had no verifiable alibi for the time of the crime and the hostile Perkins and Santo refused to testify in her behalf. In the two years she spent in prison while her case was appealed, she revealed an IQ of 114 and a fondness for poetry and classical music. She steadfastly asserted her innocence right up to the end.

Graham was scheduled to go to the death chamber on the morning of June 3, 1955, before Perkins and Santo. She dressed attractively for the occasion, had a hot fudge sundae for breakfast, and put on bright red lipstick. She appeared quiet and composed. At 9:05, a call came postponing the execution so the State Supreme Court could hear a new argument by her lawyer. An hour later, the governor telephoned personally to say the court had rejected the request. The stethoscope was being taped over her heart at 10:23 when a third call came, delaying the execution because a new petition had been filed.

"Why do they torture me?" the young woman cried. "I was ready at ten o'clock."

At 11:12, the telephone rang again; the court had turned down the last appeal. The mechanics of the execution got under way. To avoid having to see the witnesses, Graham asked for a covering for her eyes and a matron lent her a sleeping mask. At 11:32, the blindfolded prisoner walked down the carpeted corridor and into the green chamber.

In his book *I Want to Live!* (Signet Books, 1958), Tabor Rawson tells what happened next:

> Father Devers left Barbara after she was seated, and a guard fastened the strap around her chest as the guard captain fastened the strap around her stomach. This completed, they each strapped an arm, then a leg, and after the last final check the guard captain had connected the rubber tube to the stethoscope tube protruding from Barbara's harness. And then, in a quiet voice the captain had told her to wait until she heard the pellets drop before she counted to ten and—took a deep breath. That was the easiest way. . . .
>
> The men left the chamber, and the door to all that was outside was slammed shut. Then the locking wheel was spun to tighten the door in its steel frame and make it even more secure, more airtight. . . .
>
> The controls had been checked for the last time as the doctor adjusted the earpieces of his stethoscope; the beat of Barbara's heart came through hard, violent, fast. The doctor made a note on his chart—everything official and proper—as the signal had been given to the guard at the mixing room window, who opened the valves of his mixing bowls to permit the liquids to run into the receptacle below Barbara's chair. And as she heard the sound of running liquid she had probably begun to count as Father Devers—outside—continued his prayers right through the drop of cyanide eggs into the sulphuric acid where the eggs broke so that the chemicals could combine to rise around Barbara, who had to exhale soon—and inhale. . . .

At 11:42, Barbara Graham was pronounced dead. For two hours more her body remained in the chamber, her head bent forward, saliva oozing from her mouth.

For a long time afterward, prison officials remembered the last words spoken by the condemned woman as she entered the gas chamber:

"Good people are always so sure they're right."

On May 2, 1960, Caryl Chessman, the most celebrated prisoner in

California history, walked into the gas chamber at San Quentin in his stocking feet and sat down on the metal chair inside. Eight times before, he had broken appointments with death in that little room. This ninth appointment there had been no breaking—although his attorneys were at that moment still fighting desperately to win a reprieve.

Guards quickly strapped Chessman into the chair. "Too tight," he grimaced to the man securing his wrists. The two guards worked fast. Then they hastened out and the door was secured behind them.

Sixty faces watched Chessman through the glass. Two of them belonged to women reporters he'd invited. (California allows a condemned person to invite five guests to his execution.) Chessman's lips were moving, forming words with exaggerated care. It was a goodbye message for his lawyer, still pleading for his life before a federal judge.

The reporters signaled to let Chessman know they'd understood. A small smile flickered across his gaunt face.

In nearby San Francisco, just then, Chessman's attorneys suddenly won a victory. They convinced Judge Louis E. Goodman to delay the execution. It was 10:03 A.M.

At precisely 10:03:15 A.M., the executioner released his bag of cyanide pellets. Chessman heard it plop into the container of sulfuric acid beneath the perforated seat of his chair. The fumes of gas rose quickly.

Nervously Judge Goodman's secretary dialed the San Quentin number. She lost a priceless moment or two when she dialed the wrong number, had to find the right one and dial again.

She heard a voice at the other end. It was Associate Warden Louis Nelson and he sounded shocked when he heard her message. "The cyanide pellets have just been dropped," he exclaimed. "It's too late."

Chessman was still alive. According to witnesses, he was holding his breath, staving off the end as long as he could.

In a minute or two, they saw his chin begin to move up and down. His eyes were rolling. The muscles of this throat moved spasmodically.

But he was still alive.

There was still time to save him.

Or was there?

Few legal cases have unleashed so wild a furor around the world as

Caryl Chessman's. Although he had killed no one, he was sentenced to death. Although the law under which he'd been condemned was changed while he was in prison, so no one else would be executed for violating it, Chessman was deliberately excluded from its new provision.

Chessman spent more years on death row than any man before him—twice as many as Sacco and Vanzetti. The pope, leaders of other religions, Dr. Albert Schweitzer, Eleanor Roosevelt, the queen of Belgium, Pablo Casals, Aldous Huxley, and millions of others, famous and obscure, asked for mercy for him. Many were convinced of his innocence or else they felt, in the words of *Osservatore Romano*, that "anyone who has to wait eleven years for the gas chamber has expiated his guilt, no matter how grave."

To the very end, Chessman insisted he was not guilty—and to this day the evidence he presented seems so persuasive it is hard to understand why he was ever convicted and executed. But that is reckoning without the power of the circulation-hungry California press, which whipped up a campaign against him that would not be stilled until his life was.

Caryl Whittier Chessman (he was a descendant of the poet John Greenleaf Whittier) was born in 1921. He was only a boy when he suffered an almost fatal attack of encephalitis that he believed left his mental balance disturbed. When he was eight, an auto accident made his mother a helpless paralytic and left him with the humped nose of a motion-picture gangster.

Chessman's father, impoverished and neurotic, tried to kill himself twice. The boy began to steal food to feed his family and speedily graduated to more serious crime. At sixteen, he was sent to reform school, escaped, was reimprisoned, and soon after his release went back to crime. At seventeen, he was in prison again. At twenty-one, in San Quentin, he impressed Warden Duffy with his intelligence (he had an IQ of 136); he edited the prison paper, taught shorthand, and wrote scripts for the prison radio station. After another escape, he was locked up in Folsom, California's maximum-security prison, until his release in December 1947.

In January 1948, Los Angeles was startled by a series of robberies committed by a man driving a gray Ford coupe with a red spotlight. Pulling up to cars parked in lovers' lanes, he flashed his spotlight and the occupants, thinking him a policeman, lowered their windows, only to face a gun and a demand for their money. On two occasions the robber took women occupants into his car, forced them to commit fellatio, then released them. To the press he was "the red-light bandit."

Soon afterward, a police car stopped an auto that looked like the bandit's and found Chessman and another ex-convict inside with a load of stolen clothing. Chessman signed a confession that he was the red-light bandit—but later said he did so only to make the police stop torturing him.

Descriptions of the bandit were conflicting. A few of the people who'd been robbed identified Chessman; others, however, couldn't. He was charged and brought to trial before a judge who reportedly had sentenced more criminals to death than any other in the state's history.

Chessman, distrustful of court-appointed attorneys, insisted on conducting his own defense. Only twenty-seven and without legal training, he made some grave mistakes. The worst was in choosing the jury. One man and eleven women were selected—four of them with daughters the same age as the bandit's female victims.

In his defense, Chessman readily admitted his long criminal record but denied he was the red-light bandit and emphasized he had never been charged with a sex crime before. Still the jury found him guilty on seventeen counts. Two of these were for violation of the state's Little Lindbergh Law, which permitted the death penalty when a person had been carried off—even a few inches—for the purpose of robbery and had been subjected to bodily harm. For these two crimes he was sentenced to death.

Undismayed, Chessman began one of the most astonishing battles in court history. Plowing through heaps of law books, he launched one appeal after another in legal briefs that, according to attorneys, were models of style and logic. In the twelve years Chessman fought for his life on death row, his case went up to the United States Supreme Court sixteen times. So knowledgeable did he become in the law that he was able to draw up appeals for other death-house inmates that won stays of execution for them.

In 1954 Chessman told his story in a book, *Cell 2455, Death Row*, that became a national best-seller and a movie. He followed this with other books, smuggling the manuscripts out of San Quentin. His writings brought him funds to hire a team of lawyers and won sympathy for him at home and abroad.

After repeated reprieves, Chessman's execution date—his eighth—was set for February 18, 1960. Almost at the last hour a sixty-day stay came from Governor Pat Brown. It was granted at the request of the United States Department of State. The president, Dwight D. Eisenhower, was scheduled to visit South America and the government feared demonstrations by those enraged by Chessman's impending execution.

Chessman's next execution date was set for May 2. Millions of signatures urging commutation of the death sentence had been forwarded to the governor, but the California press was unrelenting in its call for Chessman's blood, and the governor decided the law must take its course.

On the morning of May 2, as one desperate appeal after another by Chessman's lawyers was rejected, he still clung to hope. When the warden came in at 9:50 A.M. to announce that no reprieve had come through and Chessman would have to go to the glass-paneled chamber down the hall in a few minutes, the condemned man showed no fear. "I just want to keep the record straight," he said. "I'm not the red-light bandit. I'm not the man."

His hair neatly combed, his face calm, he walked to the gas chamber. "Inside of me I had a feeling the court would relent and let me live," he told a guard. In his twelve years in the death house, however, he'd seen more than a hundred go for the short, final walk he was now taking.

In his imagination he'd lived through his own execution so many times it could hold few surprises for him. In *Trial by Ordeal*, he had pictured what it would be like:

You inhale the deadly fumes. You become giddy. You strain against the straps as the blackness closes in. You exhale, inhale again. Your head aches. There's a pain in your chest. But the ache, the pain is nothing. You're hardly aware of it. You're slipping into unconsciousness. You're dying. Your head jerks back. Only for an awful instant do you float free. The veil is drawn swiftly. Consciousness is forever gone. Your brain has been denied oxygen. Your body fights a losing, ten-minute battle against death.

You've stopped breathing. Your heart has quit beating. You're dead.

News of Chessman's execution was relayed to Governor Brown[5] in his office in the State Capitol at Sacramento. Outside, pickets were still marching. Their leader was a Los Angeles psychiatrist, Dr. Isidore Ziferstein. A staunch foe of capital punishment, Ziferstein had been fighting to save Chessman's life for six years.

When Ziferstein learned that Judge Goodman had granted Chessman a last-minute reprieve, but word of it had arrived too late to save the condemned man, he began to wonder: How late is too late?

The cyanide pellets had been dropped only an instant before Judge Goodman's secretary had called San Quentin. Wasn't it the duty of Warden Dickson to do everything in his power to save the man in the gas chamber?

The warden could have done much, Ziferstein concluded. He could have ordered the executioner to start the powerful blowers in the death room, drawing off the gas that had been generated and was still forming.

He could have ordered the executioner to put on a gas mask and enter the chamber, cut the straps fastening Chessman to the chair, and help him out.

Reporters had said Chessman had been holding his breath at the start of the execution. If Warden Dickson had signaled him to continue doing so while the rescue effort was being made, he might have been removed from the chamber without suffering any ill effects at all. (Will Stevens, a reporter, had prearranged a signal with Chessman that the prisoner was to give if he was in agony, and he said Chessman had given it six minutes after the pellets were dropped.)

Even if Chessman had breathed some of the gas, emergency measures could have been taken to save his life, Ziferstein discovered—including holding a handkerchief saturated with amyl nitrate to his nose and giving him injections of sodium nitrite and sodium thiosulphate. Artificial respiration could also have helped.

Why didn't Warden Dickson lift a finger to save Chessman?

The state, Ziferstein became convinced, was eager, after twelve years, to be done with the condemned man. As Warden Dickson declared in a television interview shortly after the execution, he was relieved the case "was over with, one way or another."

A day or two after the execution, Ziferstein received a letter from the dead man. Chessman had written it in the holding cell, on his final morning.

''I am sure the fact my life finally was forfeited,'' he said, ''will spur your determination to see this ugly practice of capital punishment abolished. And that makes dying easier and gives my death an affirmative meaning it otherwise would be denied.''

FIVE

Death by the Needle

Charlie Brooks was his name and he was, by his own account, a drug addict and a loser. The respectable ways of his prosperous black Texas family held little attraction for him; he felt more comfortable with heroin and criminal companions. By his thirty-third birthday he was a two-term prison alumnus.

In 1976, Brooks, with an old friend and fellow drug addict named Woodie Loudres, walked onto a used-car lot in Forth Worth. They said they wanted to buy a car, and the twenty-six-year-old salesman, David Gregory, was happy to take them for a test drive. It ended in a motel room where Gregory, bound and gagged, was killed with a single shot in the head.

When they were arrested, neither of the two buddies would say who had fired the gun. Both were charged with murder in the first degree. Brooks and Loudres were tried separately. Both were found guilty and sentenced to death. In Loudres's case, however, technical errors had been made when the jury was selected and, on appeal, his conviction was overturned. Offered a plea bargain, he settled for a forty-year prison term. With good behavior, that meant he could be out on the street in six and a half years.

Brooks wasn't so lucky. He too claimed there were errors in the selection of his jury, and for six years he made appeals on this and other grounds, but one after another his appeals failed. In his last plea to the United States Supreme Court, he won support from an unusual quarter—Jack Strickland, the prosecutor who had convicted both him and Loudres.

"Only one shot was fired," said Strickland, "and you don't know who fired it. One guy lives and one guy dies [and it] strikes the citizen as unfair."

Like so many others on death row, Brooks found a young woman to correspond with. A nurse in Fort Worth, she came to see him in the state prison in Huntsville on visiting days and they became attached to each other. They made plans to marry. Not in this world, however. Their commitment was for the hereafter.

During his long stay on death row, the condemned man found salvation in religion: he converted to Islam and became a devout believer. With its roots in the stern soil of the Old Testament, Islam holds that an eye can be paid for only with an eye, and a life only with a life. No matter how much Brooks might dislike it in his own case, as a good Moslem he could have no complaint against capital punishment. A relative who visited him in prison said, "His life has been turned over to God and he has very high hopes."

On December 6, 1982, Brooks, then forty years old, saw his last hope dissolve when the Supreme Court rejected his appeal. Eager to avoid further delay, the state authorities scheduled his execution within twenty-four hours. He would be the first black man put to death in the United States since 1967.

That same day, Brooks had a special visitor. It was Dr. Ralph Gray, medical director of the Texas Department of Corrections. The doctor's mission was to examine Brooks's blood vessels. (One prisoner out of four may have veins that are too small, covered with fat, or too scarred from drug use.) "He's got plenty of good veins," the doctor commented afterward.

Later that day, Brooks was moved from death row to the holding unit. Just a few yards from his new cell was the execution chamber. There, over the years, 361 men had sat down in the electric chair and died. But now that chair had been crated up and removed. In its place stood a gurney—a wheeled cot much like those used in hospitals, with a mattress covered with a fresh white sheet.

In his cell, Brooks took his last dinner—steak, french fries and peach cobbler. He received visitors. They didn't include his ex-wife and two sons, who said bitterly that they had not been permitted to see him. They did include an Islamic minister, Larry Sharrief. It was close to midnight when the guards came and took Brooks to the death chamber.

The chamber was small and brilliantly illuminated. With its two doctors, its medical technician and its neat gurney, it could almost have been mistaken for an emergency room in a hospital.

Brooks looked frightened, but he needed no persuasion or pressure to get up on the gurney and stretch out. Six straps were attached to the mobile cot. The guards quickly secured them—two over his torso, one above the knees, another below and two over his ankles. A board projected from each side of the gurney and to these his arms were firmly fastened.

From an opening in the red brick wall close by, two clear plastic tubes snaked. The technician took one, with a catheter needle attached, examined Brooks's left arm, swabbed it with alcohol, and inserted the needle.[1] As he did so, he might have noticed some words tattooed on the arm. *I was born to die*, they said. Another needle, to be used as a substitute if needed, was inserted in the other arm. A saltwater solution, the standard medium in giving anesthesia, began to flow into Brooks's left arm.

A mirror shone on the wall through which the intravenous tubes ran. It was a one-way mirror and on the other side, watching, stood the executioner. At a cue from the warden, he was to shoot three drugs into the IV tube. Each of the three is used every day in hospitals all over America in moderate doses. In large doses any one of them will cause death.

The first drug was sodium thiopental. A quick-acting barbiturate, its commonest use is to anesthetize patients before an operation. (It is also the "truth serum" of psychotherapy.) A dose like the one Brooks was scheduled to get—five times the normal dose—will depress the central nervous system and make the heart stop beating.

The second drug was Pavulon. A synthetic, it is often compared to curare, a plant extract South American Indians dip their arrows into to paralyze their prey. Surgeons use Pavulon to keep muscles from moving. In a heavy dose it paralyzes the heart muscles, causing suffocation.

Potassium chloride was the third member of the deadly trio. An electrolyte normally produced by the body, potassium regulates the action of the heart. Too much of it, however, will cause cardiac arrest.

A curtain ran across the death chamber, splitting it in two. It was there to give privacy while the condemned man was being prepared. When all was ready, the curtain was pulled aside. Turning his head, Brooks could see the witnesses standing nervously behind an iron railing. One of them was his betrothed, present at his invitation.

In the annals of crime and punishment the next moments would be historic. The curtain had just been drawn on what was to be the first execution by lethal injection in the United States.

The prison warden, Jack Pursley, looked down at Brooks. "Do you have any last words?"

"Yes, I do." Brooks looked over the railing and into his sweetheart's eyes. "I love you."

He had invited Sharrieff and another Islamic minister to perform a final rite. They prayed with him. "I bear witness there is no God but Allah," Brooks recited. "Verily unto Allah do we belong, verily unto him do we return. . . ."

The prayer ended. Brooks turned his face to his betrothed. "Be strong," he said.

On the other side of the one-way mirror, the man who would give the dose was watching.

It was 12:09 A.M. "We're ready," Warden Pursley said.

The executioner had been waiting for those words. One after another he worked the three big syringes. Their contents poured into the IV tube and traveled toward the figure on the gurney.

The drugs began to take effect. Brooks "moved his head as if to say no," an eyewitness would say later. "Then he yawned and his eyes closed, and then he wheezed. His head fell over toward us, then he wheezed again." His arm bounced up and down.

His shirt was open, exposing his naked torso. "Brooks's bare stomach," said another witness, "was visibly moving up and down, showing his last few deep breaths." He opened and closed his hand several times.

One of the doctors placed a stethoscope over Brooks's heart. "A couple of minutes more," he said.

At 12:16 A.M., the stethoscope was applied again. "I pronounce this man dead," the doctor said.

The witnesses, their faces ashen, began to file out. Brooks's sweetheart collapsed onto a bench and covered her face.

One of the onlookers, a sheriff, was asked about the execution. "It was very peaceful," he said. But others didn't agree. Brooks, from what they had seen, had not died easily.

Outside the prison grounds, a crowd of death penalty supporters that included members of a college fraternity were celebrating the execution. "It's too lenient," one of the students grumbled. "They've got to go out painfully."

It was an irony of the American legal system that on December 7, the day Brooks was put to death, the Fifth Circuit Court of Appeals, trying another capital case, ruled that a prisoner couldn't be executed unless the jury found that he himself, and not a codefendant, had committed the murder.

In 1977, the State of Oklahoma faced a quandary. The electric chair in the state penitentiary was in a serious state of disrepair, and estimates, reportedly, showed it would cost a cool $62,000 to get it back in shape. That seemed a high price to pay to continue a system of execution that more and more people regarded as barbarous, inhumane and out-of-date. There were fewer objections to lethal gas, but the cost of setting up a state-of-the-art gas chamber would be even greater: $200,000.

In May, Oklahoma took a step in a new direction. It became the first state to vote in a simpler, less expensive method of execution—death by lethal injection.[2]

Death by the needle, as the newspapers called it, would have much more to recommend it than cheapness and simplicity. Its supporters insisted it would be painless too, a kind of euthanasia. Reportedly, it was the method of choice of knowledgeable doctors and nurses when they committed suicide. It would be contemporary—"high tech"—a scientific method of killing for a scientific age. It would be as up-to-date as the latest issue of *The Journal of the American Medical Association*.

Death by the needle, according to its promoters, would above all be hygienic and orderly. It wouldn't be very different from procedures performed thousands of times a day in hospitals: like an ordinary patient, the inmate would lie down, have a needle stuck in his arm, and fall into a deep sleep. The only difference was that the inmate wouldn't wake up again.

When a prisoner is put to death, the law requires the presence of witnesses. At an execution by lethal injection they would see and hear nothing to disturb them. No sparks, no blood, no smoke, no stench of burning flesh; nothing to offend even the most squeamish. And, as Governor Dolph Briscoe of Texas said when he signed his state's lethal injection bill in 1977, it would, he hoped, "provide some dignity with death."

Some people, of course, would find grounds for complaint. Lethal injection couldn't be expected to satisfy hardliners, those who wanted the criminal to pay in equal coin for his crime: to suffer as much pain as he had made his victim and his victim's loved ones suffer. Still, the new method bore the endorsement of one of the strongest law-and-order men in the country. In 1973, Governor Ronald Reagan of California had indirectly recommended it with these words:

> Being a former farmer and horse raiser, I know what it's like to try to eliminate an injured horse by shooting him. Now you call the veterinarian and the vet gives it a shot and the horse goes to sleep—that's it. I myself have wondered if maybe this isn't part of our problem [with capital punishment], if maybe we should review and see if there aren't even more humane methods now— the simple shot or tranquilizer.

Only the year before, the Supreme Court had halted all executions in the United States. In a historic case, *Furman* v. *Georgia*, the court had ruled that juries were violating the Eighth Amendment prohibition against cruel and unusual punishment by sentencing criminals to death in an inconsistent and arbitrary manner. At the time, thirty-two states had death penalty statutes; every one of these was made null and void by the court's decision, and the inmates sentenced under them couldn't be executed. (Actually, there had been an unofficial moratorium on executions since 1967 as one legal challenge after another to the death sentence moved through the courts.)

Legislatures scrambled to frame new statutes that would meet the court's criticisms. In 1976 the court reinstated the death penalty. By that time six hundred people had received death sentences under the new legislation.

With the new statutes the new system of execution spread rapidly from state to state, until today it is the dominant method.

Undoubtedly, some legislators backed it because crime was on the upswing. Prisons were packed, court challenges to the death penalty were many, and the reputedly painless exit promised by the needle could make juries and judges less reluctant to hand out death sentences. Certainly one lethal-injection statute after another specified the injection should include an "ultra-short-acting barbiturate" or an "ultra-fast-acting barbiturate." As Dr. Thomas H. Paterniti, a New Jersey legislator who helped draw up his state's statute, remarked, he "wanted to put kindness in it . . . If you're on the jury, the thought of some guy in that chair sizzling is going to bother them. This way, with lethal injections, it might ease their conscience when they come up with a verdict."

Although lethal injection seemed to have so much going for it, clouds of controversy gathered swiftly. At the center of the debate were two issues: the drugs that would be used and the role that doctors would play in the executions.

In 1980, before anyone had been executed by lethal injection, death-row inmates in Oklahoma and Texas launched an unusual legal case. It began with a petition to the United States Food and Drug Administration.

Among the FDA's duties is a requirement that it make sure new drugs are safe and effective for use. After the FDA has approved a drug, it must also make sure the drug is used only for the approved purposes. The condemned men wanted a warning label placed on drugs likely to be used in a lethal injection. Those drugs had been approved for specific medical purposes, but they hadn't been approved for putting people to death. The label, said the inmates, should state that the drugs "are not approved for use as a means of execution, are not considered safe and effective as a means of execution and should not be used as a means of execution."

Injections are difficult to give to some people, the men on death row pointed out; moreover, lethal injections were likely to be given by untrained personnel. There was strong evidence that the drugs "may actually result in agonizingly slow and painful deaths that are far more barbarous than those caused by the more traditional means of execution."

The FDA replied that the "safe and effective" requirement didn't apply to drugs used in executions; it refused to intervene,[3] and the case was fought in the courts for several years.

In March 1985, the United States Supreme Court ruled against the death-row inmates. The FDA, the court held, has a right "not to exercise its enforcement authority." It was "implausible," added Justice William H. Rehnquist, who wrote the opinion, to insist that drugs used in executions meet the "safe and effective" requirement. By that time eight convicts had been executed by lethal injection.

Doctors have often been involved with executions. Two French physicians promoted the guillotine and it is named for one of them. Doctors also helped in the development of the procedures in electrocution and the use of lethal gas. Under state laws, physicians are usually required to be present at an execution to declare the inmate officially dead.

With death by lethal injection it seemed doctors might have to take a more active role. Lethal injection relies on medical technology and the use of drugs, and so would need the supervision of physicians, if not their actual participation. Wasn't that, many began to wonder, in contradiction with the Hippocratic oath doctors take that they will "above all do no harm"?

Sharp debate flared up in the medical profession. In 1980 the American Medical Association spelled out its position. "A physician, as a member of a profession dedicated to preserving life when there is hope of doing so, should not be a participant in a legally authorized execution." In an execution by lethal injection a physician should do no more than examine the convict who had been executed and declare him (or her) to be dead. The American Psychiatric Association, the American Public Health Association, and the American Nursing Association also passed resolutions against taking part.

Following the execution of Charlie Brooks, loud protests were heard that Dr. Ralph Gray, medical director of the Texas Department of Corrections, had violated medical ethics by the part he took in the execution. Gray had examined Brooks's arms to make certain he had veins that would take the needle. He had made available the drugs that were used. His office had supplied medical technicians who did the deadly work.

Doctors opposed to the death penalty led the attack. Dr. William Curran of the Harvard School of Medicine called for investigations by both the national and state medical organizations; he wanted the license of any doctor-participant in an execution to be revoked.

Dr. Ward Casscells of Massachusetts General Hospital foresaw grim possibilities. "For a doctor to be involved, even by supervising a technician, checking the veins, or getting the drugs, is a perversion of our role as a healer, comforter and caretaker." An execution might turn into a real "horror show." "It's not like a tetanus shot at the doctor's. You're inserting a plastic catheter of fairly large dimension inside a vein. If it doesn't go into the vein, it can be excruciating. And in about one in four cases, where there is no decent vein in the hands or arms, it can take hours and be a real blood bath.'' There might have to be a ''cut-down''—the skin would have to be opened and a suitable vein looked for. Physicians, the doctor feared, might be looked upon as accomplices of the executioner, and the public might come to distrust the entire profession.

Dr. Gray didn't agree. He saw nothing unethical in what he had done. Physicians, he argued, routinely cut diseased flesh out of patients to preserve their lives; similarly, when they assisted in an execution, they were helping society to cure itself of the disease of crime. Lethal injection, he said, was ''a better choice than electrocution.'' The Texas Medical Association and the American Medical Association, after studying Gray's actions, concluded they were in keeping with accepted medical policy.

Even so, some doctors refused to have anything to do with the new technique of execution. In Oklahoma the original statute for lethal injection required prison physicians to take part. The physicians raised such a ruckus that the statute was revised to free them from involvement. In Idaho doctors refused to participate and the legislature had to reauthorize death by a firing squad. In two executions in Texas no physician was present at all. In one a doctor had to be called in to pronounce the convict dead; in the other a justice of the peace performed this service.

But if some doctors had reservations about death by the needle, some inmates seemed not to. They had more than a nodding acquaintance with drugs; they had lived by the needle and they were willing to die by it. Even before the execution of Charlie Brooks they had begun to refer to lethal injection as ''the ultimate high.''

In a number of states inmates were given a choice of death by lethal injection or by some other method. Prisoners had no trouble deciding which they preferred. Arthur Gary Bishop, sentenced to die in Utah for the murder of five young boys, spoke for other prisoners when he told the judge who offered him such a choice in 1984, ''I prefer the lethal injection, your Honor.''

James D. Autry was slated to be the second person in the United States to die by the needle.

Outside the state prison at Huntsville, Alabama, on the night of October 5, 1983, a cluster of tiny flames flickered; a small band of people opposed to capital punishment were keeping a candlelight vigil. A large crowd, which included college students made boisterous by drink, were calling for his death. They carried signs. Among them was one that declared WE PAY FOR OUR BEER. NOW IT'S TIME FOR AUTRY TO PAY FOR HIS.

It was apt enough. One night three years earlier, James D. Autry hadn't paid for his beer. And because of what he had done instead, the State of Texas was about to put him to death.

On October 20, 1980, Autry had lurched into a Sak-N-Pak store in Port Arthur with a homosexual companion. Autry was drunk and on drugs and he wanted more beer. Picking up a six-pack, he set it on the counter.

"That will be $2.70," said the middle-aged clerk, Shirley Drouet, mother of five.

"Here's your $2.70," replied Autry. But instead of giving her the money, he leveled a handgun at her and shot her between the eyes. Grabbing up the six-pack, he turned to flee.

As he made for his borrowed pickup truck, Autry ran into two men. Had they seen the shooting? He wasn't taking any chances. According to the court record, he shot them both. One died; the other would live on, but with permanent brain damage.

Later, when Autry was placed under arrest and heard he was charged with killing Shirley Drouet, his reply was truthful as far as it went: "I don't know her." He denied any part in that crime, or in shooting the two men.

The prosecuting attorney was ready to make a deal. He offered the oilfield drifter a plea bargain: forty years in prison in exchange for an admission of guilt. Autry said no. He was hoping to escape punishment altogether with a little help from his friend. His friend, however, had different ideas. He accepted a plea-bargain offer, receiving a seven-year sentence for a completely different crime. (He would be out of prison before Autry climbed on the death gurney.)

Looking backward, all of Autry's life seemed like a preparation for moving into death row. He came from a broken, alcoholic home. As a child he had been arrested for shoplifting; as a teenager he had committed armed robbery. He had served three terms in reform school and two in prison before murdering Mrs. Drouet. In his small cubicle at Huntsville, he watched television, read Westerns, and begged and bartered for tranquilizers. Clergymen who called to salvage his soul were made welcome, but that was more for their company than the religious consolation they offered.

After his final appeal was denied, Autry sent his possessions home to his mother. His impending execution he seemed to regard with resignation; he was less frightened than he would have been if his sentence had been commuted and he had to face twenty years in prison. Not that he relished the idea of dying by the needle. "It ain't manly," he observed. He would prefer hanging, he said, or even the headman's ax. On death row he was known as the Cowboy.

Most of his last day Autry spent listening to country music. He spoke with his mother on the telephone and with a younger brother doing time in a Colorado prison. For his last meal, he ordered a manly one of hamburger and french fries. Shortly before 11:00 P.M., with his guards, he walked the ten steps or so to the execution chamber. On the gurney the intravenous tubes were connected to his veins and the saline solution began to flow. The lethal dose was scheduled for 12:01 A.M.

In Washington, D.C., Justice Byron White was staying late at the United States Supreme Court in case a new plea should come from Autry's attorney. (Only the day before, White had been one of the justices who rejected Autry's previous plea.) In the lobby, an American Civil Liberties Union lawyer was hastily writing an application for a stay of execution; he had come up with an argument the court hadn't heard before.

At 11:10 P.M. the handwritten plea was presented to Justice White.

At 11:30 the justice, deciding the plea merited further scrutiny, issued a stay of execution.

At 11:37 word of the justice's action reached Warden Pursley at Huntsville.

At 11:39 the warden was at Autry's side, breaking the news to him.[4]

Until 12:08 A.M. the condemned man lay bound to the gurney. Then he was unstrapped and led back to his cell. He made no comment to his guards; perhaps he was too macho.

In recent memory it was the closest a condemned prisoner had come to execution before receiving a stay. For the rest of his life Autry would relive in nightmares the horror of that hour on the gurney with the needles bristling in his veins.

The rest of his life would not be very long. The following March Autry faced the gurney again. When all other appeals had failed, his attorneys pleaded with the Supreme Court that the near-execution their client had been subjected to constituted cruel and unusual punishment. Two justices agreed he had suffered "profound psychological torment" but the rest didn't.

All hope gone, the prisoner tried to strike a blow against capital punishment: he petitioned the Texas Board of Corrections to make a public event of his execution by allowing it to be televised.

"It ain't real—all that real—to the public unless they see it on television," he said.

The board vetoed the idea.[5]

On his last morning, Autry was moved to the cell next to the death chamber. One of his callers was a priest who'd known him in reform school. "I offered forgiveness," the priest said. "He accepted it. We both cried." But the Cowboy hadn't lost all of his bravado. "Just tell 'em," he told another visitor, "I kept my cool."

He had been corresponding with a young woman in Dallas, and their relationship had become affectionate. When she visited him in the death house that afternoon, he said, "Shirley, I want to live." They wept together.

Autry had invited the woman to be present at his execution. On the gurney, he turned his face toward the witnesses and his eyes sought her out.

Hers never left him. "I love you," she said as the sodium thiopental invaded his veins. "I love you so much."

His lips trembling, he smiled wanly.

It seemed to be taking a long time. She thought he was fighting it. "Give it up," she said. "Give it up."

His labored breathing was the only sound in the tense chamber.

"I love you, baby," she said. "I'm here . . . I care."

"I love you too." His features twisted. His eyes closed. They opened again.

"You feel pain?" She blew a kiss to him. "I love you."

"My arm's hurting!" His clenched left hand opened.

"Pretty brown eyes," she said, still trying to bring comfort.

"I love you." A tremor ran through the dying man and he lay still. It was 12:36 A.M., March 14, 1984. It had taken ten minutes to kill him.

No one could say Autry's death had been easy. After, medical experts tried to figure out why it took so long.

Opinions differed. One was that the drugs had been diluted. Another was that the catheter might have been clogged. As anyone who has had injections knows, not all medical technicians are skillful in inserting needles. The death needle might have pulled loose from the vein and delivered its dose into the tissue instead, where absorption is slow.

Certainly an anesthesiologist could have done a better job. But medical professionals had taken an ethical stand: they would not participate in an execution.

A little more than two weeks after Autry's execution, it was Ronald Clark O'Bryan's turn to enter the Texas death chamber. "He made his bed, and now he is having to lie in it," said his former wife. "I have no pity for him."

The woman's wrath was understandable. A Texas jury had found O'Bryan guilty of poisoning his eight-year-old son by giving him cyanide-laced candy on Halloween in 1974. According to the prosecution, O'Bryan had killed the child because he wanted to collect $31,000 of insurance on the boy's life. Fellow inmates called him the Candy Man.

More than nine years of appeals had passed since the murder, and O'Bryan was still appealing. The prisoner's final argument was that the FDA hadn't approved the Texas death drugs as "safe and effective" for putting human beings to death and he should be reprieved until it had. The Supreme Court didn't share his view and decreed he should be executed as scheduled.

On March 31, 1984, O'Bryan, aged thirty-nine, calmly lay down on the gurney in Huntsville. He had insisted on his innocence all along. Now he forgave everyone involved in his death. "God bless you all," he said, "and may God's best blessings be always yours."

"I'll miss you, Ron!" cried an eighteen-year-old college girl, in tears; she had been corresponding with him and he'd invited her as a personal witness.

At 12:38 A.M., the executioner began the injections. "Mr. O'Bryan yawned," said *The New York Times*, "his chest heaved and his eyes rolled after the mixture of deadly drugs flowed into his veins. He gasped, and seconds later there was a gurgling, choking sound as if he was clearing his throat. He was pronounced dead ten minutes after the deadly solution began flowing into his body."

Unlike Autry in the previous execution, O'Bryan had passed into unconsciousness quickly and had apparently shown no signs of pain. In the absence of a physician, a justice of the peace pronounced him dead. An optician, O'Bryan had donated his eyes to an eye bank.

In October 1984, all was ready in Huntsville's death chamber for the execution of Thomas Andy Barefoot, who had murdered a policeman. One of the witnesses was Richard Moran of Harvard Law School, who was studying capital punishment.

The condemned man, tubes inserted in his arms, smiled at the spectators. ''I hope,'' he said, ''that one day we can look back on the evil that we are doing right now like we do the witches when they were burned at the stake. . . . I'm sorry for anything I've ever done to anybody.''

The warden gave the signal to the executioner to release his deadly liquids. Nothing changed; Barefoot seemed as alert as ever. He started to address the witnesses. He wanted them to say goodbye for him to his friends on death row. He was giving their names when all at once, according to Moran, he ''let out a terrible gasp. His neck straightened. His eyes bulged and his back arched. He lay stiff on the gurney, glazed eyes fixed on the ceiling, like a soldier standing at attention.''

Moran, previously convinced that lethal injection had taken almost all the frightfulness out of executions, now decided he was mistaken.

Four minutes later, Barefoot was pronounced dead. The prison doctor, said Moran, ''tried to close Barefoot's eyes, but the lids would not budge. He tried a second time. Still they would not move. Finally the doctor said: 'Eyes dilated, respiration stopped, heartbeat slowed. Barefoot is dead.' I thought to myself, no he isn't. His heart is still beating.''

Earlier we saw that medical men had prophesied there would be problems in implanting the death needle. In March 1985, when Huntsville was about to perform its sixth execution by lethal injection, it ran into particular difficulty.

The convict was Peter Morin, sentenced to death for the murder of a young woman in San Antonio. He had also been convicted of slaying two other young women and he was suspected of killing two more.

Morin was a longtime drug user. The medical technician made repeated attempts to insert the needle in Morin's arm and one leg but failed again and again because the veins were covered with scars. Finally the needle was successfully implanted in the convict's right arm.

Eleven minutes later the prison physician pronounced Morin dead. That was considerably less than the forty minutes it had taken to find a suitable vein and insert the needle.

"I don't know if it was the longest [execution]," said a prison spokesman, "but it was the toughest."

At 2:00 A.M., on November 2, 1984, Margie Velma Barfield, a plump fifty-two-year-old grandmother, became the first woman to die by lethal injection. She was also the first woman to be executed in the United States since 1962. The place was Central Prison, Raleigh, North Carolina.

The execution was a national event. Outside the floodlit prison yard several hundred people opposed to capital punishment, candles in their hands, had been holding a silent vigil. Reporters from around the country were taking notes. About eighty youthful supporters of the death penalty milled around. Some were chanting, "Burn, bitch, burn!" and "Hip, hip, hurray . . . K-I-L-L V-E-L-M-A!"

A look of peace on her face and a prayer on her lips, Barfield sank into unconsciousness after an apology for "all the hurt I have caused."

That hurt had been substantial. The woman had poisoned five people—most of them so they wouldn't find out she'd stolen money from them to buy drugs.

Barfield's drugs weren't cocaine or heroin. They were mostly doctor-prescribed: tranquilizers like Valium, Thorazine, and Librium, antidepressants like Elaville and Tofranil, barbiturates like Seconal; narcotics, sleeping pills, amphetamines—dozens in all. She had become addicted as a result of taking medications after a nervous breakdown, and several times she had overdosed and been hospitalized. She had also served time for fraud to get money for drugs.

In 1978 Barfield, previously twice married, was keeping company with Stuart Taylor, a widowed tobacco farmer. The small jobs she held were never enough to support her drug habit; she began to forge checks in Taylor's name to get the money she needed. Then, fearful he would find out, one night she mixed arsenic-laden rat poison into his beer and tea and went off with him to a Rex Humbard religious revival meeting.

That night, as Taylor lay twisting and turning in terrible agony, Barfield informed his family he had the flu and she would nurse him. The following day she took him to a hospital and the doctor agreed it was a flu virus, gave a prescription, and recommended lots of fluids. A few days later Taylor was dead. For the selfless way Barfield had nursed him, his relatives gave her his gold wedding band, which she had requested, and four hundred dollars.

An autopsy revealed arsenic in the dead man's body. Barfield was charged with murder. Her plea was insanity.

After being convicted, Barfield confessed Taylor hadn't been her only victim. She had also poisoned her own mother, having without her knowledge borrowed money on her house. In the same way she had murdered two old people she'd been hired to take care of. Their deaths, she insisted, were unintended. She gave the same reason for doing away with them as she had for killing Taylor: she had forged checks for small sums in their names and they had found out. "I only wanted to make them sick," she said, so she could nurse them back to health, meanwhile getting another job and returning the stolen money.

"I know that doesn't make sense," Barfield admitted later, "but to my tired, medicated brain, filled with twenty pills a day, it made perfect sense."

The body of a fifth possible victim, her second husband, also showed traces of arsenic, but she denied killing him. Later, however, in her ghost-written autobiography, published after her death, she said, "I bought a bottle of ant and roach poison. *My God! What am I doing? Stop!* I was so confused. . . . *This will make him sick. Then he'll be sorry he's caused me so much trouble, and he won't bother me anymore.*"

"Born again" as she awaited trial, Barfield, during the six years she spent in prison while lawyers tried to save her life, counseled young women inmates, read the Bible unceasingly, and prayed. She attracted the support of religious leaders; Billy Graham said she had a "big impact" and his daughter came to pray with her. Appeals made in Barfield's behalf revealed that she had been a battered child, was sexually abused by her father, and beaten by her husband.

North Carolina law gave a convict the choice of death by lethal injection or gas. Barfield chose the first. She selected the clothes she wanted to be buried in as well as the songs to be sung at her funeral. On her last day, ministers, relatives and friends visited her. She told one, "When I go into that chamber at 2:00 A.M., it's my gateway to heaven." Unable to eat her last meal, she sent a guard to buy Cheez Doodles and Coca-Cola for her. At 1:00 A.M., as execution time approached, prisoners hammered on the plexiglass windows of their cells in protest, although she had asked them not to demonstrate.

The death gurney was rolled into her cell and she was strapped to it by matrons recruited from other prisons. (The prison didn't want to use its own matrons, who were fond of her.) Stethoscope and heart-monitor leads were attached to her breasts. A diaper had been put on her; when a person dies, the anal sphincter relaxes, causing the bowel to release its contents. Dressed in her own pink pajamas, she was wheeled to the execution chamber on the top floor and positioned next to a window in the wall. Behind it was a small room where the witnesses watched.

A curtain was drawn on the other side of the gurney. The execution had been rehearsed five times so there would be no hitches. Three syringes were attached to intravenous tubes running through the curtain. While the saltwater solution flowed into the woman's arms the chaplain prayed with her. Then simultaneously the executioners pressed the plungers in their syringes.

Only two of the tubes were connected to Barfield. The third tube was a dummy, and its contents spilled harmlessly into a container near her. None of the executioners knew which tube was the dummy; thus each man could believe he had not helped to kill her. All of the executioners were volunteers from the warden's staff.

At 2:15 A.M., Barfield was pronounced dead. Outside, the protesters snuffed out their candles. The young supporters of capital punishment broke into cheers as loud "as if the home team had just scored the winning touchdown," James Reston, Jr., would report in *Vanity Fair*.

Four news people who had served as witnesses emerged and mounted a lectern. They gave a crowd of fellow reporters their impressions of what they had seen. The dead woman had written an apology for her crimes, and copies were distributed.

Velma Barfield's life was over, but not her story. She had wanted to make a more substantial apology: she had signed a paper donating her organs for transplant. It was hoped that her kidneys could be taken.

To be usable, organs like the kidneys must be removed while the donor's blood is still circulating. In a typical situation in a hospital, the body, which is brain-dead, is kept on a life-support system until the organs are harvested.

But this wasn't possible in an execution. The transplant team would have to start the woman's heart beating again no more than a few minutes after it was stopped by the lethal injection. For the best results, the doctors would need to inject a heart stimulant and use other measures to restore breathing. As long as the woman was brain-dead— as long as an electroencephalograph showed no activity—she was legally dead by medical standards.

The team's proposal had disturbed the state authorities. They had no experience with the procedure planned. One of their fears was that the dead woman might come back to life and sit up in the death chamber. They were afraid they might have to execute her again. The best solution, they decided, was not to release the body until five minutes after the heart monitor stopped showing signs of life.[6] To make matters worse, Barfield's relatives vetoed the use of a heart stimulant.

The team faced an added difficulty: they would need a hospital operating room to remove the kidneys. The prison hospital refused to allow the use of its facilities. One in the vicinity agreed to cooperate, but then reneged. The team would be obliged to use its own hospital, which was fully a hundred miles away.

After Barfield had been declared dead, prison employees rushed the gurney bearing her body out to the elevator and down to the ground floor, where the team was waiting. The doctors ran with the body to their ambulance, placed a Ambu bag on the woman's chest, inserted the attached endotracheal tube in her throat, and began to pump oxygen into her lungs while pounding on her chest. No result. By now, it was seven minutes since the body had been taken from the death chamber.

Inside the ambulance speeding through the night, a physician applied pressure again and again to the dead woman's chest. At 2:23 her gray cheeks started to show a pinkish hue.

Pressure continued to be applied over Barfield's heart. The trip to the hospital would take two hours. "After thirty minutes it was apparent that cardiac function could not be restored," the team leader would report later. The team's efforts had not produced a single heartbeat, and they were given up.

That didn't mean that all of their plans were for nothing. At the North Carolina Baptist Hospital in Winston-Salem, bone, skin and eyes were removed from the dead woman, and they were used.

In the end, Margie Velma Barfield made some amends for the lives she had taken.

SIX

███████

Firing Squad

Sheriff John Gillespie was scrawling in his journal an account of how he had put a murderer to death outside Tooele, near Salt Lake City. The man, Robert Sutton, a hostler for the Overland Company, had crept up on an ex-soldier named White, who had insulted him, and shot him dead as he lay sleeping.

"Early in the morning I pitched a small tent . . ." wrote Gillespie, "and had five men [concealed inside it] with rifles, four of them loaded with bullets and one loaded with powder, neither of the men knew who had the blank gun. I called out a company of cavalry to keep back the crowd of people, from all over the county.

"I set the prisoner on a chair about sixty yards from the mouth of the tent and covered his face and opened the front of the tent, and gave the word of command, and he was shot dead; we had his grave dug and buried him right there, dispersed the crowd and left a guard there, and moved the tent and the men that night so that no one knew who did the shooting."

That was in 1866, but death by the firing squad is still on the books in Utah and it hasn't changed very much. Nevada tried shooting too, after it grew dissatisfied with hanging. But the Nevadans shot only one prisoner, and the firing squad was actually a machine. Shooting is also the way the military punishes deserters in time of war, but out of

89

thousands and thousands of deserters, only one has been shot since the Civil War. We'll look at his extraordinary case later.

Utah was still a territory when it first provided for the death penalty. Under the 1852 statute, the court could order the doomed convict to be shot, hanged, or beheaded, or it could grant him the privilege of selecting whichever of these methods he preferred. No one ever chose to have his head chopped off, and in 1888 the state dropped the option.

But why beheading, in the first place? And why shooting?

Both beheading and shooting were originally chosen because the territory's legislators were mostly Mormon, and the Mormons—or Latter-day Saints as they also are known—believe in the biblical doctrine of blood atonement.

"Whoso sheddeth man's blood, by man shall his blood be shed," declares the Old Testament (Genesis 9: 6). Brigham Young, who led the Mormons into Utah, taught that although the blood of Jesus was shed for many sins, "yet men can commit sins which it can never remit." These sins "must be atoned for by the blood of the [guilty] man."

Blood for blood, literally: both beheading and shooting satisfied that requirement. But, recognizing that some, especially non-Mormons, might object to dying in such an unconventional way, the lawmakers also provided the more usual method, hanging. If the condemned failed to express a preference, he was shot.

Most prisoners sentenced to death in Utah—Mormon and non-Mormon alike—have chosen to die by the firing squad. The reason isn't hard to find. A volley of well-aimed bullets will kill a person faster than hanging.

In 1938 a convict's heartbeat was monitored by electrocardiograph during his execution. The heartbeat rose from a normal seventy-two beats a minute to 180 when he was strapped in the death chair. It stopped 15.6 seconds after the bullets penetrated his heart.

If a firing squad is less skillful, or less willing, or wants to inflict punishment, death comes slower. This happened in 1951, when the riflemen missed the heart-shaped target pinned to the chest of Eliseo Mares and he bled to death. Mares, an AWOL soldier, had murdered a companion. Some said the marksmen missed on purpose. The deserter mentioned earlier also took long to die.

In 1983, moving ahead with the times, Utah abandoned the hanging option and substituted lethal injection, making it mandatory if the prisoner expressed no preference. In 1987 Pierre Dale became the first prisoner to die by the new method.

Executions in Utah are carried out today at the state prison at Point-of-the-Mountain, near Salt Lake City. (They were originally done at the scene or in the county of the crime.) The sheriff used to officiate, but now it is the warden. The firing squad consists of five men. One rifle is loaded with a blank, so no member of the firing squad needs to feel any personal guilt for the killing. But canny riflemen know that the gun that fired the blank is cooler than the rest.

The squad is made up of volunteer marksmen. They are concealed from both the witnesses and the condemned man, who is usually seated in a chair and strapped to it, a blindfold over his eyes. The prison doctor, using his stethoscope, determines the exact location of the prisoner's heart and attaches a bull's-eye over it. It is his duty also to pronounce the convict dead. According to a retired guard who witnessed seven executions, "Sometimes the blood runs out the back quite strongly; other times it does not. They bleed internally."

In old Utah, rough-and-ready do-it-yourself justice was the rule. The first persons executed were Indians. Among the early Mormons, in cases of seduction, theft or the like, it was considered quite fitting for the wronged party to avenge himself; if he didn't, he might not be able to look the other members of his community in the eye again. In 1851 two husbands shot to death men who had seduced their wives, and they were promptly exonerated by the courts. Oddly, none of the guilt for the adultery fell on the women involved. Brigham Young's position was sterner. He believed the husband should kill both his wife and her seducer on the spot.

In a peaceful little valley in southwestern Utah, schoolchildren and holidaying tourists often fall silent as they read a brass tablet set close by a wall of stone. On the tablet are engraved these words:

MOUNTAIN MEADOWS

A FAVORITE RECRUITING PLACE ON THE

OLD SPANISH TRAIL

IN THIS VICINITY SEPTEMBER 7TH, 1857, OCCURRED ONE OF THE MOST LAMENTABLE TRAGEDIES IN THE HISTORY ANNALS OF THE WEST. A COMPANY OF ABOUT 140 EMIGRANTS FROM ARKANSAS AND MIS-

SOURI LED BY CAPTAIN CHARLES FANCHER, ENROUTE
TO CALIFORNIA, WAS ATTACKED BY WHITE MEN AND
INDIANS. ALL BUT 17 SMALL CHILDREN WERE KILLED.
JOHN D. LEE, WHO CONFESSED PARTICIPATION AS
LEADER, WAS LEGALLY EXECUTED HERE MARCH 23RD,
1877. MOST OF THE EMIGRANTS WERE BURIED
IN THEIR OWN DEFENSE PIT. . . .

Inside the stone wall is the mass grave of the murdered men, women and children.

The story is an astonishing one and little known. Utah, in 1857, was not a state yet, but a federal territory. Settled by the Mormons, who had built a thriving commonwealth there, it was governed by their leader, Brigham Young. The Mormons were greatly resented by some of their non-Mormon neighbors, who lodged angry accusations against them in Washington, D.C. Finally, persuaded that the members of this new religious faith were in a state of rebellion against the United States, President James Buchanan fired Governor Young and ordered an army force to invade Utah and restore federal control.

The Mormons prepared to resist. Brigham Young declared martial law. He set up a militia to fight the United States troops guerrilla-style. He called upon his people to store up supplies and prepare for a siege. War hysteria raced and raged like a fever through the territory.

That September, a large wagon train of emigrants bound for California arrived in southern Utah. They could hardly have come at a worse time. When they stopped in villages along the way to buy provisions, the Mormons refused to sell them any. They would need the supplies for themselves, they thought. Besides, they were feeling very hostile toward outsiders—gentiles, as they called them.

The emigrants responded in kind. They called the Mormon women whores (Mormons practiced polygamy at this time) and threatened to return from California with federal troops and punish the Utahans. Some of the emigrants boasted they had taken part in the murder of the Mormon prophet Joseph Smith, revered founder of the religion.

That was more than the Mormons could stand. In a vengeful mood, they turned to their friends and allies, the Paiute Indians. The gentiles, they told them, had been poisoning water holes, causing the death of cattle belonging to the Indians, and of some Indians as well. The Paiutes reached for their tomahawks and their rifles.

Traveling onward, the emigrants came to grass-covered Mountain

Meadows, where they stopped to rest and refresh their livestock. Not for long, however. The Paiutes gathered there in large numbers and swooped down upon the emigrants. The "Mericats," as they were known among the Indians, gave a good account of themselves, killing some of their attackers. Then they formed a defensive circle with their wagons, threw up earthworks, and held the Indians at bay for almost a week.

It was at this fateful moment that John Doyle Lee made his entrance upon the scene. Born in 1812, Lee had been close to both Joseph Smith and Brigham Young, and burned with religious zeal. A bishop in the Mormon church, he had been a leader in the settlement of Utah. Not only was he a major in the militia; he was also an Indian agent, responsible for dealing with the Paiutes.

Determined to make the gentiles eat their words of sacrilege, the Mormons sent a detachment of militia to Mountain Meadows. To avoid a costly direct attack, they decided to lure the gentiles out of the shelter of their wagon fort. This delicate mission was entrusted to Bishop Lee.

After a powwow with the Indians, Lee approached the gentiles under a flag of truce. He would guarantee their safety, he told them—but only if they would abandon their wagons, give up their weapons, and place themselves under his protection.

The emigrants were desperately short of food and ammunition. They swallowed the bait.

The Paiutes pretended to withdraw. Two wagons were loaded with the emigrants' smallest children, the wounded, and the elderly, and moved out with Lee in charge. Behind them trudged the older children and the women. The men, having surrendered their weapons, followed in single file. Each was accompanied by an armed Mormon.

Suddenly a command rang out: "Halt! Do your duty!"

Instantly the Mormons shot down the unarmed men they were escorting. Lee and his companions murdered the wounded and the elderly in the two wagons. The Paiutes, who had been hiding in the brush, sprang out and butchered the women and older children. The smallest children, too young to tell tales later, were spared and taken away to live with the Mormons.

Soon afterward, Lee would write later, he went to Salt Lake City and told Brigham Young the entire story of the massacre. He also gave him the names of the more than fifty Mormons who had taken part. Young told him that God had "shown him the massacre was right";

however, it must remain secret, and he was to declare it was the work of the Indians alone.

Before long, some of the true facts of the massacre leaked out. In 1859 a federal official, searching for the missing children, called on Bishop Lee.

The Mormon denied any part in the massacre. He had arrived in Mountain Meadows, he said, just after the killing had ended. According to the official, "Lee applied some foul and indecent epithets to the emigrants—said they were slandering the Mormons, while passing along, and in general terms justified the killings."

The names of some of the militiamen were known, and federal troops tried to find them, but without success. The Mormon church disavowed all responsibility. Lee's part, however, was too well known, and seventeen years after the massacre he was excommunicated. All but one of his wives (he had nineteen, who bore him sixty-four children) were automatically divorced from him.

In November 1874 a federal marshal tracked down the ex-bishop and arrested him. At his trial, the prosecution tried to show that not just Lee, but the leaders of the church—right up to Brigham Young himself—were responsible for the tragedy. The trial ended in a hung jury; the eight Mormons were for acquittal, the four non-Mormons for conviction.

The following year Lee went on trial again. This time the jury was made up exclusively of Mormons. From the start it appeared Lee was to be a scapegoat: the Mormon leaders, it was said, had made a deal with the prosecution that the ex-bishop could be convicted and executed, provided the charges against other suspects were dropped.

It took the jury just a few hours to bring in a verdict of guilty. When the judge asked Lee if he had anything to say, he remained silent. He heard himself sentenced to be executed at the scene of the massacre. Offered the choice of death by hanging or the firing squad, he replied, "I prefer to be shot."

The prisoner still had many friends. Petitions with hundreds of signatures were sent to the governor pleading that Lee was "but one of many who were equally guilty"; that the dozens of men who had taken part in the bloodshed had acted under military orders. The embittered Lee passed the months in prison writing a book called *Mormonism Unveiled*, in which he laid the blame for his crime on the church. Brigham Young, who, according to Lee, had given him a concubine as a reward for his acts in the massacre, was called "the greatest criminal of the Nineteenth-Century."

The petitions for mercy were rejected. On March 23, 1877, the day set for the execution, the condemned man was brought to Mountain Meadows in great secrecy and under heavy guard; it was feared that his sons and friends would try to rescue him if the place were known. Sentinels were posted on the surrounding hills to prevent a surprise.

The wind was icy. Lee, bundled up, sat patiently on the edge of his coffin as a photographer took pictures. He asked that copies be given as keepsakes to his wives Rachel, Sarah and Emma, who had remained faithful. Then, rising to his feet, he delivered a last message. He had tried his best, he swore, to save the emigrants. "It seems I have to be made a victim," he said. Of Brigham Young, whom he had once regarded as a father, he spoke harshly. "What confidence can I have in such a man? I have none, and I don't think my Father in heaven has any."

At the end a minister knelt on the ground and prayed. Lee asked the marshal to have the firing party shoot straight for his heart and spare his limbs. Shaking hands, he gave officials his hat, his muffler, and his overcoat to keep in memory of him. A blindfold was tied over his eyes but he asked that his hands be left unbound.

Army blankets had been drawn over the wheels of the wagon in front. They hid from view the members of the firing squad. Sitting on the coffin, Lee clasped his hands over his head. He reminded the firing squad: "Center my heart, boys. Don't mangle my body!" The five riflemen, twenty feet away, raised their rifles and took aim.

What happened next would be recalled in a brief ballad still sung in the West:

See Lee kneel upon his coffin, sure his death can do no good;
Oh, see, they've shot him, see his bosom stream with blood.

Actually, Lee was seated on the coffin, and when the bullets struck he fell back upon it.

Twenty years had passed since the massacre; Lee was sixty-four, the oldest man ever executed in Utah. At his request, his family buried him in his Mormon ceremonial robes.

More than eighty years later, in 1961, the Church of Jesus Christ of Latter-day Saints took back to its bosom the son it had cast out, authorizing "the reinstatement to membership and former blessings to John D. Lee."

In Nevada, from territorial days through the first decade of the twentieth century, convicts sentenced to death were hanged. But a wave of revulsion against the traditional method of capital punishment was sweeping across the nation in the early 1900s. In 1911, Nevada decided to liberalize its penal code. It considered allowing convicted killers to take poison, but ended by offering them the same choice Utah did: death on the gallows or by the rifles of a firing squad.

The state wouldn't have to wait long for an occasion to apply its new execution statute.

On May 14, 1912, a murder took place at the railroad depot in Tonopah. The killer was a young mine worker, Andrija Mircovich; his victim was an influential businessman, John Gregovich.

Fifteen months before, a cousin of Mircovich's had lost his life in a fire in a Tonopah mine. He left no will, and Gregovich had been appointed to administer his estate. Mircovich became convinced Gregovich was cheating him out of his proper share.

Spying the businessman on the railroad platform, Mircovich made his way toward him. He cursed Gregovich in Serbian. Pulling out a knife, he said, "I will get you, you old son of a bitch!" and stabbed him several times.

"My God, I'm cut!" cried Gregovich. "I'm dying! Take me to a hospital!" He fell to the platform.

Mircovich was disarmed and arrested. The businessman was driven to the hospital but died soon after his arrival.

Charged with murder in the first degree, Mircovich was placed on trial the following month. His command of English was poor; questions had to be put to him in Serbian by an interpreter. It took the jury no more than three days to hear the case and bring in a verdict of guilty.

Offered his choice of the two methods of execution, the Montenegrin told the judge he preferred to be shot. In his cell, he informed a reporter that death by a firing squad was swifter. He didn't really care, he said. "I am ready to go any time."

The prisoner was removed to the state prison in Carson City to await his end. He was to be the first man to be executed by rifle, and somehow people began to say that the prison guards, from whose ranks the riflemen were to be drawn, didn't relish the idea of shooting him. A reporter picked up the rumor and it spread.

It has happened many times before and since in like situations: the warden promptly heard from hundreds of people all over the country who announced they would be happy to demonstrate their marksmanship on the doomed man. Even sharpshooters in foreign countries applied.

From the warden came a quick denial that his guards were unwilling to shoot the condemned man. He also gave the lie to another report that he was trying to persuade Mircovich to change his mind and let himself be executed by the less troublesome method of hanging.

Whether or not there was any truth to these rumors, late that year the warden placed a highly unusual order with an ordnance company. It was for an execution machine.

The execution machine, or shooting gallery as journalists would call it, weighed half a ton. No one today knows how much it cost. The device, wrote Phillip I. Earl, a Nevada historian, "consisted of a steel framework hut with three small ports in front from which the muzzles of three .30-.30 Savage rifles would protrude. The weapons, equipped with Maxim silencers, were to be aimed at a steel backdrop, in front of which the doomed man would be strapped to a chair bolted to a platform. The rifles were to be pre-aimed and fired by a coiled spring mechanism set off by the simultaneous cutting of three strings, only one of which would fire the two weapons loaded with real bullets. The hut was louvered in such a way that none of the guards would be able to see the victim die."

The manufacturer worked fast, and two months later (February 1913) the machine was delivered at the state prison. The warden and his people assembled and tested the device and found it lived up to expectations. Now the only question was how long it would take for Mircovich's last appeals to be exhausted.

As expected, the appeals failed. On May 8, with only six days left to live, Mircovich was taken from his cell and into the prison yard for a rehearsal. Stoically he sat down in the chair facing the execution machine, and a heart-sized piece of cardboard was pinned to his shirt. After the rifle sights had been set on the cardboard, the prisoner was led back to his cell. The cardboard target had been removed from his shirt and fixed in precisely the same position on the chair. The rifles were fired; one bullet hit the cardboard in the middle, the other very close by.

A new warden had been appointed, Denver Dickerson. He asked the guards to write their names on slips of paper. After the names had been placed in a hat, he drew out three: their owners would take part in the execution. Dickerson also had the doorway to the execution-machine hut screened so spectators would be unable to see the guards enter or leave it.

In his cell, meanwhile, the condemned man kept muttering that the judge who had sentenced him had been unjust and Gregovich had robbed him. He often talked to himself in Serbian.

On the morning of May 14, his last day, Mircovich was visited by the chaplain, who offered him the last rites of the Episcopal Church. The prisoner said no; he was Greek Orthodox and, besides, it would be "too much trouble." He said Gregovich had gotten what he deserved. To a reporter he insisted his punishment was too severe and he should only have received two years in prison.

His time was up. Warden Dickerson asked him whether he wished to have the execution order read to him.

"I no understand very well. Maybe so," Mircovich replied. He listened alertly, running his finger over his mustache as the warden read the formal words to him slowly and carefully.

Did he want a blindfold or a black hood, the warden asked.

"No, I want to see."

"God be with you and goodbye," said Warden Dickerson, taking his hand. Like so many other wardens, he was opposed to capital punishment.

"I much obliged to you. You be good man to me."

Mircovich was led out into the prison yard.

"Now die like a soldier," said the captain of the guard. No doubt he was recalling other condemned men who had broken down. "Show the people you are brave."

"I die like soldier."

In the yard, witnesses and guards were watching behind a rope. Mircovich inspected them with curiosity, bent down under the rope, and walked over to the chair. After being strapped securely in place, he looked on calmly as the prison doctor pinned the target over his heart.

"Hold up your head," he was told.

Mircovich raised his chin. He looked at the spectators, then fastened his eyes on the openings of the hut, from which the rifle muzzles extended. The guns were swiveled until the muzzles bore directly on the cardboard target. Mircovich's expression was solemn. He squinted in the sunlight.

Warden Dickerson signaled.

The captain of the guard gave the order to fire, and the hidden guards severed the strings. Flame spurted from the rifle barrels.

Mircovich's mouth opened wide as the bullets hit. His body shook and his head slumped; the white target turned red.

After the prison physician had pronounced him dead, Mircovich's body was removed from the chair and examined. The two bullets had penetrated his heart, their points of entry less than an inch apart. Both had exited through a single hole.

Mircovich was laid to rest in the prison cemetery. The chaplain read the funeral service while a handful of guards and convicts bowed their heads. The chaplain, the warden's wife, and two guards finished the ceremony with hymns.

The execution of Andrija Mircovich was the last in Nevada for eleven years. During that period, several men on death row died of natural causes while their cases were under appeal, or their sentences were commuted. The state never employed its killing machine on any other convict, nor was anyone hanged again. In 1924, when Nevada put its next condemned man to death, it was by the innovative method of lethal gas.

What became of the execution machine? It lay forgotten for decades, gathering dust in a storage area. During World War II somebody remembered it. "In July 1942," relates historian Phillip Earl, "the old relic was included in some fifty tons of metal collected at the prison in the course of a wartime scrap drive."

The name of Joe Hill is familiar to people all over the world who know little or nothing about Joe Hill the man—least of all that he was executed by a firing squad at Utah State Prison in 1915. Much of his fame is owed to a song made popular by the singer Paul Robeson:

> *I dreamed I saw Joe Hill last night,*
> *Alive as you and me.*
> *Says I, "But Joe, you're ten years dead!"*
> *"I never died," says he,*
> *"I never died," says he.*[1]

Hill wrote songs too. Famous in his own time and later, they have been sung by unionists and left-wing groups from coast to coast in America and in many foreign countries. Best known of all is *The Preacher and the Slave*:

Long-haired preachers come out every night,
Try to tell you what's wrong and what's right;
But when asked, "How 'bout something to eat?"
They will answer in voices so sweet:
"You will eat, by and by,
In that glorious land above the sky;
Work and pray, live on hay,
You'll get pie in the sky when you die."

Sailor, stevedore, union organizer, labor journalist, revolutionary and hobo, as well as writer of songs, Hill lived a life that was brief, intense, and, for the most part, obscure. He was born in Gävle, Sweden, on October 7, 1879. His original name was Joel Hägglund. As a child, he learned to play the violin, guitar, piano and other musical instruments. When Joe was eight years old, his father died of injuries suffered in his railroad job, and the boy had to go to work. In 1902, he came to the United States, where he was known as Joseph Hillstrom and Joe Hill. A hint of his early life is suggested by John Dos Passos in his book *Nineteen Nineteen*:

A young Swede named Hillstrom went to sea, got himself cal-loused hands on sailing ships and tramps, learned English in the focastle of the steamers that make the run from Stockholm to Hull, dreamed the Swede's dream of the West:
    When he got to America they gave him a job polishing cus-pidors in a Bowery saloon.

Blond, slim, tall, with blue eyes, Hill didn't drink or smoke. With little formal education but strong intellectual leanings, he wandered across the country from job to job, writing songs on the backs of envelopes and scraps of paper, setting them to familiar tunes. By 1906 he was in California. In 1910 he became a member of the Industrial Workers of the World (IWW), a revolutionary labor union popularly known as the Wobblies. In San Pedro, as union secretary, he was active in organizing dock workers and in strike activities.

In 1911 it is said Hill joined an international brigade that fought for the rebel cause in the Mexican revolution. In 1912 he was in San Diego, where he may have been involved in a fight for free speech and was severely beaten and scarred. That same year he reportedly took part in a Wobbly attempt to set up a workers' commune in Baja California.

Blacklisted by employers up and down the West Coast, in 1913 Hill made his way to Salt Lake City. He may have worked as a miner in the Utah mountains and we know he worked for the union in an unpaid job, but much of his activity up to this time is vague and the subject of unconfirmed reports.

It is in Salt Lake City in January, 1914, that Hill's life comes into clear—and tragic—focus.

On the night of January 10, 1914, two masked gunmen burst into a grocery store brandishing guns. They confronted the owner, John Morrison, an ex-policeman, and his two young sons, who were closing up. One of the intruders called out, "We've got you now!" and began to shoot.

Both Morrison and his older son were killed, but not before the taller of the intruders was also hit. "Oh, God! I'm shot!" he cried, clutching his breast, according to the younger son, who survived. Then the two ran from the store. They took no money, leading the authorities to label the incident a revenge killing.

Two hours later, Joe Hill staggered into a doctor's office just four blocks away. He was bleeding from a bullet wound in his lung. The doctor dressed the wound, and when he helped his patient put on his shirt, a shoulder holster with a gun in it dropped from his clothing. Hill explained he'd been shot in an argument with a friend over a married woman and he'd taken the gun from him. While being driven home from the doctor's office, Hill flung the gun out of the car window.

A day or so later the doctor read about the Morrison killings and reported his late-night visitor to the police. Going to Hill's apartment to change the dressing, he gave Hill a morphine injection to ease his pain and to put him to sleep. Then, by prearrangement, the police came in. In the excitement, the half-unconscious man was wounded.

Charged with the two Morrison killings, Hill denied any knowledge of them and repeated his story about how he had been shot; he also steadfastly refused to name the woman involved or the man who had wounded him. A friend, Otto Applequist, who shared his room and was suspected of having been his accomplice, had disappeared and was never found. Neither was the gun Hill had thrown away.

The Morrison boy who had survived couldn't identify Hill. The evidence against Hill was purely circumstantial. IWW people acquainted with him insisted he couldn't have committed such a brutal crime. Others, however, suggested that Morrison, in his days on the police force, might have killed a friend of Hill's, and been killed himself in revenge.

During his trial Hill refused to testify and provided little information to his lawyers. In the middle of the trial he fired them. The IWW hired a highly experienced labor attorney to replace them, but Hill was found guilty and sentenced to death. Offered the choice of being shot to death or hanged, he replied, "I'll take shooting. I'm used to that."

Appeals were carried to the Utah Supreme Court and the board of pardons. Discrepancies in Hill's story and the sudden disappearance of his roommate didn't help his case. The board offered to free him if he would tell his lawyer, in complete privacy, how he had come by his wound. He refused. "If I can't have a new trial," he said, "I am willing to give my blood as a martyr that others may be afforded fair trials."

Both Hill and the IWW insisted he had been framed because of his union activities, and for almost two years the case was appealed. Meanwhile, the IWW waged a worldwide campaign to arouse sympathy for him. Thousands of people demonstrated in the streets of New York and Minneapolis. Governor William Spry was snowed under with letters. The Swedish government and Samuel Gompers of the American Federation of Labor tried to win a new trial for him. Helen Keller sent a telegram to President Woodrow Wilson asking him to save Joe Hill. Two days before the execution date, Wilson wired the governor and asked him to intervene; the governor, an avowed enemy of the IWW, angrily rejected this "unwarranted interference" in the state's affairs.

In prison, Hill wrote songs as well as articles for IWW newspapers. A visiting journalist was profoundly impressed by his calmness in the face of death.

The night before the execution, Hill sent a telegram to William Haywood, head of the IWW:

Goodbye, Bill. I die like a true-blue rebel. Don't waste any time mourning—organize! It is a hundred miles from here to Wyoming. Could you arrange to have my body hauled to the state line to be buried? I don't want to be found dead in Utah.

Later he gave a guard a poem he had written:

MY LAST WILL

My will is easy to decide
For there is nothing to divide.
My kin don't need to fuss and moan,
"Moss does not cling to a rolling stone."
My body?—Oh!—if I could choose
I would to ashes it reduce
And let the merry breezes blow
My dust to where some flowers grow.
Perhaps some fading flowers then
Would come to life and bloom again.
This is my Last and Final Will.
Good luck to all of you.

Joe Hill

On the morning of his execution, November 10, 1915, Hill barricaded himself in his cell by tying the door shut with bedding and forcing his mattress up against it. He broke a broom and used the handle to fend off the guards when they began to force their way in. Finally, he surrendered with these words: "Well, I'm through, but you can't blame a man fighting for his life."

According to Olive Woolley Burt, the ballad collector, years later she was told by the prison doctor that he had said to Hill, "You have a pretty stiff ordeal ahead of you. How about a slug of whiskey?"

"I don't want no whiskey. I ain't never drunk the stuff and I don't intend to start now."

"Perhaps you're right, Joe," replied the doctor. "It might be habit forming."

Taken to the prison yard, Hill was strapped to the death chair. About twenty feet away, the firing squad was hidden behind a canvas drape. Holes had been cut into it for five rifle barrels.

"I'll show you how to die," Hill said. "I have a clear conscience."

A blindfold was tied over his eyes. The prison doctor used a stethoscope to locate the exact position of his heart and a white target was pinned over it. Hill leaned back and tried to see under the blindfold.

"I'm going now, boys," he cried. "Goodbye! Goodbye, boys!"

The officer in charge called to the firing squad: "Ready—aim—"

"Fire—go on and fire!" interrupted the prisoner, grinning.

"Fire!" called the officer, and the bullets pounded into the target.

The smile vanished from Hill's face. His chest sank as if it had been hit by a heavy weight. Blackened circles appeared on the white target and blood oozed from them. A few minutes later, he was pronounced dead.

Hill's songs, his final telegram to Haywood, and the widespread belief that he had been framed, helped to make him a hero of the labor movement. Like Sacco and Vanzetti, he was enshrined as a martyr. Huge crowds demonstrated when his coffin was carried through the streets of Salt Lake City and Chicago. Afterward, his body was cremated in a blast furnace.

On May Day, 1916, Joe Hill's ashes were scattered in many foreign countries and in all of the states, with one exception, Utah.

The place they chose was Ste. Marie aux Mines, a small town in eastern France. The United States Military Government obtained a house with a good-sized garden surrounded by a stone wall. To ensure privacy, the Army took possession of the properties around the house. The execution, after all, was nobody's business but the Army's.

In front of the stone wall at the rear, they set up a post. Behind that was built a barrier of heavy lumber. Bullets that passed through the prisoner's body and the lumber and bounced off the stone wall would ricochet off the barrier and not harm any of the witnesses.

Slovik was a coward, and the Army figured he might pass out on the way to the post. So a large board was prepared to which he would be strapped if necessary; it would be propped up against the post so the execution might proceed without delay.

Twelve riflemen, all crack shots belonging to his division, the 28th, were selected for the firing squad.

Some of the men didn't like the idea of shooting one of their own, but they were told they had to do it—or else.

The commanding general, Norman D. Cota, addressed them. He pointed out Slovik not only was a deserter, but had a criminal record in civilian life. Father Cummings, the chaplain, told the riflemen that no guilt could attach to them; they would simply be obeying orders.

The Army doctor decided he wouldn't pin a target to the prisoner's chest. Instead, choosing one of the marksmen, he pointed out on him which part of the body they should aim at. Then, with Major Fellman in charge, the riflemen marched out into the chilly garden and went through a rehearsal of the execution step by step, down to the last detail. The Army didn't want any slip-ups.

On January 30, 1945, the night before the execution, there was a fierce snowstorm. Private Eddie D. Slovik, his ankles tied, his wrists in manacles, was being driven from the prison in Paris to Ste. Marie by MPs. A slightly built man with blue eyes and sandy hair, he was almost, but never would be, twenty-five years old.

En route, they stopped for refreshments and Slovik begged the MPs to do him a favor. He wanted them to let him run from the vehicle, and he wanted them to shoot him down as he ran.

The guards were sympathetic, but they told him they couldn't; he had to be executed officially, as a warning to would-be deserters. They told him he shouldn't worry, it would all be over in a matter of hours.

At 7:30 A.M., on January 31, they delivered him in Ste. Marie and he was taken to the closely guarded house. He was still wearing his uniform, but every bit of insignia had been stripped from it.

In a room apart, an altar was set up and the businesslike Catholic chaplain, Father Cummings, listened to the prisoner's confession and his act of contrition. The United States Army wouldn't grant Private Slovik absolution but the priest did. Then he handed the condemned man a thick packet of letters from his wife. Tears rolled down Slovik's cheeks as he read them; Antoinette didn't even know what was happening to him.

With only minutes left to live, Slovik asked Father Cummings to tell the men of his regiment that on that day at least he wasn't afraid to die. What he had feared most about combat was the anxiety, the never knowing if and when he'd be blown to Kingdom Come. He asked Father Cummings to tell the firing squad he didn't hold what they were going to do to him against them—and, above all, to shoot straight.

In another room, the firing squad's twelve M1 rifles had been laid on a table. Two officers were loading them methodically, in private. Eleven got live ammunition; the twelfth received a blank. None of the riflemen was supposed to know who got the gun with the blank.

In the snow-covered garden outside, a large group of soldiers of all ranks were stamping their feet and trying to keep warm. Most were enlisted men, chosen from different units of the 28th Division to witness the execution; the Army wanted them to bring back to their buddies a firsthand account of what happens to a man who shirks his duty. More than two dozen officers were also present.

A sergeant began to tie Slovik's wrists. Slovik told him he wasn't being shot for desertion; everyone knew thousands of GIs had deserted and not one of them had been shot. No, he was going to die because the Army needed to execute someone as an example, and they had chosen him because he had a criminal record in civilian life, although all of his crimes were pretty small ones.

Then they were outside in the garden. Bareheaded, trembling in the bitter cold in spite of the blanket thrown over his shoulders, Slovik listened as Major Fellman read the execution order to him. The blanket was pulled off and Slovik, praying with Father Cummings, was strapped tight against the post.

A sergeant stood waiting with a black hood. The chaplain asked Slovik to say a prayer for him in heaven. He would, Slovik said; he'd pray the priest wouldn't have to join him up there too soon.

The execution moved along like clockwork. The prisoner's head disappeared under the hood. In quick step, the riflemen marched out into the cold and faced the man strapped to the post. Major Fellman looked up and down the line. "Squad," he ordered rapidly, "ready—aim—fire!"

The twelve rifles roared. Slovik slumped. Then he seemed to struggle against his bonds.

Fingering his stethoscope, Dr. Rougelot strode forward, leaned over, and listened to Slovik's heart.

It was beating faintly and erratically, but still beating.

All eleven bullets had hit the prisoner, Rougelot observed, but none had entered the heart. The riflemen must have been rattled at having to shoot a fellow soldier, he decided; he really should have pinned a target over Slovik's heart.

The witnesses watched uneasily as the doctor continued to listen through his stethoscope. It looked as if they would have to go through the whole shooting again.

A young lieutenant passed along the line of marksmen and started to insert bullets in the M1s. The riflemen looked away.

But before the lieutenant had loaded the last bullet Slovik's heart gave up. Knives quickly cut down the body, it was anointed by the chaplain, and the soldiers pulled a mattress cover over it.

Later, the men who had witnessed the execution would say the deserter had not died like a coward. Why, they wondered, had someone like that been afraid to go into combat with them. Of all the men in the garden that morning, Slovik, Father Cummings would say, had shown the least fear.

During World War II, forty thousand servicemen deserted. Of these, only forty-nine (some of them officers) were sentenced to death for desertion. Only one, Private Slovik, was actually executed. Since then the military legal process has changed. It appears unlikely that a deserter will be executed in the foreseeable future.

Edward Donald Slovik was born in Detroit in 1920, the son of an auto worker. When he was only twelve he had his first run-in with the law; he and some friends broke into a brass foundry and started a fire. A policeman saw the smoke and pulled the boys in. Eddie caught a year's probation.

Eddie dropped out of school when he was fifteen. He kept bad company. He was nabbed for breaking and entering, disturbing the peace, petty theft—usually with buddies. In 1937, while he was clerking in a drugstore, he admitted he had stolen change, cigarettes and candy adding up to $59.60 over a six-month period. Charged with embezzlement, he was sentenced to six months to ten years. After a year in the Michigan Reformatory he was released on probation.

In 1939 Eddie and some friends went for a joy ride in a car that didn't belong to them and smashed it up. That earned him another term in the reformatory. Agreeable, eager to please, he made lots of friends: his supervisor was especially fond of him. Later, this man would recall what an insecure person Eddie was, and how easily he was frightened.

In 1942, when Eddie was paroled at age twenty-two, the United States was at war. As an ex-convict he was considered ineligible for the draft, and he was placed in Class 4-F.

With the help of his sister and a friend of hers named Antoinette, Eddie got a job working for a plumber. Antoinette was five years older than Eddie, she had a physical handicap, and she was subject to epileptic fits. That didn't stop him from falling in love with her and they were married later that year. Both worked hard to furnish their apartment and save for a car. Determined to make something of himself, Eddie got a better job in an auto plant.

By 1944 they had the car, but they wouldn't keep it for long. The draft boards were scraping the bottom of the manpower barrel; Slovik was placed in Class 1-A and inducted.

The letters Eddie wrote from camp to Antoinette reveal what a tragedy it was for him. After years of drifting and being in trouble he had found stability: a woman who loved him, a steady job, a home and a future. Now suddenly all of these had been wrenched from him. He was desperately unhappy and insecure.

Misfortune dogged Antoinette as it was dogging Eddie. She had a miscarriage. She began to have severe epileptic seizures, her eyes started to fail her, and she couldn't work anymore. Going to the Red Cross, she begged for a hardship discharge for her husband. The Red Cross turned her down.

Meanwhile, the Army was determined to make Private Slovik into a rifleman. Scared of guns and the noise they made, he kept failing at target practice. He was sent back to the rifle range so often his arm got sore and his cheek swollen. His letters to Antoinette reflected his misery: "You have so many troubles . . . but I have more troubles than you . . ." And: "Without you and your love I will die."

In August 1944 Eddie was shipped overseas; his division was engaged in bloody, bitter battles in northern France and it needed many replacements. As he, a buddy named Tankey, and other soldiers were being trucked to their outfit, they came under heavy shelling in the town of Elboeuf and were ordered to dig in.

Later an order was given to move out, but apparently Eddie and Tankey never heard it. Separated from their group, they fell in with Canadian troops, who adopted them and put them to work as foragers and cooks. Weeks passed before they caught up with their own division and rejoined it. This was on October 8.

Slovik's troubles were about to begin in earnest: he would have to move into the line and use the rifle he hated and feared.

On the way up he had told Tankey he would never fire it. Now he went to his company commander and informed him he was gun-shy—too frightened to go into combat. He asked for duty in the rear; if he didn't get it, he said, he'd run away. His request was denied.

"If I leave now," Slovik asked, "will it be desertion?"

He was assured it would, and he promptly disappeared from his company.

Slovik's desertion lasted all of a day. On October 9 he came back and turned himself in. To the officer in charge he gave a sheet of paper on which he had printed by hand:

I Pvt. Eddie D. Slovik #36896415 confess the Desertion of the United States Army. At the time of my Desertion we were in Albuff [Elboeuf] in France. I come to Albuff as a Replacement. They were shilling the town and we were told to dig in for the night. The following morning they were shilling us again. I was so scared nerves [nervous] and trembling that at the time the other Replacements moved out[2] I couldn't move. I stayed their [there] in my foxhole till it was quite [quiet] and I was able to move. I then walked in town. Not seeing any of our troops so I stayed over night at a French hospital. The next morning I turned myself over to the Canadian Provost Corp. After being with them six weeks I was turned over to American M.P. They turned me lose. I told my commanding officer my story. I said that if I had to go out their [there] again Id [I'd] run away again. AND ILL RUN AWAY AGAIN IF I HAVE TO GO OUT THEIR.

—Signed Pvt. Eddie D. Slovik
A.S.N. 36896415

If you withdraw your confession and go back to your company, Slovik was told, your offense will be forgotten; if you don't, it could go hard with you. Slovik refused, and he was placed under arrest.

A month later he was court-martialed. In the trial, which lasted less than two hours, he declined to testify.

The jury's decision was unanimous: Slovik was sentenced to be shot to death. His division was engaged in heavy fighting and the jurors felt he should be punished for declaring, at a time when so many of his comrades were risking their lives, that he would "run away again if I have to go out their." From past experience the jurors believed the sentence would be reduced and Slovik, after a few years in prison, would be a free man. Evidently he shared that belief.

Next, the case moved up to the division commander, General Norman D. Cota, for review. Here the clemency Slovik was depending on could be recommended.

Now a new and devastating element entered the case. The Federal Bureau of Investigation had forwarded to Colonel Sommer, the division's advocate general, a copy of Slovik's criminal record in civilian life. Minor though the crimes were, with Colonel Sommer they carried great weight. He also had been appalled by the bluntness of Slovik's confession.

Judges will sometimes show mercy to a lawbreaker who is penitent. But Slovik hadn't asked for mercy at his trial. He not only had freely admitted his act of desertion, but also had the effrontery to state in writing that he would continue to desert.

After reviewing the case, the colonel refused to recommend clemency. (Years later, Sommer told William Bradford Huie, who wrote a notable account of the case called *The Execution of Private Slovik*, that he never believed Slovik would actually be executed.) He included

Slovik's criminal record in his review—where from now on it would count severely against the prisoner.

General Cota approved his advocate general's review of the sentence, and the papers were forwarded for final approval to the commander of the European Theater of Operations, General Dwight D. Eisenhower.

Now at last Slovik began to realize how grave his situation was. His act of desertion, committed to save his life, could cause him to lose it.

In prison the private penned a long letter to General Eisenhower, begging for mercy. Here it is, just as he wrote it:

Dear General Eisenhower:

I Private Eddie D. Slovik ASN 36896415 was convicted on the 11th day of November year 1944 Armistic Day by General Court Martial to be shot to death for desertion of the United States Army.

The time of my conviction or before my conviction I had no intentions of deserting the army whatsoever. For if I intended too I wouldn't have given or surrendered myself as I did. I have nothing against the United States army whatsoever, I merely wanted a transfer from the line. I asked my CO when I came back if their was a possible chance of my being transferred cause I feared hazardars duty to myself and because of my nerves. I'll admit I have some awfull bad nerves, which no doubt in my mind we all have. I was refused this transfer.

I must tell you more about my past. I assume you have my records of my past criminall life in my younger stage of life. After being released from jail I was put on a two year parole after spending five years in jail. In them two years I was on parole I got myself a good job cause I was in class 4-F, the army didn't want anything to do with me at the time. So after five months out of jail I decided to get married which I did. I have a swell wife now and a good home. After being married almost a year and a half I learned to stay away from bad company which was the cause of my being in jail. Then the draft came. I didn't have to come to the army when they called me. I could of went back to jail. But I was sick of being locked up all my life so I came to the army. When I went down to the draft board, I was told that the only reason they were taking a chance on me in the army was cause I got married and had a good record after being out of jail almost two years. To my knowledge sir I have a good record in the past two years. I also have a good record as a soldier up to the time I got in this trouble. I tried my best to do what the army wanted me to do till I first ran away or should I say left the company.

I don't believe I ran away the first time as I stated in my first confession. I came over to France as a replacement, and when the enemy started to shelling us I got scared and nerves and I couldn't move out of my fox hole. I guess I never did give myself the chance to get over my first fear of shelling. The next day their wasn't any American troops around so I turned myself over to the Canadian MPs. They in turn were trying to get in touch with my outfit about me. I guess it must have taken them six weeks to catch up with the American troops. Well sir, when I was turned over to my outfit I tried to explain to my CO just what took place, and what had happened to me. Then I asked for a transfer. Which was refused. Then I wrote my confession. I was then told that if I would go back to the line they would destroy my confession, however, if I refused to go back on the line they would half to hold it against me which they did.

How can I tell you how humbley sorry I am for the sins Ive committed. I didn't realize at the time what I was doing, or what the word desertion meant. What it is like to be condemned to die. I beg of you deeply and sincerely for the sake of my dear wife and mother back home to have mercy on me. To my knowledge I have a good record since my marriage and as a soldier. I'd like to continue to be a good soldier.

Anxiously awaiting your reply, which I earnestly pray is favorable, God bless you and in your Work for victory:

> I remain Yours for Victory
> Pvt. Eddie D. Slovik

General Eisenhower, enmeshed in the Battle of the Bulge, with the lives of many thousands of Americans at risk, had no time to spare for Slovik's pathetic letter. The case was turned over for a final review to lawyers on his staff.

The lawyers fastened on Slovik's list of peacetime offenses. In them they found a "persistent refusal to conform to the rules of society in civilian life, an imperviousness to penal correction and a total lack of appreciation of clemency; these qualities the accused brought with him into his military life. . . ." They concluded: "He has directly challenged the authority of the government . . . If the death penalty is ever to be imposed for desertion it should be imposed in this case . . . to maintain that discipline upon which alone an army can succeed against the enemy."

General Eisenhower confirmed the sentence and the provost marshal ordered it to be carried out on January 31, 1945.

Antoinette Slovik was never notified of her husband's desertion or trial, his sentence, or his impending execution, only of his death. Later, she would complain that she had never had an opportunity to appeal to the President for clemency, as the wives of condemned soldiers did to Abraham Lincoln during the Civil War, sometimes with merciful results.

Private Slovik was buried in the Oise-Aisne American Cemetery, near Château-Thierry. Thousands of American soldiers who fell in France were laid to rest there. But Slovik was buried apart from the others. He lay in a plot he shared with ninety-five other Americans executed during World War II. Those ninety-five, found guilty of raping or murdering civilians, or both, all suffered death by hanging. Slovik was the only military offender executed by a firing squad—the first American put to death for desertion since the Civil War.[3]

On January 18, 1977, a small chartered airplane with an unusual cargo flew over the rugged, windswept landscape near Provo, Utah. Its passengers had just come from a memorial service there, and the strains of *Amazing Grace* and *Flow Gently, Sweet Afton* still echoed in their ears. About a quarter of a mile above the ground the pilot lifted a plastic bag and emptied it out of the window. In an instant the gray ashes—all that was left of Gary Mark Gilmore—scattered in the wind.

All that was left? Not quite. For not far away, in a hospital, a physician unwrapped bandages from the eyes of a youthful patient. "My God," the patient exclaimed, "this is wonderful. I can see!" The newly transplanted corneas that gave him the gift of sight were the same ones through which Gilmore, only the day before, had calmly looked into the muzzles of the rifles that took his life.

It was a tranquil ending to a criminal saga that had both sickened and intrigued millions. At its center was the grotesque, malevolent, yet somehow romantic figure of a man who had spent eighteen of his thirty-six years behind bars—and finally, without rhyme or reason, shot two young men to death in cold blood. After fighting off repeated efforts to save his life, he had sat down cheerfully in front of a firing squad and become the first person to be executed in the United States in ten years.

Born in Texas, Gilmore was one of the four sons of a man given to heavy drinking and violent rages. The family was constantly on the move, its home life unstable. In Oregon, at twelve, the boy became a runaway. At fourteen he stole a car and was shipped off to reform school for eighteen months. One run-in with the law led to another. Gilmore's gaunt face became a familiar one in the courts as he was convicted of charges that ranged from robbery, assault and statutory rape to shooting a friend with a stolen gun during a drunken spree.

Prison psychiatrists came to know Gilmore too. In him they recognized the classic profile of the sociopath—egotistical, antisocial, cunning, indifferent to the pain he inflicted on others. At the same time they found a completely different side to him. He possessed a high IQ, read widely, and had above-average talent as an artist and writer.

In 1963, with an old prison buddy, Gilmore mugged and robbed a man. Thirty minutes later he was in handcuffs. He pleaded insanity (he had twice spent time in mental hospitals) and slashed his wrists in a suicide attempt. The court, unconvinced, bundled him off to the state prison, where he would serve nine years.

Behind bars, Gilmore sometimes showed signs of depression (real or feigned) that sent him to the mental ward. His violent nature continued to erupt. Hard and domineering, he earned a reputation as a cell-block enforcer, boasting of brutal exploits that included paralyzing a fellow inmate for life with a hammer blow. He organized a suicide club (his own suicide attempt was faked) and was a leader in a riot and in hunger strikes. He kept bouncing into and out of solitary confinement.

Given an opportunity to escape from his pattern of self-destruction, Gilmore would foul up. Once, for example, a sympathetic warden agreed to let him out of prison to attend a class in sign painting. Gilmore repaid him by cutting the class, going on a drinking binge, and holding up a service station. Promptly nabbed by the police, he was transferred to a federal prison.

In 1976 Gilmore was released on parole; a kindhearted uncle in Provo had offered him a room and employment in his shoe repair shop. The ex-convict quickly failed at that job and the next one.

Thrown out by his uncle for drunkenness, he went hitchhiking, supporting himself by stealing. Again the police caught up with him, but his probation officer helped him stay out of prison.

He took up with an attractive woman named Nicole Barrett. Only twenty, she had already been married and divorced three times and had two children. The affair was stormy and brief. Drinking constantly and popping painkillers, Gilmore abused her and her children, and in short order she walked out on him.

In a murderous fury, Gilmore went to look for Nicole at her mother's house. She wasn't there. Instead, he found her younger sister, fresh out of a mental hospital, and lured her away with him. Driving to a gas station, he robbed it and shot the unresisting attendant dead in cold blood with a stolen gun. Then he took the disturbed girl to a motel.

Early the next morning she found her way home. "Momma," she moaned, "I almost got my head blew off."

The following night, after another fruitless search for Nicole, Gilmore robbed a motel in Provo and, without any provocation, murdered the night clerk. When he attempted to hide the gun, it went off, wounding him in the hand. The bloody hand drew attention to him: before the night was over, he was back in jail.

Gilmore's trial took no more than three days. Charged with just the second of the murders, he told the jury the killing was "something that couldn't be stopped." The jury found him guilty and sentenced him to death.

The condemned man was offered Utah's choice of execution by hanging or the firing squad. Of the forty-four criminals Utah had executed in the past, thirty-eight had chosen to be shot. Gilmore was to become the thirty-ninth. He was transferred to a maximum-security unit at Utah State Prison, near Salt Lake City.

Before his trial, Gilmore had been examined by psychiatrists to determine whether he was legally sane. In the killings, one psychiatrist stated later, the convict had been driven by a death wish.

I think that shortly after Gary got out of prison he knew within himself that he wasn't able to make it in society. Knowing he didn't want to return to prison, he took the steps necessary to turn the job of his own destruction over to someone else . . . He went out of his way to get the death penalty; that's why he pulled two execution-style murders he was bound to be caught for.

Gilmore might not have disagreed. Before his conviction, he had told a relative, "I would definitely prefer a quick death to a slow life in the joint . . . My soul is on fire and is screaming to be released from this ugly house I've built around it."

After he was sentenced, his lawyers, without consulting him, appealed to the Utah Supreme Court and won a stay of execution. Gilmore flew into a rage, and fired them. He called the court "silly," and engaged a new lawyer to persuade it to have him put to death as soon as possible. In an obliging mood, the court restored the original death date, November 15.

Now the governor, Calvin Rampton, intervened, imposing another stay; he wanted the state board of pardons to review the case. Gilmore was indignant.

Since the law was moving so slowly, Gilmore decided to take matters into his own hands. He had patched up his romance with Nicole Barrett. Now he convinced her that she ought to join him in a suicide pact.

On November 16 a guard found Gilmore unconscious in his cell from a drug overdose. The prisoner was rushed to a hospital; he could not be allowed to take his life himself when it was forfeit to the state. That same day Nicole was discovered in a coma in her apartment. Gilmore's photograph lay on her bosom.

How had the convict obtained his drugs? Nicole had a prescription for Seconal sleeping capsules and she had visited him the previous day. A matron had searched her and found nothing. It was theorized she'd hidden the capsules in a body opening and slipped them to her lover during a last embrace. In any event, Gilmore's recovery was rapid—he'd evidently taken just a small dose—but Nicole's coma lasted several days. To prevent any more suicide attempts, he was removed to the prison infirmary and kept under close watch. He began a hunger strike.

The day of Gilmore's appearance before the state board of pardons finally arrived. He pleaded to be executed without delay, and the board set an early date. But appeals were still under way to save him. His mother was behind one of them; behind another were two fellow inmates of death row who feared his execution—the first since 1967—would open up the way for their own. Organizations opposed to capital punishment had also filed appeals.

By now Gilmore was big news. His notoriety was bringing in a flood of television, book, movie and interview offers, and he had acquired a literary agent to handle them. Hundreds of letters, some with offers of marriage, poured into the prison for him. A song had been written about him, "The Ballad of Gary Gilmore."

> *What's to become of Gilmore,*
> *the killer who wanted to die?*
> *Will they just do away with Gilmore,*
> *or will they give him another try?*

Gilmore's date with death was finally set for December 17, at sunrise. The night before, he was in high spirits: he joked with relatives and danced to country music with a cousin. His merriment faded when he was told a federal judge had just issued a stay of execution. He swore he would kill himself, and he had to be calmed with sedatives. In the middle of the night, state attorneys flew off to the district court in Denver to get the stay overturned by dawn. Gilmore, more hopeful, had a last supper of hamburger, eggs and potatoes, posed for photographs, and fortified himself with smuggled bourbon.

Shortly before sunrise, Warden Samuel Smith brought the good news: the stay had been vacated and the execution would go ahead in minutes.

The morning was frosty and bright. On the prison grounds stood an empty warehouse of gray concrete blocks. Once it had been a cannery. On this day, however, it would be a place of execution.

Arrangements had been made in a hurry. A barrier of plywood, half an inch thick, had been erected not far from the door. Piled high in back of the barrier were dozens of sandbags and an old mattress to receive the bullets, presumably to keep them from ricocheting off the wall behind. Immediately in front of the barrier, on a low platform, was an expendable office armchair with a leather seat and back. It was illuminated by a powerful light.

Ten yards in front of the chair, the executioners were seated on a bench. They were hidden behind a blind formed of sheets of green sailcloth stretched over a framework of two-by-fours. Their weapons were high-powered .30-caliber Winchester rifles, and in front was a railing to support them. Openings for the rifle barrels had been cut three feet apart in the cloth. To one side, peering through a hole higher up, was the squad captain.

Only the warden knew the names of the executioners, but they were

In 1857 Mormon Bishop John D. Lee played a key role in the massacre of 123 emigrants passing through Utah. (Utah Historical Society)

Lee, at left, sits on his coffin while preparations are completed for his execution by firing squad in 1877 at the scene of the massacre. (Utah Historical Society)

In 1913 Nevada undertook its one and only execution by firing squad. The "squad" consisted of three rifles mounted on a pedestal and fired automatically. (Nevada Historical Society)

Joe Hill (also known as Joseph Hillstrom), after his arrest for murder in Salt Lake City.

The holes made by four dumdum bullets in Hill's body can clearly be seen after his execution by firing squad in 1915.

Gary Gilmore became the first man executed in the United States in ten years when he sat down before a Utah firing squad in 1977. (Portland Bureau of Police)

In 1862 thirty-eight Sioux are swung into eternity at Mankato, Minnesota—the biggest mass execution in American history.

Until the introduction of the electric chair in 1890 most condemned criminals were put to death by hanging.

Major John André, young British officer, sentenced to a spy's death in 1780.

André in a self-portrait in pen and ink made shortly before he was marched off to the gallows at Tappan, New York.

CONFESSION;
OF
George Brown, *alias* **W. T——.(†)**
LATE MATE OF THE
SCHOONER RETRIEVE,
WHO WAS
Executed this day, on board said Vessel,
IN THE EAST RIVER,
OPPOSITE BROOKLYN HEIGHTS,
For Mutiny and the Murder of
Captain JOHN LEWIS,

While on a Voyage from Cadiz to Vera Cruix, with a short account of his Trial before his Hon. Judge Livingston, at the City-Hall of this City, on the 5th September last ; the sentence of the Judge, and some particulars of his conduct subsequent to his condemnation, and prior to his execution

(†) Brown is an assumed name, motives of delicacy, and a wish not to wound the feelings of an amiable mother, who resides in the City, &c. his real name.

New-York, Oct. 22. 1819.
For sale at the *Printing Office.* No. 9 Wall-st. third floor.

In keeping with an old tradition of the sea, George Brown was executed on the ship on which he committed murder.

On June 21, 1877—Pennsylvania's Day with the Rope—ten Molly Maguires were hanged in the state's coal-field wars.

In 1887 Chicago executed the four so-called Haymarket conspirators, who came to the gallows dressed in their shrouds. Their guilt was never proved.

In New York's Tombs Prison Captain Nathaniel Gordon faces his doom in 1862, the only American to die for transporting slaves.

Known as the Prince of Hangmen, George Maledon constructed the gallows at Fort Smith and hung at least sixty-seven men.

Newspapers traditionally devote considerable space to executions. Perhaps the most startling headline of its kind was this one in the Chicago *Times* of November 27, 1875.

Isaac C. Parker, the Hanging Judge, sent eighty-eight men to the gallows and wept as they were strung up.

Charles Thiede, executed in Utah in 1896, was hung by a mechanism that jerked him up into the air by the dropping of a counterweight.

William Calder, a ranch hand, looks uneasy as the sheriff checks the noose moments before hanging him in Lewistown, Montana, in 1898.

When Minnesota abolished the death sentence in 1911 this cartoon appeared in the *Minneapolis Journal* under the heading "Spring Fashions for Minnesota."

John Brown in 1859, shortly before he made his raid on Harper's Ferry. (Library of Congress)

Surrounded by rank upon rank of soldiers, Brown is trussed up for hanging. Southern states vied to supply the rope.

Crawford Goldsby, known as Cherokee Bill (center), had killed thirteen men before he turned twenty.

The hanging of Black Tom Ketchum in New Mexico in 1901. Next to Butch Cassidy, he was the most wanted criminal in the Southwest. Here a lawman fits the noose around his neck.

Hanging is a fine art, but the hangman here was no artist. When Ketchum fell through the trap his head was torn off.

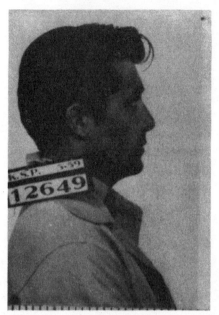

Perry Smith (*top*), thirty-six, and Richard Hickock, thirty-three, hanged in 1965 in Kansas for the killing of the Clutter family. (Kansas Bureau of Investigation).

believed to be law officers, and every one a crack shot. Reportedly each man would be paid $175.

Behind a green line stood the witnesses, about twenty of them. They heard a car drive up. Gilmore, tall and rawboned, his wrists in shackles, strode in with his guards and headed for the chair. He was wearing a black T-shirt, white prison trousers and tennis shoes. He had hoped to face the firing squad on his feet, unshackled, but now he was strapped to the chair.

A guard led four witnesses Gilmore had invited over to him—his uncle, two lawyers, and Larry Schiller, his literary agent.[4] He had also invited Nicole, but she couldn't be present; she was confined to a mental hospital. Smiling, Gilmore shook hands and said goodbye. To one of his lawyers, who was partly bald, he joked, "You can have my hair when it's over." Then the four were led back behind the green line. Cotton had been handed to the witnesses and they packed it into their ears.

Gilmore, a Catholic, had not wanted a priest, but one was present, and he recited a last prayer with the condemned man. "*Pax vobiscum*," Gilmore said at the end.

The convict was trying to see the faces behind the row of openings in the green blind. Warden Smith read the death warrant to him. Did he have any last words, the warden asked.

"Let's do it!" replied Gilmore firmly.

A hood of black corduroy was fitted over his head.

"He did not quiver or deny its coverage," Schiller said later. "A black target with white circle was then pinned to Gary's black T-shirt. The priest and others moved away."

The rifle muzzles could be seen protruding from the blind. Warden Smith made a slight signal with his left hand.

"One—two—" counted the firing squad captain behind the blind; "—THREE!"

Four bullets ripped into Gilmore's heart. Blood seeped out of the white circle on his chest and his body quivered. Two minutes later he was pronounced dead.

Utah, with its heavily Mormon, law-abiding population, has had relatively few murders and executions compared with many other states, and it has never executed a woman. Still, a number of highly curious incidents have occurred in capital cases. For the unusual stories that follow, the author is greatly in the debt of Professor L. Kay

Gillespie of Weber State College in Utah. The facts are gleaned from a work in progress by Dr. Gillespie, to be called *Utah's Executed Men*.

In 1857, during the trouble between the United States and the Mormons that came to be known as the Utah War (the massacre at Mountain Meadows was an incident in it), Warren Drake, a member of the Mormon militia, was on duty in Echo Canyon. Accused of bestiality with a mare, he was tried by a court-martial and sentenced, with the mare, to be executed. Drake was excommunicated from the Mormon Church, but wasn't put to death; instead, his sentence was commuted to exile from the territory.

The mare, however, was not so fortunate. In her case the sentence was carried out. Bizarre though this may sound to modern readers, in earlier times it was not uncommon for animals to be tried for crimes and executed.[5]

The youngest person Utah has put to death was Chauncey W. Millard, executed in 1869 at the age of eighteen. Millard actually traded his body to the attending physician for a pound of candy. After reading the seventh chapter of Matthew, the prisoner was eating his candy at the very moment the bullets ended his life.

Wallace Wilkerson, executed in 1879, made one of the oddest—and most sadly mistaken—remarks by a condemned person at the point of death. Here is an excerpt from a newspaper account of what happened after the target was pinned over his heart. (Apparently he wasn't tied to the chair.)

> The instant the bullets struck him he raised on his feet, turned partially to the south, and as he was pitching forward, took two steps and fell on his left side on the ground. On the instant of striking the ground he turned on his face, exclaiming, "My God! My God! They missed it."

Patrick Coughlin, a horse thief, faced a firing squad in 1896. Appropriately enough, one of the five rifles with which he was shot was his own; it had been used by him in an exchange of fire in which two law officers, Dawes and Stagg, were killed. Asked what he would like for his last meal, he said, "I'd like to have a little Dawes or Stagg on toast."

Enoch Davis, father of nine children, murdered his wife and buried her in a potato hill. After first telling his children their mother had left him, he changed his story, saying she had committed suicide. "She died like a lady and I buried her like a gentleman,'' he lied. He was convicted with the help of his children.

Davis was executed on a ranch in 1894, with some of his children present. The witnesses' sympathy for him quickly changed to scorn when he asked if there were "some prostitutes on the ranch." Six rifles were used by the firing squad, all of them loaded with bullets. For a target the doctor attached a prescription blank to the prisoner's chest. Only four bullets hit it.

One of Utah's most pathetic murder cases concerned another uxorcide, Franklin Pierce Rose. In bed with his wife, Rose angrily complained about her extramarital carryings-on and told her she would have to stop.

"Well, there's only one way to stop it and that is for you to kill me," she said.

Getting his revolver, Rose shot her behind the right ear. She didn't lose consciousness, but, as he would relate later, "She asked me to put a wet towel around her head and rub the place where the bullet had entered."

He did so. Then she asked him to kiss her and bring their two-year-old baby to her. He placed the child in her arms and she kissed it while it fondled her.

Lying down next to his wife, Rose watched as she died. Then, after a drunken binge that lasted two days, he went to the police and confessed. The baby was found hungry but well.

Rose was executed in 1904, after confessing he had murdered ten men. Before facing the firing squad he said, "I feel sorry for my little baby but not for the woman. If I had it to do over again I would do it."

Another wife-killer was Howard DeWeese, a thief. Mrs. DeWeese had left her first husband to marry him, but he murdered her not long after, stealing her diamonds. Before his execution, in 1918, he asked that a white silk handkerchief be placed under the target on his chest and delivered after his death to his wife's first husband.

DeWeese's last words were: "Tell 'em to go to hell."

SEVEN

To Hang by the Neck

It was the greatest mass execution in our history.

Never has the United States put so many people to death at a single time as it did on December 26, 1862.

On that day, near Mankato, Minnesota, the United States Army marched thirty-eight Sioux warriors, decked out festively as for a celebration, up onto an enormous scaffold. Standing on four great trapdoors, they chanted and swayed, the white hoods of death pulled down over their faces.

A drum beat a tattoo. A knife flashed. The trapdoors fell. The Indians danced on air.

The Sioux had been found guilty of taking part in the bloodiest massacre of the West. Four months earlier their war parties had swept through the Minnesota settlements and, according to President Abraham Lincoln, slaughtered eight hundred innocent men, women and children. President Lincoln himself wrote out the warriors' death warrant.

The great Sioux uprising, which took so many lives, was not the result of a carefully hatched plot. An outburst of blind fury, it was a spontaneous, passionate act of vengeance against the United States because it had cheated the Sioux out of their birthright.

In 1862 many of the Sioux were living on a reservation in southern

Minnesota. It had been established eight years earlier as part of Washington's plan to "civilize" the Indians—to persuade them to put on trousers, cut their hair, go to church, and till the soil like the white settlers moving in all over the region.

Most of the Indians, however, found it hard to change their ways. Out of ten Sioux only one was willing to become a "pantaloon" or "Dutchman" and adopt the customs of the whites. The other nine, the "blanket Indians," continued on the nomadic path of their ancestors. They hunted, they fished, they trapped. The trouble was that the game had become scarce, for the tribes had surrendered their choicest land to the settlers.

In compensation for the millions of acres they had ceded, each Sioux was paid a small sum of money every year. In 1862 the Civil War held up the payments. In need of the barest necessities of life, the Indians asked the white traders on the reservation for credit.

In the past the Sioux had often complained about the way the traders cheated them. Now they had another complaint: The traders refused to sell them anything unless they paid for it on the spot. The Sioux were hungry and they were furious.

On August 17, 1862, four young warriors had been out hunting for days without finding game. After riding past the prosperous settlements of the white man and grumbling about their own hard lot they finally made their kill: four unsuspecting whites and a girl.

Next morning, many of the tribes on the reservation, exhilarated by the hunters' daring, took to the warpath. With rifle, tomahawk and firebrand, they overran the towns and homesteads of southern Minnesota. No one knows exactly how many whites they shot and butchered. Some put the number in the thousands.

Colonel (later General) Henry H. Sibley was ordered to suppress the uprising. With sixteen hundred troops, he marched on the Sioux, survived an ambush, and routed them. Most of the leaders of the revolt—those guilty of the most brutal murders and rapes—fled to Canada or the western plains and escaped punishment.

Among the Indians who remained, many were persuaded to turn themselves in; told they would be prisoners of war and treated with mercy, they surrendered willingly. Others were taken prisoner when soldiers surrounded their encampments. Sibley placed four hundred in irons.

To try his prisoners Sibley created a "military commission" of five officers. No defense counsel was appointed for the Sioux. The Reverend Stephen Riggs, a missionary who knew them well, served as interpreter and chaplain. He was the grand jury too, interrogating the survivors of the massacre and drawing up the charges.

Any warrior who admitted he had been present at a battle—whether he had killed anyone or not—was found guilty of a capital crime. As many as forty were convicted in a day, some after just a five-minute trial. Three hundred and six were sentenced to hang. Each condemned man was given a number, and the names and numbers were telegraphed to President Lincoln.

The convicted Indians were locked up in a stockade at South Bend, near present-day Mankato. Chained in pairs, they whiled away their days smoking and chatting as they awaited the President's final decision.

On December 4 a crowd of saloon patrons marched from Mankato to the stockade. They demanded that the imprisoned Indians should be turned over to them. When their demand was turned down they assaulted the guards. Soldiers took the lynch mob in custody, releasing them later.

In Washington the President had many questions about the Indians and their trials. Above all he didn't want the South to accuse him of executing prisoners of war. A detailed record of the trials was requested of General Sibley. When it reached the White House, Lincoln told two assistants to determine which Sioux were guilty of actual crimes and which simply of taking part in battles. The result was that the President confirmed less than one sentence in eight.

On December 23 the missionary Riggs entered the stockade. In his hand was a letter from the White House. The Indians fell silent.

"I have known you for many years," said Riggs in their language. "I have pointed you to the Cross and prayerfully endeavored to convince you allegiance to God and the Great Father at Washington was your duty. With a broken heart I have witnessed your cruelty to inoffensive men, women and children—cruelty to your best friends. You have stained your hands in innocent blood and now the law holds you to strict accountability."

As the clergyman completed each sentence, the Indians grunted; it was their traditional way of showing they understood.

Riggs unfolded President Lincoln's death warrant and read the names of the warriors who were to die. No Indian grunted now. The guilty, Riggs told them, had just four days left to live.

A former Indian agent from the reservation stepped forward and, one by one, identified the prisoners named in the order. He didn't know every one by sight. Some had similar names, and whether all he identified were actually the ones named in the document would always remain a question.

Soldiers promptly separated the men under sentence of death from the rest. Placed under guard, they were led to a stone house and locked up.

That evening the condemned warriors began to sway and stamp their feet. "Hi-yi-yi," they chanted, "Hi-yi-yi."

It was the Sioux death wail. The guards had never heard anything like it before. Fearful the prisoners might be preparing to attack them and break out of prison, they called for help. Soldiers poured in and each Indian's chains were secured to the floor.

Some of the doomed men had friends and relatives among those detained in the stockade. On Christmas Eve, they were brought in to say goodbye. The prisoners gave them many of their possessions: clothing, money, knives, trinkets.

On Thursday, Christmas Day, the women who cooked for the prisoners—some of them were also relatives—were admitted to the stone house. The warriors gave them most of their remaining possessions, as well as locks of hair, to be delivered to friends and relatives who were elsewhere. To the women they also entrusted messages for their loved ones.

Friday morning came. Doomsday. The prisoners decked themselves out as for a festival. They arranged their hair. They decorated themselves with beads, feathers and paint, glancing at little pocket mirrors they carried.

A priest, Father Ravoux, and some newspapermen were admitted. Those of the Indians who had no relatives made these white men presents of their possessions. Ravoux, who had baptized many of the Sioux during their imprisonment, gave them the last rites and exhorted them to meet their end with courage.

"While Father Ravoux was speaking to them," the *St. Paul Pioneer* would report, "old Tazoo broke out in a death wail in which one after another joined until the prison room was filled with a wild, unearthly plaint which was neither of despair nor grief but rather a paroxysm of savage passion, most impressive to witness and startling to hear. During the lulls in their death-song they would resume their pipes, and with the exception of an occasional mutter or the rattling of their chains, they sat motionless and impassive until one among the elder would break out in the wild wail, when all would join again in the solemn preparation for death.''

White hoods were placed on the Indians' heads, rolled up so they could see. Their chains were struck off, and their hands were crossed in front of them and tied securely. They continued to listen to the priest. Some twisted their way over the floor to get closer to him.

The provost marshal, Captain Redfield, appeared in the doorway. He whispered to the priest. His words were translated into Sioux and the prisoners rose to their feet and fell in behind him. The warriors appeared eager to leave the room. As they moved out into the sunlight their ominous chant began again.

The scaffold was a huge square structure, with a wide platform on each side and steps in front. Over each platform, from a notched beam, hung ten ropes. The Indians knew well enough what the structure was; they had watched from the stockade while it was being erected.

Facing the scaffold, on every side, stood file upon file of infantrymen gripping muskets with bayonets fixed, and mounted cavalrymen with drawn sabers—more than fourteen hundred men in all. Outside the ranks of the soldiers, filling the roofs and windows of buildings as well as the river bank close by, was a great crowd of settlers. Many had suffered at the hands of the Sioux and had come to see the score settled. Inside the stockade, the reprieved prisoners were watching too, through chinks between the logs.

Captain Redfield mounted the scaffold steps. The Indians crowded up after him.

Each Indian was guided to his position on one of the platforms, and stood submissively as a noose was placed around his neck. A few wriggled and squirmed: the rope was too tight. The white hoods were drawn down over their faces.

"Hi-yi-yi," the death wail continued, broken from time to time by piercing shrieks. Even on the gallows the Indians stamped their feet and swayed in rhythm.

The scaffold trembled. Under the impact of so many feet, it began to shake. The provost marshal roared a command and the Indians stopped.

The warriors were standing very close together on the four platforms. Although they were bound, they attempted to reach out and grasp each other's hands. A few succeeded and swayed together as they chanted. "One old man," reported a newsman, "reached out on each side but could not grasp a hand. His struggles were piteous and affected many beholders.'' Each man shouted his own name and that of a nearby friend as if to let him know he was not alone at this terrible moment.

After the provost marshal had checked that everything was in order, a drum began to boom slowly. The stays supporting the platforms were knocked away.

William Duley, a settler who had lost two sons in the massacre, was standing close to the scaffold. A grim expression was on his face, a long knife in his hand. At a signal he sliced through a tightly stretched rope.

Instantly the four platforms crashed downward. The Indians flailed the air with their legs. From the onlookers a muffled cheer rose.

One rope snapped, and the prisoner it had supported fell to the ground. His neck was already broken, but another rope was placed around it and thrown over the beam. He was hauled back into the air.

For half an hour the thirty-eight bodies hung from the gallows. Then they were cut down and Army doctors moved from one to another and pronounced them dead. Soldiers lifted the bodies onto wagons and they were hauled to the sandbar below the river bank. There a shallow hole was waiting. The corpses were dumped into it, lined up and covered with blankets. Finally, the hole was filled in.

Cadavers have always been needed for the teaching and study of anatomy. In earlier times, executions often supplied them. That night, physicians from nearby towns drove to the sandbar with wagons, helped themselves to bodies, and carted them away.

One of the body snatchers was Dr. William Mayo, who had treated settlers maimed or wounded in the massacre. The corpse he took with him was that of a notorious murderer named Cut Nose.

Back home, Dr. Mayo removed the flesh from the body and mounted the skeleton. Later on, when his sons, Charles and William, showed a desire to follow in his footsteps, he used Cut Nose's skeleton to teach them about bone structure. In time the two younger Mayos would found the celebrated medical clinic that bears their name in Rochester, Minnesota.[1]

The hanging of the thirty-eight Sioux was big news in 1862. For twenty-four hours it virtually crowded the Civil War off the front pages. Today, of course, hardly anybody knows the story. Hanging itself, once America's favorite method of capital punishment, is disappearing. In only a few of the states is it still part of the criminal code.

Brought over from England by the first settlers, the gallows was used to punish some one hundred and sixty felonies, including blasphemy, witchcraft, slave rebellion, spying, piracy, treason, bearing false witness, robbery, kidnapping, counterfeiting, arson, adultery, homosexuality, bestiality, rape and murder. The more crimes, the more culprits. In 1967 sociologists Negley K. Teeters and Jack H. Hedblom estimated sixteen thousand men and women had been executed by the rope in America.

No doubt one reason for the widespread, long-lasting popularity of hanging was its cheapness. All that was needed was a stout rope and a sturdy branch on a tree. After forming a noose with a slipknot at one end of the rope and pulling it tight around the prisoner's neck, the hangman simply threw the other end over the branch and hauled, usually with some help. This was the method favored by the followers of Judge Lynch.

Another method in Colonial days required the use of a ladder. After it had been placed against a tree branch, the condemned was forced to climb up with the noose around his neck; after he had gone up high enough he was turned off the ladder. Still another method was to stand the noosed prisoner on a cart beneath the bough and draw the cart away from under his feet.

There was another good reason for the widespread use of hanging: It was terribly cruel. As a rule death did not come rapidly. Usually it took the prisoner twenty minutes or longer to strangle to death. Meanwhile, he would writhe and twist in agonized convulsions. People believed a criminal should die hard, and many came from a considerable distance to watch him fulfill that obligation.

Over the years, much human ingenuity has been expended in developing new and improved kinds of gallows. The simplest and probably most familiar type consists of two upright posts with a crossbeam connecting them; the hanging rope is thrown over this beam. In time, a platform was added, with a trapdoor supported by a catch of bolts. At the fatal moment, the trapdoor would be released and the criminal, who had been standing on it, would plunge through and "dance on air," as people used to say. If the prisoner was sick or weakened by a suicide attempt, as sometimes happened, he could be carried to the trap on a chair, and man and chair would fall through together. There were a number of more ingenious hanging mechanisms, on some of which the prisoner was even obliged to be his own executioner.

Hanging developed into a science not in America but in Great Britain. Britain's master hangmen, in the last century, found that the key to a successful hanging was the "long drop"—a fall long enough to break the prisoner's neck so he would die quickly. William Marwood, the nation's official executioner from 1874 to 1883, is credited with introducing this improved method. It was later refined by his successor, James Berry.

About six feet on the average, the long drop varied inversely with the prisoner's weight. For example, Berry's formula allowed an eight-foot drop for a person weighing 196 pounds. He added two inches to the drop for every seven pounds lighter that the prisoner was, or shortened it two inches for every seven pounds heavier.

Actually, figuring out the correct drop is somewhat more complicated. Besides knowing the inmate's height and weight, the hangman has to take into account his age, his physical condition, and his musculature. A younger, stronger prisoner might require a longer drop than a prisoner who is old and weak. Too short a rope may not break the neck but result in protracted strangling; too long a rope may rip off the head.

Hanging ropes have to be of prime quality. (The wrong kind of rope might break and the prisoner would have to be suspended again.) Traditionally the ropes have been made of hemp, are round and smooth, and are close to three quarters of an inch in diameter. A typical rope is twenty-five or thirty feet long or longer and made up of four or five sections, with one of these the heart section and the others wound around it. The number of loops securing the noose may vary, but seven appears to be a frequent number.

In the heyday of hanging, ropes were frequently supplied by the manufacturer with the noose already made. At San Quentin, when hangings were performed there, new ropes were suspended from the ceiling for two years with 150-pound weights attached to eliminate any spring or bounce, since slack in the rope might result in incomplete strangulation.

"Get your rope working easily through the knot by rubbing a little mutton tallow on it," wrote J. A. Johnston, warden of San Quentin, in 1916 to a New Mexico sheriff new to hanging. "Avoid getting any kinks on your noose, as they will cause the body to spin around when you drop it.'' He also advised that, just before springing the trap, the noose should be drawn ''with a quick pull as tight as possible.''

In this country, hanging has generally been considered the most barbarous of the accepted methods of executing a condemned prisoner. (Earlier we saw it was the gruesomeness of hanging that led New York and other states to turn to electrocution.) Not so in Great Britain. The British Royal Commission on Capital Punishment, after considering alternate methods in 1950, decided that hanging was the least objectionable. (In 1969, the United Kingdom turned away from capital punishment altogether.)

Evidence has been presented time and again indicating that when hanging is performed correctly, the condemned feels no pain. The only credible testimony on the subject would have to come from executed criminals, who cannot supply it. Certainly the psychological terror they must suffer is acutely painful. A number of people who have been partly hanged or who have attempted suicide by hanging have testified they didn't feel physical pain, but their statements have been questioned. What may not be questioned is the testimony of hundreds who have seen hangings performed incorrectly in which the prisoner clearly suffered terrible pain while slowly strangling to death.

H. L. Mencken, who as a newspaper reporter witnessed nine hangings, considered this a ''humane method of putting criminals to death *provided it was competently done.*'' (Author's italics.) In a competent hanging, when the condemned falls through the trap, he experiences a terrible jolt on coming to the end of the long drop. This jolt breaks the neck vertebrae and severs the spinal cord. The convict doesn't die instantly but is said to become instantly unconscious. The flow of oxygen-rich blood to the brain is cut off and the prisoner dies of asphyxia or cerebral anemia.

To achieve these results the knot of the noose must be in a position to jerk the prisoner's head sideways and dislocate the vertebral column. ''We have to put it on the left lower jaw,'' declared the British hangman Albert Pierrepoint, ''and if we have it on that side, when he falls it finishes under the chin and throws the chin back [thus breaking the neck]; but if the knot is on the right-hand side, it would finish up behind the neck and throw the neck forward, which would be strangulation. He might live on the rope a quarter of an hour then.''

The hangman's job calls for thorough experience, yet even a highly competent man may botch a job for unpredictable reasons. In this country hangmen have rarely taken pride in their work, as British hangmen used to. At San Quentin the names and pictures of the hangmen were never made public, and in the prison itself they were pariahs. Early American hangmen were mostly unknown; they might wear masks or blacken their faces so they wouldn't be recognized.

Perhaps the best known of American hangmen was George Maledon, who worked for the famous "hanging judge," Isaac Parker, and put sixty men to death. His story is told later. One hangman became a national figure, although not for his skill with the rope. This was Grover Cleveland, who hanged two men in 1872 and 1873 while serving as sheriff in Erie County, New York. The job of hanging a condemned criminal often fell to the sheriff. Most sheriffs hated it; they did it rarely, and seldom with notable skill.

New York had a celebrated hangman in the second half of the nineteenth century. His actual identity was never made public; the press baptized him George or Monsieur New York (after the executioner in Paris, known as Monsieur de Paris). A former butcher's assistant, he applied for the job in 1850 when the regular hangman quit, and he soon acquired a reputation for exceptional competence. He was paid one hundred dollars a hanging, with additional sums for the rope and the building of a gallows when needed.

Monsieur New York's skills brought requests for his talents from other places. The Army called on his services occasionally, as when he was asked to hang Captain Robert C. Kennedy, a Confederate secret agent, for his part in a daring plot to set New York on fire in 1864. A perfectionist, one time when Monsieur New York was a guest at a hanging in New Jersey he became so disturbed by the executioner's fumbling that he charged up to the scaffold and took over the hanging. He plied his craft for close to thirty years.

Probably the most practiced American hangman of all time was John C. Woods of San Antonio. An executioner in civilian life and a master sergeant in the Army, he hanged 347, including the ten Nazi leaders condemned to death at the Nuremberg trials. After that hanging it was charged that the prisoners' necks hadn't been broken properly and he had bungled, but he insisted the medical officer had told him the opposite and he had done a good job. He died in 1950.

Hanging, we've seen, has gone out of style. One of the few places it is still on the books is the State of Washington. Early in 1989 Charles R. Campbell, a triple murderer, was scheduled for execution in the Walla Walla state penitentiary. The state hadn't hanged anyone in twenty-six years and it had no executioner. A spokesman for the Department of Corrections declared there were only two hangmen left in the United States, and one of them had suffered a nervous breakdown.

Dozens of Washington's citizens volunteered to dispatch Campbell, including some women, but none proved to be technically competent. Finally a qualified person was found outside the state who agreed to do the job for fifteen hundred dollars. Two days before the execution, the convict was granted a reprieve.

Clinton T. Duffy has given us a detailed picture of prison hangings as they were practiced at San Quentin prior to the change to lethal gas. Before the execution the condemned person was taken to a holding cell. Here he was issued his last outfit: jeans, a white shirt and slippers. When the time came, his wrists were strapped together and a belt was fastened around his waist. Three officers (including the hangman) accompanied him to the gallows room; one walked on each side, holding an arm; the third, behind, held the man by the belt.

Thirteen steps led up to the gallows. (The number of steps had no special meaning; other gallows have had more steps or fewer.) In the platform were two traps, in case of a double execution, and the condemned was placed on one of these. The hangman set the noose around his neck, positioning the knot behind his left ear. Meanwhile a guard bound the inmate's ankles with a strap. The other guard placed a black hood over the head.

Three guards sat at a table in a hidden booth nearby. In front of each was a string that extended out of eye range. One of the strings released the trap, but which string that was only the hangman knew. At a signal from the warden, the hangman motioned to the three guards and simultaneously they cut the three strings.

According to Duffy, after falling through the trap the prisoner jerked convulsively. In a few minutes the jerking ceased. A guard opened the convict's shirt and the prison doctor checked the body for signs of life. When he found none the body was removed, to be buried in the prison cemetery if no one claimed it.

Many hangings have been botched, especially in the years before the long drop became standard practice. Here we shall look at a few of the many different kinds of problems that gave hanging a bad name.

In 1876, James Murphy was scheduled to be executed in Ohio for the stabbing murder, while he was intoxicated, of Colonel William Dawson in Dayton. One reporter present was Lafcadio Hearn, later to become famous for his writing about Japan. According to Hearn, the rope had been tested with a keg of nails and other heavy weights but had weakened. Made of unbleached hemp, it was three-eighths of an inch in diameter; it seemed no thicker than a strong clothesline.

On the scaffold Murphy delivered a last speech. It was in the classic vein of the age. "Gentlemen, I want all young men to take warning by me. Drink and bad company brought me here today."

When the trap was sprung, the rope snapped at the crossbeam. The witnesses were appalled to see the prisoner crash to the floor below.

"My God, my God," cried the deputy sheriff, "give me that other rope quick!"

His face hidden beneath the hood, the noose around his neck, the prisoner lay on his back, apparently unconscious.

Hearn ran up and knelt beside him. He felt his pulse. "It was beating slowly and regularly. . . . Then a pitiful groan came from beneath the black cap.

" 'My God! Oh, My God! Why, I ain't dead—I ain't dead!'

"The reporter [Hearn], who still kept his hand on the boy's wrist, suddenly felt the pulsation quicken horribly, the rapid beating of intense fear; the youth's whole body trembled violently. 'His pulse is one hundred and twenty,' whispered a physician."

The prisoner was carried back up the scaffold. He clutched the deputy sheriff's coat in deathly fear.

"Let go, my son; let go, like a man; die like a man," said the Irish priest.

Murphy was held upright on the trap at arm's length, till it could be sprung again. Only after seventeen minutes was he pronounced dead.

A somewhat similar case occurred in Minnesota. A murderer named William Williams was hanged on February 13, 1906. After the trap was sprung, the prisoner fell through to the floor. The sheriff had failed to take into account that both the rope and the prisoner's neck could stretch. Three deputy sheriffs rushed to the platform and pulled on the rope, keeping Williams's feet above the ground for fifteen minutes, while he strangled to death.

Minnesota was appalled by the horror of Williams's execution.

During the next five years, although prisoners were sentenced to death, nobody was actually hanged. Finally, in 1911, the state enacted a law substituting life imprisonment for capital punishment. A newspaper celebrated the event with a front-page cartoon showing a noose with the caption "This necktie will not be worn in Minnesota hereafter."

On August 1, 1884, Alexander Jefferson was hanged in Brooklyn, New York, for two murders. The method used (we'll talk more about this later) was to shoot the prisoner upward by dropping a heavy weight attached to the other end of the rope.

When the weight fell, the prisoner was pulled five feet in the air. His legs hadn't been pinioned and, writhing, he raised his knees almost to his chin. He succeeded in freeing his hands, tore off the black hood with a moan, and reached out his arms pleadingly to the witnesses. Clutching at the noose, Jefferson tried to loosen it but was unable to. His face was terribly distorted. After eight minutes of torment, his movements slowed and finally stopped. The sheriff was in tears.

On June 20, 1890, a husband and wife, Josiah and Elizabeth Potts, were hanged in Elko, Nevada, for the murder of Miles Faucett. They were convicted on circumstantial evidence after Faucett's body was found buried in the cellar of their former home.

Before the black hoods were put on, the pair managed to kiss.

"Goodbye, Elizabeth," Potts said. "I'm sorry. I love you."

"I love you, Josiah," she answered. "God knows we are innocent."

The sheriff cut a cord, springing the trap, and both fell through. As the woman, who was quite heavy, came to the end of her rope, an artery broke in her neck and a thick jet of blood spurted under the hood, pouring down over her dress. One of the witnesses fainted. The husband's end was slower; he struggled almost a quarter of an hour before being declared dead.

According to Phillip I. Earl, the Nevada historian, "it was found that her excessive weight on the five and half-foot drop had almost severed her head from her trunk, the rear neck muscles alone supporting the connection."

Even more gruesome was the execution of Black Jack Tom Ketchum on April 26, 1901. Ketchum, one of the most wanted men in the

Southwest, was captured during a one-man train robbery in New Mexico. While awaiting execution he put on considerable weight.

Black Jack was eager to be on his way. He leaped up the gallows steps. Once there, he didn't make the speech that he had promised. (Instead, in a letter made public by his lawyers, he had advised "all boys not to steal a sheep, cattle or horses, but if they must steal, to rob a bank or a railroad train. He . . . never had murdered anybody.")

The prisoner good-humoredly helped the inexperienced hangman adjust the noose around his neck. "I'll be in hell before you start breakfast," he told the witnesses.

There were several delays while he was waiting on the scaffold and he became nervous. "Let 'er go, boys," he urged. As the *New Mexican* reported it, "When they were quite ready, he again shook hands with them and repeated: 'Let 'er go, boys.' Sheriff Garcia, at 12:17 P.M., cut the rope and the body shot down. The fall severed his head from his body. He alighted on his feet and his headless trunk stood for an instant upright, then swayed, then fell and great streams of blood spurted out from the severed neck. The head, remaining in the black cap, rolled to one side and the rope, released, flew high in the air."

Horrible accidents continue to happen, even when the hangman is skilled in his craft. In the early 1960s, at the Washington State Prison in Walla Walla, a convict's head was nearly ripped off, spraying the witnesses in the front row with blood. A large sheet was hung from the gallows platform to the floor to prevent such accidents.

In the effort to make hanging more efficient, gallows of many different types have been developed. In the last century, machines were invented that, instead of dropping the prisoner, raised him into the air with a jolt to assure his neck would be broken. These devices enjoyed a wide vogue across the United States.

One of the most notorious criminals to die on this kind of hanging machine was Gerald Chapman, executed in Wethersfield, Connecticut, on April 6, 1926. Chapman had begun his journey to the gallows in boyhood by robbing neighbors. In time he became a bootlegger and a safecracker, and took part repeatedly in crimes of violence, one of which, a mail robbery, netted him and a partner $2.4 million. He was executed for the murder of a police officer while robbing a safe.

At the state prison in Wethersfield, a weight, at the end of a fifty-foot rope, was suspended three feet above the floor. This weight was connected by a steel rod to a lever close to the deputy warden's foot. Seconds after the noose was placed around the killer's neck, the deputy pressed the lever. With a click the mechanism released the weight, and Chapman shot twelve feet into the air. His neck was broken instantly.

Oddly enough, the hanging machine had been "improved" for Chapman's execution. Previously, it had been operated by buckshot. The prisoner had been led to a small metal trap set in the floor. When he stepped on the trap his weight caused a container that held fifty pounds of buckshot to open. The pellets, released, rolled rapidly down an incline until their increasing weight pressed a trigger. The trigger in turn released a heavy weight suspended six feet above floor level. As the weight fell, it hoisted the prisoner six feet, fracturing his neck vertebrae. This device, first used in 1894, was the brainchild of a prisoner, who was given his freedom as a reward. After using it for more than thirty years, the state decided it was illegal because it forced the prisoner to commit an unlawful act: suicide.

A similar machine, used in Idaho to execute two prisoners, was worked by water instead of buckshot. It was abandoned, reportedly, because the authorities feared the water would freeze in cold weather. These devices for self-execution seem to have been developed by the state to minimize the feelings of guilt associated with putting a convict to death.

Hangings were public events in the United States until the mid-nineteenth century. Often they were held in town squares or on city commons. Or they might take place on some other piece of public property where the hanging might be seen from afar—a "gallows hill," for example. People would come from great distances to witness the event, especially in the case of a well-known criminal. Depending on how the citizenry felt about the convict and the crime, the execution might be an occasion for cheers or tears. More usually it was the former.

Other favorite places for hangings in earlier times were islands. Piracy wasn't uncommon in those days, and an island in a highly visible situation seemed a logical place to put a pirate to death. Bedloe's Island in New York Harbor was such a spot. In 1860, Albert Hicks, who had seized a sloop and murdered its crew of four, was strung up there in full view of ten thousand spectators on hundreds of small vessels. Today the island is the site of the Statue of Liberty.

Nix's Mate Island in Boston Harbor was famous as a place where the bodies of executed pirates were exhibited and buried. One of the better known of these buccaneers was William Fly. A boatswain on an English slaver, Fly hated his villainous captain, and with fellow mutineers flung him and his mate overboard. Captured after a brief career as pirates, Fly and two others were sentenced to die in Boston on July 12, 1726. A nosegay in his hand, joking and smiling, Fly faced death without flinching. When the hangman, presumably inexperienced, was having trouble with the knots, Fly scolded him for "not understanding his Trade, and with his own hands rectified matters," an eyewitness wrote.

In his last words the unrepentant Fly, according to the *Boston News-Letter*, "advised Masters of vessels not to be Severe and Barbarous to their Men, which might be a reason why so many turn'd Pirates: the other Two seem'd Penitent, beg'd that others might be warn'd by 'em."

After, the bodies were taken by boat to Nix's Mate Island. Fly, the principal villain, was hung up in irons as a warning to seafaring men; his companions were simply buried there. Two hundred years later Edward Rowe Snow, a writer-historian, found a fragment of an iron band and some links of chain near where the corpse had been exhibited.

Fly's body is described as having been "hung in chains." This was a practice called gibbeting, carried out as an added punishment. (Another might be dissection—turning the body over to surgeons to be anatomized or used for experiments.)

In gibbeting, the cadaver would be placed inside a metal framework and hung up in a public place. (Sometimes this would be done while the convict was still alive.) The body might be left hanging for years, until it fell apart. Occasionally it might be dipped in tar to make it last longer. Pirates and slaves were the most frequent victims of gibbeting.

One of the most famous cases of gibbeting took place in Massachusetts in 1755. Two slaves, Mark and Phillis, were found guilty of poisoning their owner, Captain John Codman. Mark was hanged at Cambridge, and about ten yards away Phillis was burned at the stake,[2] after considerately being partly strangled into unconsciousness, as was the custom. Mark's body was then gibbeted on Charlestown Common.

Three years later an army surgeon saw Mark's remains still hanging on the common. The location became associated with the gibbeted slave. When Paul Revere was recalling his celebrated midnight ride of 1775 long after it took place, he mentioned coming to a point "opposite where Mark was hung in chains."

Public hanging, originally considered a deterrent to crime, came to be viewed with distaste as time went by. In Britain, the novelist Charles Dickens waged an eloquent campaign against it, and it was finally prohibited, the last public hanging occurring in 1868. In the United States, Pennsylvania became the first state to pass a law (in 1834) prohibiting public hanging. State followed state, with Missouri being the final one; the last person it executed publicly was Roscoe Jackson, in 1937, after which it turned to lethal gas. Executions were banished to county or other prisons. Today, all executions are carried out in state prisons.

Souvenirs from hangings were once in great demand. After a public execution, there would often be a mad rush to obtain portions of the hanging rope once the body had been cut down. Sometimes they might be sold by the sheriff. Superstitious people believed they could ward off bad luck and cure illness.

Souvenirs of many kinds were sought after. Following the execution of the Lincoln conspirators, the ropes and the scaffold were cut up and distributed to eager recipients. Pieces of a dead criminal's clothing might be torn from his body for souvenirs. After Rainey Bethea, a black, was hanged in Owensboro, Kentucky, in 1936, people fought over the death hood and attempted to hack off pieces of his flesh in a scene reminiscent of old slave executions. Twenty thousand were present at his hanging.

Occasionally the actual bodies might be exhibited, with a fee charged to view them. Dummies made to look like well-known executed criminals were popular in sideshows. Before Albert Hicks was put to death, P. T. Barnum paid him for the right to make a cast of his bust for a dummy, and traded him a new suit of clothes for his old one, in which the dummy was to be exhibited in the Barnum Museum in New York City. Hicks complained that the clothing was shoddy and didn't fit properly, but it was too late for alterations and he was hanged in it.

For well over half of our history, hanging was America's usual method of capital punishment. More convicts have died by the rope than by any other means. Most, of course, were common criminals. Others, however, were not. Some, because of the dramatic times they lived in, the words they uttered, the reasons for their sentence, and the manner of their dying, have won a significant place for themselves in the American story. In this chapter and the next we shall pay particular attention to a number of these remarkable people.

Earlier we looked at the stories of those who were the first to die by electrocution, lethal gas and lethal injection. It is impossible to find who was the first to die by the rope, for early records are fragmentary. They do, however, mention a Daniell Frank, put to death in Virginia on March 1, 1622. His crime was theft; he had stolen a calf and other property. That was fifteen years after the colonists landed in Jamestown, so perhaps he wasn't the first to die on the gallows.

We know more about the man who presumably was the first to hang for murder. This was John Billington, one of the Pilgrim Fathers. Contrary to popular belief, there were hell-raisers and troublemakers among the Pilgrims, and Billington was one of the worst. "He is a knave," wrote Governor William Bradford of Plymouth in 1625, "and so will live and die." His words were prophetic.

A Londoner with a wife and two sons—"one of the profanest families amongst them," according to Bradford—Billington was a signer of the historic Mayflower Compact but he was no Puritan. Like many of his fellow Pilgrims, he came to America to find, not religious freedom, but his fortune. On the voyage over, he became involved in a mutiny. He locked horns with Captain Miles Standish when he refused to perform sentry duty, abusing the captain with "opprobrious speeches." His punishment was a painful one—his neck and heels were tied together. Billington suffered such agony that pity was taken on him; he was allowed to apologize and was released. In 1624 he seems to have participated in a revolt that threatened to tear Plymouth apart.

In 1630 Billington undid himself. After an argument with a new arrival, John Newcomen, he waylaid this young man and blasted him to death with a blunderbuss. The evidence against Billington was clear-cut. Both a grand jury and a petty jury found him guilty of willful murder.

What to do with the criminal was the question. The Pilgrims felt that he deserved to die. Billington himself was convinced he wouldn't be executed because the colony was short of settlers and its authority to inflict capital punishment had never been spelled out.

Unsure of their ground, the colonists decided to consult the founders of the newly settled Massachusetts Bay Colony; it had a grant from the

Crown and was believed to have greater power. Governor John Winthrop and other Massachusetts Bay leaders, who had a better knowledge of British law, "concurred with them that he ought to dye and the land to be purged from blood." On September 30, 1630, Billington, aged forty, became the first of the Pilgrims to suffer death on the gallows.

Eight years later, in 1638, the first woman was hanged in America. Her name was Dorothy Talby and she was executed in the Massachusetts Bay Colony for murdering her little daughter. Reportedly she had previously tried to kill her husband and commit suicide, so she may have been unbalanced.

Although the Puritans came to New England because they wanted to be free to worship God in their own way, they didn't believe in extending that privilege to others. Anyone who challenged the tenets of their faith might suffer the harshest punishment they could inflict, including hanging.

Those they punished most severely in the 1650s and '60s were the Quakers. For a long time, members of the Society of Friends made vigorous attempts to put down roots in Massachusetts and spread their doctrines, and just as vigorously the Puritans suppressed them. Quakers might simply be banished—but first they might suffer punishments ranging from whipping to having their ears cut off or their tongues pierced with a hot iron. If they persisted in coming back from exile, they faced the hanging tree.

In 1659 three determined Quaker missionaries—Mary Dyer, William Robinson and Marmaduke Stephenson—who had returned to the colony, were sentenced to hang. On October 27 they were led from the jail by a detachment of a hundred soldiers armed with muskets and pikes. When the prisoners tried to speak to the crowd of spectators, drummers drowned out their words.

On their way to the place of execution, Boston Common, Mrs. Dyer, her chin high, walked between Stephenson and Robinson and held their hands. Wasn't she ashamed to walk like that, the dour Puritan marshal asked her.

"It is the greatest joy and honor I can enjoy in this world," she replied proudly.

The gallows was most likely a tree. Robinson climbed the ladder, which probably was propped against a branch. The crowd pressed in against the ring of soldiers to hear his last words. He and his companions, he declared, weren't evildoers; the light of Christ burned in them.

"Hold thy tongue, be silent, thou art going to die with a lie on thy mouth," thundered the Reverend John Wilson.

"I suffer for Christ, in whom I live and for whom I die." Those were Robinson's last words. "This day shall we be at rest with the Lord," said Stephenson. "This is an hour of the greatest joy I ever knew," said Mary Dyer. Early Christians about to be crucified couldn't have sounded very different.

The ladders on which the two men stood were turned and they hung in the air, strangling.

Mary Dyer was bound, a handkerchief borrowed from the preacher Wilson was placed over her face, and she was told to climb the ladder. As she stood on it with the noose around her neck, she was informed she had been reprieved. The halter was removed but Mary remained on the ladder; perhaps she was reluctant to have her martyrdom snatched from her. Finally she was taken back to prison.

The ropes from which Stephenson and Robinson dangled were cut and their bodies fell to the ground. Their clothing was removed (clothing was a valuable commodity in old New England) and their naked bodies dragged to a hole and buried.

Mary Dyer was sent back to relatives in Rhode Island. But she had her mission; she returned to Boston and once more was sentenced to death. On June 1, 1660, at the place of execution, a reprieve was offered her if she would go back home. She wouldn't, and she was hanged. A statue of her stands today on Boston Common.

Quaker missionaries continued to come to Massachusetts, despite the threat of death. One of them, William Leddra, was asked if he would be willing to sail to England if the court released him. "I have no business there," he replied. On March 14, 1661, before he was turned off the ladder, his last words were, "Lord Jesus, receive my spirit."

In England the Quakers, long in disfavor, finally won the ear of King Charles II, and the Massachusetts colony was ordered to stop putting them to death. No more would die on the hanging tree. Instead, the Puritans tied them to the end of a cart, tore off their upper clothing, men and women alike, and flogged them through the streets.

One of the greatest miscarriages of justice in America's history took place in Salem, Massachusetts, in 1692. In that year nineteen men and women were hanged for witchcraft. Another person, charged with the same crime, refused to plead. He was slowly pressed to death.

Shocking as it seems today, three hundred years ago almost everybody in the Christian world believed in the reality of witches and of Satan. They believed that great numbers of people—but mostly women—had made a pact with the devil to do his wicked work.

"Thou shalt not suffer a witch to live," declares the Bible. In England it has been estimated that thirty thousand men, women and children were burned at the stake or hanged as witches. When Englishmen landed in the New World they brought this belief in witches with them. In America they didn't burn their witches—although many people believe they did—but simply hanged them.

Even on shipboard supposed sorceresses turned up. In 1654, Mary Lee, and in 1658 Elizabeth Richardson, on their way to Virginia, were charged with black magic: raising storms that endangered the ships on which they sailed. Both were executed.

Aside from one hanging in Maryland, the only American colonies that put people to death for witchcraft were Connecticut and Massachusetts. At least thirty-six persons were executed as witches. Many more were charged in these and the other colonies but escaped with their lives. Some died in prison. Some, while under sentence of death, won reprieves or else were spirited away by relatives or friends.

The outbreak of witchcraft in Salem began in February 1692. Two preadolescent girls, Elizabeth Parris, aged nine, and her cousin, Abigail Williams, eleven, showed signs of demonic possession.

Elizabeth was the daughter of the Reverend Samuel Parris, who had lived in Barbados and had brought to New England two West Indian slaves, Tituba and her husband, John Indian. Tituba read the palms of the girls and their friends and told them tales of voodoo magic and witchcraft. Before long the children believed themselves bewitched. "Sometimes they [Elizabeth and Abigail] were taken dumb, their mouths stopped, their limbs wracked and tormented." Abigail, in addition, ran around on all fours and made barking or braying sounds.

Fearing the children were possessed, Parris took counsel with other men of the cloth and they prayed for the girls. The belief grew that the Evil One was making an all-out attack on New England. To purge the Puritans' wicked hearts the General Court ordered a fast to be held all through the colony. The publicity these measures gave to the girls' mania inevitably caused it to spread; soon, close to forty people were complaining they were bewitched. Some of these were normal, respectable members of the church.

With the backing of two leading Puritan divines, Cotton and Increase Mather, Sir William Phips, governor of the Bay Colony, set up a court to inquire into "what witchcraft might be at the bottom." Jurors were empaneled. Asked who was tormenting them, the girls had begun to name names.

The accused were brought in. Some were old, frightened, confused or demented. Some were very young—one was only four. Determined prosecutors, convinced the prisoners were guilty, subjected them to cruelty, both mental and physical. Traditional legal safeguards were ignored; the accused were allowed no attorneys. Forty-seven, prodded by the prosecutors, confessed they were witches. Some named others as their confederates.

According to the witches, the devil, sometimes taking the form of a little black man, had made them give him their souls in exchange for supernatural powers. In their own forms or those of animals, they tormented their neighbors. They rode on sticks, they flew to witches' sabbaths, they cavorted with Satan and his imps.

Two committees were appointed, one of men, one of women. They were ordered to examine the bodies of accused witches of their own sex for "preternatural excrescences"—small growths, especially on the breasts or genital areas. These were witches' teats, used for suckling Satan's imps. Such growths, which aren't uncommon, particularly in older people, were absolute proof their possessor was a witch.

Accusations multiplied. They spread from Salem to Newbury, to Andover, to Boston. Ministers named longtime members of their congregations as witches. Many accused their neighbors. Children complained their mothers and fathers had bewitched them. The circle of girls who had surrounded Tituba enjoyed extraordinary power: they could cause terrible damage to anyone they chose.

What was the fate of those who confessed?

Tituba was the first. After repeated beatings by her master, Parris, she knew what was expected of her. Taking cues from the magistrates, she embroidered a confession so weird it held the courtroom spellbound for three days. After thirteen months in prison she was set free.

Like Tituba, no one who confessed was executed.

Without exception, those who refused to confess were hanged.

On June 10, 1692, the first of the condemned witches was put to death. This was Bridget Bishop, a tavern keeper. She was a flashy dresser who had a way with men, so it is hardly surprising some complained she had afflicted them. A large crowd watched as the sheriff carted her up Gallows Hill and hanged her from the branch of a great oak tree. The hill was a high one; people who didn't join the throng could observe the proceedings from their windows.

On July 19, in a mass execution, five more women were hanged on Gallows Hill. One of these, a poor creature named Sarah Good, was urged by Nicholas Noyes, a local minister, to confess and save her soul. She knew very well, he told her, that she was a witch.

"You're a liar!" she cried angrily. "I'm no more a witch than you are a wizard—and if you take away my life, God will give you blood to drink!"

After the hanging, the bodies of the executed were buried in a crevice on a rocky outcropping on the hill.

On August 19 five more who had steadfastly refused to acknowledge their guilt were executed. Of the four men in the group the most outstanding was George Burroughs, a Harvard graduate and former minister. A contemporary account gives a dramatic picture of his ending:

> Burroughs was carried in a cart with the others through the streets of Salem to execution; when he was upon the Ladder, he made a Speech for the clearing of his Innocency, with such Solemn and Serious Expression, as were to the Admiration of all present; his prayer (which he concluded by repeating the Lord's Prayer) was so well worded, and uttered with such composedness, and such (at least seeming) fervency of Spirit as was very affecting, and drew Tears from many (so that it seemed to some, that the Spectators would hinder the Execution). The accusers said the black Man stood and dictated to him . . .
>
> Being mounted on a horse, Mr. C. Mather addressed himself to the People, partly to declare, that he (Burroughs) was no ordained minister and partly to possess the People of his guilt; saying, That the Devil has often been transformed into an Angel of Light; and that did somewhat appease the People, and the Execution went on . . .

Burroughs dead was treated no better than Burroughs alive. Evidently his shirt and breeches appealed to someone, perhaps the executioner. The same account relates:

When he was cut down he was dragged by the Halter to a Hole
. . . between the Rocks, about two feet deep, his Shirt and
Breeches being pulled off, and an old pair of Trousers of one
Executed, put on his lower parts; he was so put in, together with
Willard and Carryer, and one of his Hands and his Chin and a
Foot, of one (of) them being uncovered.

On September 19 one of the accused, Giles Cory, eighty years old
and a man of property, was pressed to death. He appears to be the only
person in American history who suffered such a punishment.

In England, pressing was inflicted when a prisoner, ordered to plead
guilty or not guilty, refused to do either. It consisted of placing weights
on him, one by one, until the pressure forced him to plead. Very few
could resist this compelling procedure.

Cory was one of them. He felt he had a good reason. In all cases
(except treason), when a person failed to plead, he couldn't be tried
and convicted—and thus his possessions could not be confiscated as
part of the penalty.

Cory's wife, Martha, had already been found guilty of witchcraft,
and was awaiting execution. At first the deluded old man had believed
the allegations against her; he had testified she was a witch. Now,
facing the same charge himself, he realized how terribly mistaken he
had been. If he were placed on trial, he saw he too would be condemned. Deciding that if he couldn't save his life he could at least save
his property, he drew up a deed transferring it to those of his sons-in-
law who believed Martha innocent.

On September 19 Cory was hauled out to an open field next to the
jail. An old ballad tells what happened next:

> *They got them a heavy Beam,*
> *They layde it on his Breast,*
> *They loaded it with heavy stones,*
> *And hard upon him presst.*

> *"More weight!" now sayde this wretched Man,*
> *"More weight!" again he cryde,*
> *And he did no Confession make*
> *But wickedly he dyed.*

The record tells us that when poor Giles thrust out his tongue in pain, the sheriff pushed it back in with his walking stick.

A few days later, on September 22, Giles's wife, with seven others, bounced up the rough road to Gallows Hill. During the ascent the cart got stuck in the mud. Some of those who had accused the condemned said that Satan himself was hindering it. But the forces of good evidently won out, for the cart finally began to roll again.

One of the witches was a man, Samuel Wardwell. Under relentless cross-examination he had been persuaded to confess, but later he had recanted and been sentenced to hang. From the ladder he tried to address the onlookers and protest he was innocent. The sheriff was smoking a pipe right by him and the smoke choked Wardwell so, he couldn't go on. Some people said it was the devil himself who stopped him.

When the last of the prisoners had been turned off the ladder, a minister, Nicholas Noyes, said unctuously, "What a sad thing it is to see eight firebrands of hell hanging there!"

Such a spectacle no one would see in America again.

By early 1693 eight more witches had been condemned and their graves already dug when Governor Phips reprieved them. Cotton Mather and other ministers wanted to continue with more prosecutions, but the climate had changed. People who earlier had believed the spectral evidence against the witches now understood it was a web of lies and hysterical imaginings.

The minister Parris, in whose house the scare had begun and who had been a diligent persecutor of the accused, was dismissed from his post. Cotton Mather was censured repeatedly and rejected for the presidency of Harvard, which he coveted. Jurors apologized publicly for their part in the witch trials.

Nothing could be done to bring back to life the guiltless dead. But some steps were taken to make amends. In a number of cases the sentence of excommunication that had been passed on the condemned was blotted out in church records. So were convictions for witchcraft in court records. And in some cases, when families prosecuted their claims vigorously enough, the province paid them small sums in compensation.

Nathan Hale, the twenty-one-year-old schoolmaster spy, has passed into legend. Because his short life ended on the gallows and not many know the actual facts, his story is well worth telling here.

Born in Conventry, Connecticut, in 1755, at eighteen Hale was graduated from Yale. He had an outstanding record as a classical scholar, orator and writer, and especially as an athlete. "I have seen him follow a football and kick it over the tops of the trees in the Bowery at New York," a friend would recall.

Hale was teaching school in 1775 in New London when news came of the bloody fighting at Lexington, the first battle of the American Revolution. At a town meeting, the young man made a fiery speech for freedom and independence. Commissioned a lieutenant in the Continental Army (five of his nine brothers also served), he took part in the siege of Boston. When the American army moved to New York he was already a captain.

Hale longed to do some signal service for his country. In September 1776 George Washington desperately wanted information about the British fortifications on Long Island. The officers of Hale's company, Knowlton's Rangers, were asked if any would volunteer to obtain it, but no one stepped forward; spying seemed disgraceful to them. Hale, still weak from an illness, came in late and accepted the assignment.

A friend tried to dissuade him.

"For a year, I have been attached to the army," Hale explained, "and have not rendered any material service." Now at last he had his opportunity.

Pretending to be a schoolmaster looking for a post (he carried his Yale diploma to support his story), he set out from camp on Harlem Heights on September 12 and crossed Long Island Sound by boat from Norwalk, Connecticut. Making his way through the territory held by the British forces, and gathering information wherever he could, he had reached upper Manhattan, close to the American lines, when he was seized. His family always believed he was betrayed by his cousin Samuel Hale, a Tory in the service of the British commander, General William Howe.

Hale was taken directly to General Howe. The evidence against him was damning and he knew it: sketches of the British fortifications and other detailed information had been found on him. Calmly he gave his name and rank and admitted what he had been up to. According to a British officer present, the "manly bearing and the evident disinterested patriotism of the handsome young prisoner, sensibly touched a chord of General Howe's nature; but the stern rules of war concerning such offenses could not allow him to exercise even pity."

Sentenced to hang the next day, Hale was placed under close guard in a greenhouse. When he asked for a clergyman and a Bible, both were denied him by the vengeful provost marshal (who fifteen years later would himself be hanged for forgery in London).

Next morning, September 22, while the final preparations for the execution were being made, a British captain offered the prisoner the hospitality of his tent.

"Captain Hale entered," the officer reported; "he was calm and bore himself with gentle dignity, in the consciousness of rectitude and high intentions. He asked for writing materials, which I furnished him; he wrote two letters, one to his mother and one to a brother officer." They were never delivered.

Only a handful of soldiers and camp followers witnessed the execution. "He behaved with great composure and resolution," the British captain related. After being pinioned, he made a "spirited and sensible speech" about a soldier's duty to obey his orders, ending with the heroic words "I only regret that I have but one life to lose for my country" (This sentence, permanently linked with Hale's name, he adapted from an English classic, *Cato*, by Joseph Addison.)

Hale's body, it is said, was left to dangle for a while as a caution to other would-be spies. British soldiers added their own personal touch: they found a sign with a picture of a soldier (perhaps from some inn), lettered the name of General Washington on it, and strung it up next to the dead man.

The site of the execution was close to where Grand Central Terminal stands today in New York City and is marked by a plaque.

Other spies were captured and "exalted upon the gallows" (to use George Washington's phrase) by both sides during the Revolutionary War. One was Edward Jones, a Connecticut Tory, condemned to death in 1779. Jones was standing on a ladder with a noose around his neck under a tall gibbet when something curious happened: the executioner, who probably had been drafted for the job, suddenly couldn't be found. An angry General Israel Putnam ordered the prisoner to jump. It is hardly surprising that Jones didn't obey. Finally, someone turned the ladder, throwing him to his death.

Another odd case involved a courier carrying a silver bullet. This was Daniel Taylor, a young British officer, and hidden inside the bullet was an important military message. Taylor was captured in 1777 and, obeying orders, swallowed the bullet. A very powerful emetic was forced on him. No sooner had he vomited up the bullet than he swallowed it again. Threatened that his stomach would be slit open, he reluctantly accepted a second dose, producing the evidence that convicted him. After he was hanged, Americans joked that the secret agent had been condemned "out of his own mouth."

Of all those executed for espionage, no one died a more moving death than John André, the British counterpart to Nathan Hale. "Young, handsome, brilliant, charming, loyal, high-minded, he was to be the sacrifice to evil, or to fate, that mythology demands," observe two noted historians, Henry Steele Commager and Richard B. Morris. "He is, indeed, so nearly legendary a character that had he not existed, legend must inevitably have created him."

Major John André died on the gallows at Tappan, New York, in 1780. A British Army officer, he was executed as a spy on the direct order of General George Washington, who nevertheless sympathized with him deeply. His last meal was carried to him from Washington's own table.

Born in London in 1761, André was endowed with literary and artistic gifts. A fine soldier, he rose rapidly in the military. In 1779 Sir Henry Clinton, commander-in-chief of the British forces in America, made him his adjutant general, or chief administrative officer.

In 1780 Benedict Arnold, American general commanding the fort at West Point, was planning to go over to the enemy and betray the fort to them. Major André, his "handler," set out to negotiate with him. Sailing up the Hudson River from British-held New York City on a sloop of war, André went ashore in uniform, met Arnold, and made arrangements with him.

To André's misfortune, his sloop was driven away by American cannon fire. Forced to spend the night behind the American lines, the major let himself be persuaded to take off his regimentals and put on civilian clothes. Arnold wrote out a pass for him under an assumed name and gave him confidential papers, including the plans of the fort. These André hid in the feet of his stockings.

With the sloop gone, the young officer traveled south on horseback toward the British lines. Near Tarrytown, New York, three irregulars rushed out of the woods and seized his horse. They led him to believe they were British, and he happily informed them he was a British officer. That he had made a tragic error dawned on him when he found himself looking into the muzzles of their firelocks. A search of his person revealed the hidden papers. Taken to General Washington's headquarters at Tappan, he was confined under guard at a tavern.

Washington could have had André shot summarily. Because of the prisoner's rank, however, Washington convened a court of inquiry. Its fourteen members, all generals, included Nathanael Greene, the Marquis de Lafayette, and Baron von Steuben. The British officer, who viewed himself as General Clinton's deputy, readily admitted what he had done but insisted he was no spy. The court disagreed with him and its verdict was death.

Resigned to his fate, André still hoped he wouldn't have to meet it on the gallows. Writing to Washington, he mentioned his high military position twice and asked to be shot as a soldier, not hanged like a spy and a criminal.

To spare the young officer's feelings, the general didn't reply. André thus could go on hoping he would die before a firing squad. ("The practice and usage of war," Washington would notify Congress, "circumstanced as he was, were against the indulgence.")

At the first word of André's capture, Benedict Arnold had fled to the British. Itching to get their hands on him, the Americans wrote General Clinton that they would exchange their prisoner for the traitor. The British commander refused, and André's last hope was gone.

As his end approached, André didn't ask for a clergyman or even a Bible; he was ready to meet death "like a Roman," as Thomas Paine put it. His final hours were spent making sketches with pen and ink. His orderly had arrived from New York with André's regimentals, so he could die as an officer of the British Army.

October 2 was warm and summery. Five hundred troops were stationed around the tavern where the prisoner was confined. Civilians were arriving in large numbers to witness the execution.

André dressed with particular care. "Leave me till you can show yourself more manly!" he ordered his servant, who was crying. "I am ready at any moment to wait on you," he told the two officers guarding him.

The sound of music was heard outside. It was noon, the time set for the execution. Linking arms with the two officers, he ran out the door with them. He smiled at the column of armed men drawn up in front and took his position in their midst. With a drum and fife corps playing the "Dead March," the column moved toward the place of execution.

Keeping step, André marched as on parade. "I am much surprised to find your troops under so good a discipline,''he told the officers, ''and the music is excellent.'' He was very pale but he smiled and bowed to those he recognized.

Close to the top of the long hill, they came to an open field. It was packed with spectators. A cluster of high officers were sitting on their horses. André recognized the generals who had condemned him and he bowed to each of them, receiving their bows in return. ''Such fortitude I never was witness of,'' said a medical officer. ''To see a man go out of time without fear, but all the time smiling, is a matter that I could not conceive of.'' General Washington, perhaps not surprisingly, was nowhere to be seen.

The gibbet came into view. André started.

''Must I die in this manner?'' he asked.

He was told it was unavoidable.

''Gentlemen, I'm disappointed. I expected my request would have been granted.'' His voice rang loud and clear. ''I am reconciled to my fate but not to the mode.'' Head erect, he strode forward.

Around the gallows, their backs toward it, stood three circles of soldiers, one inside the other, with bayonets fixed. A wagon was waiting with a black coffin on it. A heap of fresh earth showed André where his grave had been dug.

The death warrant was read. As André listened, his face flushed and he pushed a stone about with his foot. He seemed to have trouble swallowing. He looked up at the gallows. ''All the spectators seemed to be overwhelmed by the affecting spectacle,'' said an army officer, ''and many were suffused in tears.''

The reading over, at an order André climbed onto the wagon. ''It will be but a momentary pang,'' an army surgeon heard him say to himself.

Getting on the coffin, he walked back and forth on it. He took off his hat and placed it on the black box. People commented on his hair, long and beautiful, wound with a black ribbon in the fashion then current, and hanging down his back.

Removing his neckcloth, André turned back his shirt collar.

The executioner was a captured Tory; he was to be released in exchange for hanging the prisoner. He had blackened his hands and face to make himself unrecognizable. As he awkwardly made ready to place the noose over André's head, the condemned man seized it from him and positioned it with his own hands, setting the knot below his right ear.

André took a handkerchief from a pocket and fastened it over his eyes.

He was asked if he had any last words.

He lifted the blindfold. "I have nothing more than this: that I would have you gentlemen bear me witness that I die like a brave man." He pushed the blindfold back.

The executioner was told to tie his arms. From his pocket André brought forth another handkerchief and the executioner fastened it above his elbows behind his back. He waited quietly.

An order was given. A whip cracked, and the wagon rolled away from under the young man's feet.

The rope made a great swing, and in that swing he seemed to die.

The entire British Army mourned the death of Major André. Washington, who declared him "more unfortunate than criminal," was widely criticized for executing him. American officers, who had known him for just a few days, expressed their sorrow. "Never, perhaps, did a man suffer death with more justice, or deserve it less," wrote one of them, Colonel Alexander Hamilton, who thought Washington had dealt with André too harshly.

Close to half a century afterward, in 1821, André's remains were dug up and taken to Britain. They were reburied in Westminster Abbey, where a handsome monument was dedicated to his memory. At Tarrytown, in the place where he was captured, a monument was raised to the three irregulars who took him prisoner.

EIGHT

From Nat Turner to the Clutter Killers

Nat Turner, who died on a gallows tree in 1831, has been called the most famous slave rebel in American history. Anathematized by whites in his own time, revered as a martyr-hero by blacks in ours, he was a strange figure about whom a controversy still rages.

Turner was born in 1800 on a cotton plantation in Southampton County, Virginia. The son of a woman brought over from Africa, like other slaves he took the family name of his master. He was sold several times. Exceptionally bright, as a boy he received a rudimentary education from his master's son, and early showed an intense interest in religion. A foreman on the plantation, "Preacher Nat," as he came to be called, was permitted to hold church on Sundays and acquired a strong influence over other slaves in the neighborhood.

A mystic, from childhood on he saw visions. On March 12, 1828, he would relate later,

> I heard a loud voice in the heavens, and the Spirit instantly appeared to me and said the Serpent was loosened, and Christ had laid down the yoke He had borne for the sins of men, and that I

should take it on and fight against the Serpent, for the time was fast approaching when the first should be last and the last should be first.

Convinced that God had chosen him to be a prophet and lead the slaves out of bondage, he waited for a sign from heaven. It came in 1831 in the form of a solar eclipse. On August 13, when an atmospheric disturbance made the sun grow dim and seem to change colors, he was sure the day of deliverance was at hand.

In the early hours of August 22, with six loyal followers, Turner began his revolt by butchering his current master, Joseph Travis, and his family in their beds. Like John Brown after him, he confidently expected blacks everywhere would join his rebellion and slavery would fall. Recruiting other blacks—they finally numbered about sixty—he set out to slay one white family after another. Here is part of his account of how they proceeded:

> I took my station in the rear, and as it was my object to carry terror and devastation wherever we went, I placed fifteen or twenty of the best mounted and most to be relied on in front, who generally approached the houses as fast as their horses could run, this was for two purposes, to prevent the escape of and strike terror into the inhabitants—on this account I never got to the houses . . . until the murders were committed. . . . I sometimes got in sight in time to see the work of death completed, viewed the mangled bodies as they lay in silent satisfaction, and immediately started in quest of other victims.
>
> Having murdered Mrs. Waller and 10 children, we started for Mr. William Williams'—while engaged in killing him and two little boys that were there, Mrs. Williams fled and got some distance from the house, but she was pursued, overtaken, and compelled to get up behind one of the company, who brought her back and after showing her the mangled body of her lifeless husband, she was told to get down and lie by his side, where she was shot dead.

By the end of forty-eight hours, the group had beheaded, hacked to pieces, or shot dead fifty-five whites: twenty-four children, eighteen women, thirteen men. The prophet allowed no rapes and sprinkled his supporters with the blood of the slain. According to his confession, he killed only one person, a woman, whom he beat to death.

Among those the rebels killed were some slaves who refused to join them and died defending their masters.

At the first news of the revolt, the whites began to organize armed parties. Reinforced by two thousand militia and eight hundred federal troops, they trailed the insurgents and attacked them, killing a large number of blacks throughout the countryside, including many who had taken no part in the rebellion, and mounting the heads of some on posts. They brought back dozens as prisoners, but not Turner, who remained at large.

The trials of the insurgents were held at the county seat, Jerusalem. The slaves were defended by local lawyers.

Meanwhile, Turner had hidden himself in a hole he'd dug in a field, coming out only at night to steal food. Substantial rewards were offered for his capture.

To help identify the fugitive, a description was prepared. It read:

He is between 30 & 35 years old—five feet six or 8 inches high—weighs between 150 and 160 rather bright complexion but not a mulatto—broad-shouldered—large flat nose—large eyes—broad flat feet rather knock kneed—walk brisk and active—hair on the top of the head very thin—no beard except on the upper lip and tip of the chin. A scar on one of his temples produced by the kick of a mule—also one on the back of his neck by a bite—a large knot on one of the bones of his right arm near the wrist produced by a blow.

After six weeks in hiding, Turner was taken prisoner. Under interrogation, he answered every question forthrightly. Entering a plea of not guilty, he said he was "in particular favor with heaven" and had done nothing wrong. Feeling ran high against him: special deputies had to be hired to protect him from lynching.

Declaring Turner was in "a state of fanatical delusion," the judges sentenced him to die on the gallows. A value of $375 was placed on him; the state would have to pay that sum to his late owner's estate in compensation for his loss.

November 11, 1831, was the end for Nat Turner. At noon, with armed horsemen riding before and behind, a wagon brought him in chains to a field outside Jerusalem. The county seat had no gallows; an old tree served the purpose. Eating, drinking, and in a festive mood, a great mass of people was waiting.

The sheriff asked the prisoner if he wanted to make a last statement. "I'm ready," he said, and that was all. His voice was strong.

Calm and unafraid, the prisoner looked up at the sky, ignoring the noisy crowd, while the sheriff drew a heavy hemp noose tight around his neck. The other end of the rope was flung over a sturdy branch.

Highly appreciative of the honor, several men lustily hauled Turner up into the air with a jerk. Onlookers cheered.

If they expected to see a death struggle they were disappointed. The doomed man might have been dead already. "Not a limb nor a muscle was observed to move," an eyewitness said.

What happened to Turner's body next wasn't uncommon for executed slaves. It was turned over to physicians, who dissected it for medical study. "They skinned his body and made grease of the flesh," wrote W. S. Drewry in his account of the Southampton insurrection.

Twenty-one of the slaves who took part in the rebellion, including one woman, died on the gallows. Turner had a wife and daughter, and they were sold to slave traders. New, more stringent slave codes were passed to prevent such a revolt from happening again in the South— which from that time forward lived in fear that one would.

In June 1859, a gaunt man with the long gray beard and hypnotic eyes of an Old Testament prophet rented a farm in Maryland close to the Virginia border. Farming, however, was the furthest thing from his mind. He was about to carry out a mission—a mission he was certain God had chosen him for—one he believed would set the nation on its ear.

Instead it would lead him directly to the gallows.

Rifles, pistols, pikes and ammunition started to arrive secretly at the farm and the Old Man hid them. A handful of devoted young followers arrived too. He hid them away as well. If the neighbors saw them and became suspicious, the jig would be up.

October 16 came. It was The Day.

In the morning the Old Man read to his young disciples from the Bible, about the enslavement of the children of Israel by the Egyptians. In the evening, heavily armed and under cover of darkness, he and eighteen of his followers (three were his own sons and five were black) set out in a wagon and on foot. Their destination: the little town of

Harper's Ferry in Virginia (West Virginia today). On the way they cut the telegraph wires.

Crossing the Potomac River, the insurgents swooped down upon the unsuspecting town. In a short while fifty of its citizens (they were to be used as hostages), the federal arsenal, the armory and the rifle works were in their hands.

The taking of Harper's Ferry, with its great store of weapons, was to be only the first shot in the Old Man's campaign. He firmly believed that when the slaves in the area heard what he had done, they would throw off their chains and flock to his banner. "When I strike," he had told the black leader Frederick Douglass, "the bees will begin to swarm." More and more would revolt and join his forces until he had an army behind him. The abolitionists of the North would rise up and add their strength to his. The slave system of the South would crumble.

It was a bold dream, but only a dream. As the hours went by, not one slave came forward to join the insurgents. A dozen were "freed" and pikes were thrust into their hands; frightened, they got rid of them as soon as they could. The first person killed by Brown's forces wasn't a plantation owner. It was Shephard Hayward, a free black man who worked as baggagemaster at the railroad depot.

Word of the raid traveled fast. Local citizens reached for their rifles and came running. In Charlestown, the militia armed themselves and headed for Harper's Ferry. So did the militias of half a dozen other towns, some coming from as far away as Baltimore. They pinned down the handful of raiders in a fire-engine house and cut off all chance of escape.

In Washington, Colonel Robert E. Lee was hastily summoned by President Buchanan. With a force of ninety marines and two howitzers, he was rushed to Harper's Ferry, and early on October 18 his troops stormed the fire-engine house. The Old Man was shot, stabbed and slashed. About half of his followers were killed (two of his sons among them), and he was captured. On the other side, soldiers and civilians were killed and wounded.

Interrogated by his captors, the Old Man told them he had acted as an "instrument of God." He and those of his men who hadn't escaped or been killed were carried off to Charlestown and lodged in the jail. The governor ordered them tried under the laws of Virginia. The charges: "treason, conspiring and advising with slaves and other rebels, and murder in the first degree."

Depending upon how they felt about slavery, Americans either admired, hated or feared the Old Man. Born in Connecticut in 1800, John Brown had inherited his antislavery sentiments from his father. In Pennsylvania, Brown started a project to educate young blacks. He operated a "station" on the underground railroad. The father of twenty children, he worked at farming, tanning and sheep rearing, but never very successfully; he was always running off to meetings to organize opposition to slavery.

In 1855, Brown joined some of his sons living in the Kansas territory, near Osawatomie. Kansas had become a bloody battle-ground; pro- and antislavery forces were wrestling to win it for their cause, and Brown went there to help in the struggle. In 1859, with his sons, he attacked and killed five proslavery men in Pottawatomie to avenge the murder of abolitionists. A revolver in each hand, he tried to defend Osawatomie against a horde of proslavery Missourians, losing a son. He became widely known as Osawatomie Brown.

At about this time, Artemus Ward interviewed John Brown. He found him

> a medium-sized, compactly built and wiry man, and as quick as a cat in his movements. His hair is of a salt and pepper hue and as stiff as bristles. He has a long, waving, milk-white goatee [it would shortly become a full beard], which gives him a somewhat patriarchal appearance. His eyes are gray and sharp. A man of pluck is Brown. You may bet on that. He shows it in his walk, talk and actions. He must be rising sixty and yet we believe he could lick a yard full of wild cats before breakfast and without taking off his coat.

Osawatomie Brown's trial began on October 25, 1859. His attorneys obtained affidavits proving insanity ran in his mother's family. They urged him to plead insanity as his defense—newspapers all over the country, after all, were calling him a madman. He refused.

Weak from his wounds, Brown was carried into court on a cot. Sometimes he would leap from it to raise objections. He defended himself rationally and with dignity, speaking passionately of his efforts to help the slaves.

On October 31, the jury needed just forty-five minutes to reach a verdict of guilty, and he was sentenced to hang. His followers, tried later, received the same sentence.

Slightly more than a month of life remained to Osawatomie Brown. He spent a good part of it corresponding with friends and receiving visitors. Everything that was happening to him, he told them, had been ordained before the beginning of time. His letters revealed a martyr's willingness to sacrifice his life. Writing to his wife and children, he declared, "I can trust God with both the time and the manner of my death, believing, as I now do, that for me at this time to seal my testimony for God and humanity with blood will do vastly more toward advancing the cause I have earnestly endeavored to promote than all I have done." He believed that "nothing that either I or all my family have sacrificed or suffered will be lost."

Brown's supporters were eager to help him escape. He told them not to try. He "would not walk out of prison if the door was left open."

To prevent any attempt at a rescue, Governor Wise ordered Charlestown to be filled with armed troops. The town presented, according to one newspaper, "the unusual scene of a military encampment in time of national peace."

Brown's wife pleaded to be allowed to come from her home in New York State to see him. After repeated refusals he finally gave in.

Mary Brown arrived the day before the execution, and her carriage was escorted to the jailhouse by cavalry. She was overcome at first, according to the Baltimore *Sun*, but Old Brown was "firm as a rock." When she left, a detachment of twenty mounted men escorted her back to Harper's Ferry.

On the following day, December 2, after a peaceful night's sleep, Brown rose early. About a third of a mile in back of the jailhouse, on a common, he could see carpenters building the scaffold on which he would hang. Calmly, he completed a task he had set himself: marking off in his Bible the passages that had most influenced his life. He wrote a final letter to his wife. He had a will drawn up providing gifts of Bibles to his children and rifles to the sheriff and jailer, who were friendly to him.

With just half an hour left, Brown visited his followers, who were locked up in the same jail awaiting execution. He said goodbye to each, shook hands, and gave them the money in his pocket.

"If you must die," he told them, "die like men."

He had refused the visits of southern ministers; if they supported slavery, he said, they weren't men of the spirit. The books in his cell he gave to his guards. To one he also gave a sheet of paper on which he had written this prophetic statement:

I John Brown am now quite *certain* that the crimes of this *guilty land; will* never be purged *away*; but with Blood. I had *as I now think: vainly* flattered myself that without *very much* bloodshed; it might be done.

It was time to go, they told him. Wearing a black suit, a slouch hat, and carpet slippers, he walked out into the bright sunlight. His hands were bound at his sides.

It was a moment that would be celebrated in words and pictures. A few weeks later, in New York City, John Greenleaf Whittier would publish a poem that included these lines:

> *John Brown of Osawatomie,*
>   *They led him out to die,*
> *When lo, a poor slave-mother*
>   *With her little child pressed nigh.*
> *Then the bold, blue eyes grew tender,*
>   *And the old hard face grew mild,*
> *And he stooped between the jeering ranks,*
>   *And kissed the negro's child.*

A Currier & Ives print would show Brown gazing compassionately at a black mother and child. The painter Thomas Hovenden would portray the scene of Brown kissing the child in a colorful, dramatic picture presently in the Metropolitan Museum of Art in New York City. The actions attributed to Brown would have been true to his character, but unfortunately none of them could have taken place. The entire area was under tight military control. No unauthorized civilian could have gotten near the condemned man.

Outside the jail a wagon was waiting; Brown could see his coffin in the back. Companies of infantry, with bayonets fixed, were standing in front of the wagon, at the rear, and on both sides.

The sheriff and the jailer helped Brown up into the wagon. He seated himself on the coffin and the procession got under way. Along the route infantrymen and cavalry stood guard.

At the foot of the steps of the scaffold, the wagon came to a halt and Brown was helped down. Companies of soldiers stood rigidly all about, sunlight glinting on their bayonets. Cannon had been placed at strategic locations and squads of soldiers were stationed in the distance.

The prisoner climbed the steps rapidly. As he went up he saw the attorney who had prosecuted him, and he bowed to him. On the platform he thanked the sheriff and the jailer for the kindness they had shown.

The sheriff asked if he wanted a handkerchief in his hand to drop as a signal when he was ready.

"No, I don't want it, but don't detain me longer than is actually necessary."

A white hood was pulled down over his head and his ankles were tied. The noose was adjusted around his neck. (The rope had been exhibited in town for several days; southern states had competed to supply it, and Kentucky had won.)

Now a curious military maneuver began. Governor Wise had called for strict security; the soldiers on the common were to form two squares, one within the other, about the scaffold, so they could better stand off any attack. Ten or twelve minutes went by as they marched and countermarched before they were all in position.

The jailer asked Brown if he was tired.

"No. But don't keep me waiting longer than necessary."

At a quarter past eleven the hangman sprang the trap. "A slight grasping of the hands and twitching of the muscles and then all was quiet," reported a newspaper. "The body was examined several times and the pulse did not cease beating for thirty-five minutes. Then the body was cut down and placed in the coffin." Surrounded by companies of soldiers, it was taken back to the jailhouse, where it was examined again. It looked remarkably lifelike; reportedly, the doctors wondered whether Brown's followers wouldn't be able to bring him back to life with a galvanic battery. Finally, satisfied, they signed the death certificate.

At Harper's Ferry the coffin was turned over to Mrs. Brown. Distrustful, she opened it to make the sure the body inside was actually her husband's.

The coffin was brought home by train and ship. As it passed through northern cities bells were rung. In New York City it was taken to a funeral home, where the coffin was changed—Mary Brown didn't want her husband to be buried in a southern coffin. A long line of visitors called to pay their respects to the old warrior.

Brown was buried in a funeral plot on his farm in North Elba, New York, close to a huge granite rock, on which his name was carved. In just a few years a song about him would rise from the throats of thousands and thousands of Union soldiers as they marched off to battle in the bloody struggle he had foretold.

Many condemned prisoners have sought to escape the shame of execution by taking their own lives. One of the most sensational of these attempts was made by a young New England sea captain, Nathaniel Gordon. On February 21, 1862, after swallowing poison, Gordon had to be half-carried to the scaffold to be strung up. His crime was piracy.

Gordon was far from a pirate in the traditional sense: he was a sailor engaged in transporting slaves from Africa to the West. As early as 1794, Congress had passed a law that made it illegal for Americans to carry slaves to foreign countries, and a later law forbade transporting them to the United States. But there was good money in slave trading, and the traffic went on. After 1819, some—but not many—American naval vessels patrolled the African coast and searched ships suspected of transporting slaves. Then, in 1820, Congress went further: it classed slaving as a form of piracy and made it punishable by death.

From time to time, the Navy would overtake a slave ship, seize it, and bring the captain back to the United States to stand trial. But courts didn't view the crime as gravely as the law did; usually the captain was given a light sentence or the case was dismissed. Nathaniel Gordon was the only exception in American history. He had the singular bad fortune to come to trial at the wrong time and it cost him his life.

A native of Maine—he was born in Portland in about 1835—Gordon was the son of a sea captain. Starting as a cabin boy, he rose to captain while still in his twenties. Not he, but the owners of his ship, the *Erie*, were the actual owners of the black cargoes he carried. He made several successful voyages as a slaver and, for his skill in eluding United States patrols, earned the sobriquet of Lucky Nat.

On August 8, 1860, Lucky Nat's luck ran out. On the previous day, at the mouth of the Congo River, he had taken aboard his ship a cargo of 897 blacks, more than half of them children. Setting sail for Cuba, he was about fifty miles out when he was overtaken by the U.S.S. *Mohican*, a steam-powered war sloop. A search party came aboard and the *Erie* was seized and escorted to Liberia. On the fifteen-day voyage, more than two dozen blacks died of disease; the rest, all of whom reportedly had running sores, were set free.

Gordon and his vessel were taken to New York City. Turned over to the federal authorities, he was charged with piracy.

The prisoner was placed on trial in Manhattan Federal Court. The jury couldn't reach a verdict and a second trial was ordered. By the time it began, November 6, 1861, the North and the South were at war. Hatred of slavery and those who profited from it was running high. A new prosecutor, George Pierce Andrews, recently admitted to the bar and eager to make a name for himself, pursued Gordon with zeal. Gordon, for his part, loyally refused to reveal the names of his employers, who would have faced the same penalty that he did. In just two days the trial was over and the jury found the prisoner guilty.

"Think of the cruelty and wickedness of seizing nearly a thousand human beings, who never did you any harm," the judge summed up, looking at Gordon, "and thrusting them between the decks of a small ship, beneath a burning tropical sun, to die of disease or suffocation, or to be transported to distant lands and consigned, they and their posterity, to a fate more cruel than death." Gordon was sentenced to hang.

On February 20, 1862, the day before the execution, two women made an urgent visit to Washington, D.C. They were Gordon's wife and mother, and they wanted to see President Lincoln and beg for a stay of execution. Their timing was unfortunate. The President's beloved son, Willie, had died that day and Lincoln would see no one. Heartbroken, they returned to New York.

That night the two women paid Gordon a farewell visit in the Tombs Prison and brought him a gift of cigars. After they left, Gordon was granted the condemned man's privilege of walking up and down the corridor. He bantered with the guards, quite unlike a man who was facing the scaffold, and diverted them with Portuguese songs. Locked up in his cell, he smoked and wrote until midnight, then turned in.

At about three o'clock Gordon started suddenly up from his bed, peered at his watch, muttered something, then lay down again, facing the wall.

An hour later his guards noticed he was writhing and tossing about. Thinking he was having bad dreams, they tried to wake him but couldn't. The prison doctor was summoned. By the time he arrived, Gordon's convulsions were more terrible than before and he was raving. The doctor applied a stomach pump to the prisoner and gave him stimulants. At one time, rolling about on the floor, he cried, "I've cheated you! I've cheated you!"

He suffered episodes of lockjaw. For half an hour at a time his jaws were clamped so tight he couldn't speak or even manage a groan; his face was livid and the slightest touch or noise sent him into paroxysms.

His pulse was feeble and he barely breathed. For hours he was in terrible pain—worse pain, it seemed to those present, than he could possibly suffer on the gallows.

The doctor kept giving him whiskey, hoping to keep him alive until 2:00 P.M., the hour set for the execution. Gordon, the physician said, had probably taken strychnine during the night when he woke up; perhaps it had been smuggled to him by the women in the cigars they had brought.

Gordon spoke sometimes when the lockjaw let up. "He said that he had suffered a thousand deaths since he took the poison," *The New York Times* would report the following day, "and begged that he might be allowed to die and end his suffering." Instead the doctor gave him more whiskey.

At 11:00 A.M., the gates of the prison yard swung open and in marched a company of marines, muskets with fixed bayonets on their shoulders. With them came a marine band playing military music. Rumors were circulating that a mob would attempt to set Gordon free; apparently the marines had been sent to prevent such an incident. While they stood guard, the executioner tested the scaffold and made the noose ready.

At a quarter past eleven the condemned man's attorney came rushing in. He asked the federal marshal, Murray, to delay the execution; Governor Morgan, he related, had sent a wire to President Abraham Lincoln requesting a reprieve. (Later it was said that powerful people connected with the ship's owners had induced the governor to telegraph Lincoln.) The marshal's reply was no.

At noon Marshal Murray appeared at the door of the condemned man's cell and said it was time to go—apparently he had advanced the time of execution, fearing Gordon might die of the poison before he could be hanged. Gordon grumbled about the change in schedule, but he let a deputy marshal help him dress and accepted a large drink of whiskey. His arms were tied and a black hood was placed carelessly on one side of his head. He was carried out into the corridor and set on a chair.

Marshal Murray took out the death warrant. Gordon was helped to his feet and the marshal, who appeared deeply moved, read it to him.

Raising his head, the prisoner began to speak drunkenly but with passion. "I die with the conscience of a man who has done, intentionally, no wrong. When a man [Andrews, the prosecutor] gets up in court and says to the jury that if they will only convict a man for him he will do everything to get that man pardoned and then goes to the President and begs him to hang the man, it's very mean and contemptible. Such a man would do anything to promote his own ends. He is a mean fellow.''

Gordon asked for, and was given, another drink. The death procession began to move solemnly toward the scaffold, with the prisoner supported by the marshal. They came to a halt under the gallows.

"Well, a man can't die but once," Gordon said. "I'm not afraid.''

Those were his last words. While a deputy held him upright the black hood was drawn over his pale, exhausted features and the noose placed around his neck and tightened.

Then, according to the *Times*, "with a jerk, he went high into the air and fell to the length of the rope. . . . The body swayed hither and thither for a few moments and then all was quiet. At the proper time, the physicians examined the body and pronounced him dead with a broken neck.''

His court-martial had just begun. Captain Henry Wirz, former commandant of the infamous Andersonville death camp, could hardly doubt how it would end. He would be found guilty and sentenced to hang.

An impressive figure, almost six feet tall, with a full beard and graying hair, Wirz was housed in the Old Capitol Prison in Washington, D.C. General Lafayette C. Baker was in charge. It was Baker's responsibility to see that nothing happened to his prisoner until he stood face to face with the hangman.

Wirz showed signs of strain, but otherwise he seemed normal enough. It was only when the prisoner's wife came to visit him for the first time that the general noticed something odd: neither Wirz nor his wife showed the slightest trace of affection for each other.

Arriving for her first visit, Mrs. Wirz said, "How are you, Wirz?''

"Well," he replied gloomily, "I am getting along pretty well.''

She looked at him. "When did you have on a clean shirt last? I never saw you look so dirty in my life.''

Wirz began to complain about his misfortunes. In a short while she said goodbye and left.

The woman's coldness was just as marked on her second visit. The general found her conduct exceedingly strange.

On her third visit the suspicious Baker was taking no chances; he stayed in the cell right beside the couple. As Mrs. Wirz rose to leave, he was surprised to see her lean forward to kiss the captain.

The general's eyes were fastened on their mouths. Their lips, as they came together, moved in a highly unusual way.

Thrusting the woman aside, Baker leaped at Wirz and seized him by the throat.

"Open your mouth!" the general commanded.

Wirz had no choice. As his lips parted, he spat something to the floor.

The general picked it up. A small ball of something, partly crushed. Smaller than an acorn, and coated with licorice.

Baker scraped off the black coating. Beneath it he saw a thin wrapping of oil silk. He pulled it apart carefully.

Strychnine. And in a moment it would have been in the prisoner's stomach, dissolving.

You will never be permitted to visit your husband in his cell again, Baker told the woman angrily. She went away, and in a short while left the capital.

When the Civil War ended in April 1865, many in the North demanded that the leaders of the Confederacy be arrested, tried and summarily hanged. The Union Army resisted, but the demands continued unabated. One of those whose heads were called for was Captain Henry Wirz. He was only small fry among many big fish, but the authorities finally decided to sacrifice him.

A native of Switzerland, Wirz had come to the United States in 1849. Settling in the South, he practiced medicine in Louisiana. With the outbreak of the war he enlisted in the Confederate Army and was a clerk in a Richmond military prison. In 1863 he fought in the battle of Seven Pines, where he was wounded. Later he served as a Confederate agent on missions in Europe, and in 1864 was named commandant of Andersonville.

Andersonville, a hastily built military prison, was the worst hellhole of the Civil War. Enclosed by a high stockade of pine logs, it covered twenty-six acres in the Georgia swamps. It had no barracks—prisoners slept in tents on the ground or in rude huts. Built to hold ten thousand prisoners, at its peak the camp had more than three times that number. Sanitary conditions were atrocious. The water was polluted. Overexposure was common. With food and medicines in short supply, starvation, infected wounds, typhoid and typhus took a heavy toll. In the thirteen months the prison was in operation, thirteen thousand Union soldiers died there.

Appalling stories of the horrors of Andersonville had reached the North, and when the survivors, diseased and emaciated, came home at war's end, there was a loud outcry for vengeance. Wirz was arrested and charged with cruelty and murder. Although his lawyer presented evidence that he had done his best to help the prisoners, he was quickly convicted and condemned to death.

After Wirz's attempt to take his life, the authorities proposed to place a few men in his cell to keep an eye on him, as well as to help him pass the time.

Wirz objected. "I'm not going to commit suicide. I'm not afraid to die and I will not save the government the expense of hanging me. I'm damned if the Yankee eagle hasn't turned into what I expected—a damned turkey buzzard."

At 10:00 A.M. on November 2, 1865, the prison yard was teeming. Two hundred soldiers stood guard with muskets. Reporters were jotting notes, artists were sketching, photographers were readying their cameras. Outside, tree branches, windows and roofs that overlooked the yard swarmed with spectators. In the distance, on the dome of the Capitol, the figure of Liberty glittered in the brilliant sunlight.

In a few minutes Wirz appeared, a strange-looking figure in a gown of black cambric with a cowl at the shoulders. Two priests walked with him. Moving rapidly, he mounted the steps to the platform and sat down on a stool in the middle. The dangling rope touched his head.

An Army major began to read the charges. The list was a long one. Wirz listened patiently, but from time to time he looked up and shook his head in dissent, flashing a defiant smile.

When the major concluded, Wirz rose to his feet and stood calmly as his arms were bound to his sides. His manner was manly and self-confident.

The noose was placed around his neck. "This is too tight," he complained. "Loosen it a little." Then he spoke his last words: "I am innocent. I will have to die sometime. I will die like a man. My hopes are in the future."

The cowl was drawn over his head. Standing silent and motionless, he looked like a monk out of the Middle Ages.

At 10:32 the bolts were drawn and Wirz plunged through the

trapdoor opening. The crowd of watchers outside the prison yard burst into cheers so loud the dying man could have heard them as he swung around, his legs moving convulsively. In the yard itself no one uttered a sound.

In its account of the execution, the *New York Tribune* observed that the prisoner was to be buried next to the Lincoln conspirators, hanged a short while before.

"Wirz's life," the paper concluded, "was not worth much to him or his death worth much to the nation. Many a greater criminal has been pardoned and many better men hanged. The public conscience will probably be satisfied as if a great act of justice had been done."

Many years later, a historian would note that Wirz's was the "sole execution because of the war."

Who were the Molly Maguires? Not many remember today. Yet in Pennsylvania a century or so ago, just the mention of that name was often enough to make coal-mine owners uneasy and policemen reach for their pistols.

All of that came to an end between 1877 and 1879 when, after being found guilty of a long series of murders, twenty unrepentant Mollies mounted the scaffold, kissed the crucifix, and gave up the ghost. They had been convicted on evidence provided by a spy, born in Ireland and a Catholic like themselves, whom they had treated as a brother.

The Mollies were Irish-Americans. A clandestine insider group within the Ancient Order of Hibernians, they were active in the anthracite mining district around Scranton. Their name they had borrowed from Ireland, from an old secret society set up to resist and harass the agents and process servers of the oppressive landlords. The original Molly Maguire, tradition says, was a poor widow evicted from a small farm in 1839. The young Irishmen who first used her name disguised themselves in women's clothing and bullied and beat landlords' agents and government officials.

The coal barons of eastern Pennsylvania controlled not just the mines but the economic and political life of the region. Working conditions in the mines were outrageous, and in the 1860s and '70s the Mollies waged a war against the mine owners with strikes and terrorism. The owners fought back with every means at their disposal.

In 1873, after repeated unsuccessful attempts to destroy the Mollies, the mine owners turned to the Pinkerton detective agency. James McParlan, an Irish-born detective with a brogue, was sent into the region. Pretending to be a counterfeiter hiding from the law, he gained admission to the order. McParlan won the members' trust and was elected secretary of one of the most criminal lodges. In this position, he was able to gather information about the Mollies' illegal activities. After two years, he turned it over to the authorities and the arrests began. Large numbers of the Mollies were sentenced to prison or death, and the society's power was broken forever.

June 21, 1877, has been called "Pennsylvania's Day with the Rope" and "Black Thursday." On that day the first two groups of condemned Mollies mounted the scaffold—six in Pottsville and four in Mauch Chunk (later renamed Jim Thorpe, for the famous athlete).

Outside the Pottsville jailyard, standing in the rain, a crowd of relatives and friends of the condemned loudly protested their innocence. Three gallows had been erected side by side in the yard, each furnished with two hanging ropes. In front of the scaffolds a long rope stretched across the yard, holding back the crowd of spectators.

At 10:50 A.M., an iron gate creaked open and the first pair of prisoners appeared, James Boyle and Hugh McGehan, each accompanied by a priest, with prison guards following. They mounted one of the scaffolds.

"The degree of nerve displayed by both men, particularly by Boyle, was extraordinary," the *New York Tribune* reported the following day. "At times his manner seemed to indicate a feeling of utter indifference to his surroundings . . . as the religious services proceeded he occasionally inhaled the perfume of a beautiful red rose which he held in his hand and applied to his nostrils. He responded to a remark of his attending priest, with, 'I ain't a bit sorry.' "

Both men had been found guilty of killing Benjamin Yost, a policeman. "I only ask forgiveness of the whole world if I have done wrong to them," were McGehan's final words. Boyle echoed him. "Goodbye, old fellow, we'll die like men!" he added. Leather straps were fastened around their limbs and at 11:11 the trap was sprung. The red rose Boyle had been holding fell to the ground.

Two by two, the four other condemned men followed Boyle and McGehan to the gallows. None of them showed any fear. Meanwhile, at Mauch Chunk, on a scaffold built for them, four more Mollies were hanged for the murder of two mine bosses, and their bodies were brought by special train to Pottsville.

The execution of two other Mollies, Charles Sharpe and James McDonnell, at Mauch Chunk on January 14, 1879, is worth noting because of some unusual incidents. The men had been convicted of the murder, sixteen years earlier, of George K. Smith, a mine operator, on the testimony of other Mollies who turned state's evidence.

It was customary at this time and place for the hanging ropes to arrive from the manufacturer with the nooses already made. When the sheriff opened the box, however, he saw the ropes had no nooses. From 9:00 to 10:00 A.M., he was busy getting the ropes ready. As he was making his final preparations, a telegram arrived from Pottsville, saying McDonnell's wife and children were on their way to the prison to say goodbye to him. The authorities had agreed with the priests that the execution would take place at 10:30; now they feared the train would be late—and even if it weren't, the arrival of the family would unnerve the condemned man. They decided to start promptly.

"A short service was at once begun," the New York *World* reported, "and in their responses the prisoners exhibited a firmness of tone that was lacking in the priests."

"I declare I am as innocent of the murder of George K. Smith as the child unborn," said Sharpe. He turned to his companion. "James McDonnell, you are innocent of the Smith murder." Both men thanked the sheriff and his family for their kindness.

It had been agreed, with the consent of the prisoners, that Father Bunce would drop a handkerchief as a signal.

"Just as the sheriff descended from the platform," the *World* said, "a telegraph boy with a reprieve rang the front door bell but neither the prisoners nor the executioner heeded the sound. Bunce's handkerchief dropped, the sheriff pulled the rope [that released the trap] and Sharpe and McDonnell fell with a heavy thud. Their bodies twirled until the twist was out of the rope. Sharpe struggled violently for a minute and then both men hung as limp as wet rags. All at once there was a slight commotion and the word reprieve was on everybody's lips. The news of the receipt of the dispatch nearly crazed the brothers of Sharpe and McDonnell, who had stood almost unconcernedly throughout the whole proceedings, the nearest men to the scaffold. They called the sheriff a murderer and denounced the authorities generally."

In the eyes of labor's left wing, the twenty Mollies who were executed were martyrs. According to Eugene V. Debs, labor leader and Socialist presidential candidate, "Not one of them was a murderer at heart. . . . To resist the wrongs of which they and their fellow workers were victims and to protect themselves against the brutality of their bosses, according to their own crude notions, was the prime object of the organization of the 'Mollie Maguires.' ''

It was called the Indian Country. Home of the Cherokee, the Creek, the Choctaw, and other tribes, to it had fled the worst riffraff of every state in the Union—robbers, rapists, murderers. The only law known there was the law of the gun.

In 1875 justice finally came to the Indian Country. In that year President Ulysses S. Grant named Judge Isaac Charles Parker to head the court of the recently created Western District of Arkansas. Before long, newsmen were calling it the Court of the Damned, and Parker the Hanging Judge.

Born in Ohio in 1838, Parker had practiced law in St. Joseph, Missouri, served in Congress, and held a number of political appointments. He was a federal judge in Missouri when he was called to the bench in Fort Smith, Arkansas.

Determined to stamp out crime, Parker held court from eight in the morning to dusk every day of the week except Sunday; it is said he never took vacations. His deputy marshals were kept on the move: in his twenty-one years in the district, sixty-five of them were killed. He tried thousands and thousands of cases. He pressed his juries to convict, and most of the time they obliged.

Given a choice between sentencing a man to prison or the gallows, the judge chose the gallows. For the first fourteen years, he had absolute power of life and death; there was no appeal from his sentence. One hundred and seventy-two people received death sentences from him, a record number. Of these, eighty-eight were hanged. (The rest escaped the gallows because their sentences were commuted or they won new trials.)

Parker's appearance belied his grim reputation. "He was," wrote Paul I. Wellman, historian of the West, "plump, even rotund, and in his later years his snow-white hair and white beard, with his bulbous nose and pink round cheeks, gave him more the look of a jovial Santa Claus." A deeply religious man, he was considered good-hearted and kindly by his friends, who pointed out that he wept when he sentenced a prisoner to death or saw him hang. To the criminals who came before him, however, and to much of the American public, he seemed a heartless sadist.

Parker was a fervent believer in the deterrent effect of punishment consistently applied. Memorable is this brief but pointed statement he made when he called on the grand jury to indict one of the most notorious killers in the Southwest, Cherokee Bill:

It is not the severity of punishment but the certainty of it that checks crime nowadays. The criminal always figures on the chance of escape, and if you take that away entirely he stops being a criminal. The old adage of the law, "Certainty of punishment brings security," is as true today as it ever was.

Although Parker wept when he sentenced a criminal to death, that didn't prevent him from subjecting the culprit to a prolonged tongue lashing. Even a hard case like Cherokee Bill couldn't remain indifferent when he heard these words from the angry judge:

"The crime you have committed is but another evidence, if any were needed, of your wicked, lawless, bloody and murderous disposition. It is another evidence of your total disregard of human life; another evidence that you revel in the destruction of human life. The many murders you have committed, and their reckless and wanton character, show you to be a *human monster*, from whom innocent people can expect no safety!"

The condemned man's only hope, Parker used to say, was in repentance and the consolation of religion. "Your fate is inevitable," he told one prisoner. "Let me, therefore, beg of you to fly to your Maker for that mercy and pardon which you cannot expect from mortals . . . and endeavor to seize upon the Salvation of His Cross."

Parker's good right hand in seeing justice done was George Maledon, called by newsmen the Prince of Hangmen. Of German descent, Maledon was a lean, short man with straggling whiskers and a somber stare. During the Civil War, he had served in the Union Army. Afterward, as a deputy marshal at Fort Smith, he regularly volunteered his services as a hangman for extra compensation. When Parker came to the district, Maledon became his official hangman. The pay was one hundred dollars an execution, a remarkably good fee at the time.

Maledon had an expert knowledge of his craft. His ropes were woven of choice hemp in St. Louis and he treated them with a special preparation of pitchy oil to keep them from slipping. He hung a sandbag from a new rope to stretch it to its limit, so it wouldn't stretch during the execution. To form the noose, he wound the end of the rope around thirteen times. The knot he placed in the hollow in back of the convict's left ear. The drop was eight feet; when he pulled the lever the force of the fall broke the convict's neck like a matchstick. "I never hanged a man who came back to have the job done over," he commented laconically.

Maledon executed at least sixty men, reportedly more than any other hangman in America. To this number must be added two that he shot dead when they tried to break out of jail.

At Fort Smith, it used to be quipped that Judge Parker sentenced men to death and Maledon "suspended" sentence. The district gallows was built under his supervision and was big enough to meet all emergencies. The double-leafed trapdoor had room for twelve men standing one next to the other. Twelve steps led up to the platform. After trussing up the condemned man and placing a hood over his head, the hangman would walk down and release the trap.

A number of Maledon's executions were multiple. Twice, the Prince of Hangmen executed six men at a time. The first of these executions took place in 1875, not long after Parker began to dispense justice at Fort Smith. The six condemned men, a particularly hardbitten lot, were all killers: one had murdered his eighth victim, another had killed a nineteen-year-old for his boots. People came by the wagonload to witness the event; the crowd, which numbered five thousand, included newsmen from the East, who named the hanging the Dance of Death.

Four clergymen officiated. "The entire lot of six convicted felons," wrote S. W. Harman, a journalist and friend of the judge, "were lined up with their feet squarely across the line where met the two planks forming the death trap, and after prayer and the singing of gospel hymns, the last farewells were spoken, the black caps were drawn and at the word all were shuffled off together." Their necks were broken instantly.

Across the country, people read about the execution and were revolted by it. Forever after, Parker was known as the Hanging Judge.

The killer that Maledon wanted most to execute he never got a chance to. The executioner had a daughter, Annie, who at eighteen was considered a beautiful woman. Her virtue, however, didn't match her good looks, and she became the mistress of George Carver, a gambler. She proved unfaithful to him, and Carver, in a drunken rage, shot her dead. Convicted of murder, he was sentenced to hang by

Judge Parker. Maledon was making plans for the execution when the convict's sentence was commuted to life imprisonment on the ground that the killing had not been premeditated.

Another murderer Maledon never got to hang was Cherokee Bill, for the hangman had already resigned by 1896, when Bill mounted the gallows. Bill's real name was Crawford Goldsby. Of mixed race, he was a member of the notorious Cook gang and was only twenty when he paid for his crimes. He had a feud with Judge Parker, who took special pleasure in sentencing him to death. The man chosen to spring the trap was a guard Cherokee Bill had attempted to kill while in prison.

Thousands turned out to witness the hanging of this celebrated criminal. Even the condemned man was impressed.

"Hell, look at the people," said Bill. "Something must be going to happen."

He was asked if he had any last words.

He shook his head. "No. I came here to die, not to make a speech."

Later that year Judge Parker's court was abolished. He died not long afterward. The scaffold being no longer needed, Maledon tried to get possession of it, but the city had it burned.[1] The hangman did, however, end up with six of his hanging ropes, part of the main beam, and some of the hardware. For a while he traveled about with these relics, entertaining the public with demonstrations of how he had plied his trade and exhibiting old newspaper clippings and photographs of his victims. Later he became a farmer. He died in 1911.

In Chicago's turbulent history, May 4, 1886, occupies a special place. On that day a bomb was thrown in Haymarket Square, causing the death of twelve people. No one ever found out who made the bomb or who flung it—but that didn't save four men from dying on the gallows for the crime.

The incident, known as the Haymarket Square riot, capped a period of intense labor trouble in the city. During the 1880s the demand for an eight-hour workday had begun to sweep across America. In 1886, at the McCormick Reaper Company plant in Chicago, union members and unorganized workers clashed frequently. A general strike for the shorter workday idled more than fifty thousand workers.

Anarchists, many of them German, were especially active in the city. In a fracas between locked-out employees and those still working at the reaper plant, the police were called in and shots were fired. The anarchists charged that workmen had been killed. "Revenge! Workingmen, to Arms!" they proclaimed in an inflammatory circular. They called for a protest meeting the following day in Haymarket Square, and urged the demonstrators to bring weapons.

On the night of May 4, some fifteen hundred people turned out in the square. A speaker delivered a fiery harangue. The police, present in large numbers, began to close in. The police captain ordered the crowd to disperse.

"We are peaceable!" the speaker cried.

As if the words had been a signal, at that instant a bomb was thrown into the massed ranks of the police. A volley of shots came from armed members of the crowd. The police, opening fire, charged. Eight of the police officers and four demonstrators were killed or mortally wounded; more than a hundred suffered injuries.

Eight of the anarchists were rounded up. They were charged with murder, as accessories before the fact.

Labor historians would call the trial a travesty. No evidence was produced that any of the accused had manufactured or thrown the bomb, but in the climate of fear of the "red terror" and the desire for revenge that gripped the populace they were found guilty. One received a fifteen-year prison term; the other seven were sentenced to hang.

Later, the sentences of two of the condemned were commuted to life imprisonment. Another, Louis Lingg, killed himself in jail by exploding a dynamite cap in his mouth. The remaining four—August Spies, Albert Parsons, George Engel and Adolph Fischer—waited on death row and hoped.

Their hopes were disappointed. Petitions for clemency, one signed by eminent writers like Oscar Wilde and Bernard Shaw, were turned down. So were appeals to higher courts.

On November 11, 1887, close to two hundred people (more than a quarter or them journalists) filed into the jail gallery. The scaffold, which extended twenty-five feet between the wall and the second tier of cells, had a five-by-fifteen-foot trap. Four ropes with running nooses dangled from the crossbar overhead. At the rear of the platform was a wooden compartment in which the attendant who would spring the trap was concealed.

"Hats off, please, gentlemen," Chief Deputy Cahill ordered at 11:45 A.M., and everyone uncovered.

A dozen deputy sheriffs came in and took up their positions. Then, one by one, the anarchists appeared. The four were dressed in white shrouds, with their hands manacled behind them. Each man took his place behind a rope.

Spies looked at his noose and smiled. He showed no fright as the noose was drawn over his head and the knot fixed under his left ear. The others were also made ready for execution.

Spies was the first to have the death cap pulled over his head.

"Why, this is queer! What are you putting this on for now?" he asked the deputy. Apparently he'd been prepared to make a speech from the gallows.

Through his death cap, Engel said goodbye to Deputy Peters, who had shown him much kindness. "Give my love to my family. It is the last thing I shall ask."

A deputy was drawing the death cap over Fischer's face. "Don't draw it so tight," said Fischer with a smile. "I can't breathe."

"For a moment or two," reported the *Chicago Tribune*, "the men stood like ghosts. The bare neck of each showed oddly between the white cap and the white shroud beneath. Necks could hardly be more unlike. That of Spies showed round and full veined. The neck of Fischer was large, muscular and astonishingly long. Engel's neck was short and thick. The neck of Parsons appeared small enough to span easily with the fingers. Suddenly from beneath the cap of Spies came the words in a thick voice: 'Our silence will be more powerful than the voices they are going to strangle today.' "

Spies's voice was muffled, but Fischer's was loud as a trumpet. "Long live Anarchy!" Engel echoed him: "Long live Anarchy!"

"Hurray for Anarchy!" Fischer cried out. "This is the happiest moment of my life!"

"Shall I be allowed to speak?" asked Parsons. "O men of America," he began. His inflection changed. "Let me speak, Sheriff Matson," he pleaded. "Shall the voice of the people be heard? O—"

But his next word was lost in the loud crash of the descending trap, and he shot through the platform with his companions.

It was a drop of four feet. The bodies twisted convulsively, then grew still. A physician stood next to each man, studying his pulse. The heart of the giant, Fischer, was the last to stop, seven minutes and forty-five seconds after he fell through the trap.

"The necks of the dead men appeared horribly elongated," wrote the *Tribune* reporter, who had an eye for picturesque but grisly detail, "and had changed from the ruddy hue to a blue white which almost matched the shrouds and caps."

Many prominent persons in Chicago and elsewhere, convinced the anarchists had been improperly convicted, petitioned for the release of the three in prison. In 1893, after seven years behind bars, they were granted pardons by John P. Altgeld, governor of Illinois.

"Much of the evidence given at the trial," wrote Governor Altgeld, "was a pure fabrication."

During World War I, the United States Army hanged at Fort Sam Houston in San Antonio what was probably the second largest number of prisoners ever executed at one time in America—thirteen black soldiers. Civil rights activists promptly labeled it a military lynching.

Stationed at Camp Logan, near Houston, the soldiers of the 24th Infantry were, according to the black writer Langston Hughes, "desperate over the brutalities of the Houston police and the taunts and insults of white civilians," who resented the idea of black men bearing arms. All that was needed to set the soldiers' fury ablaze was the right incident, and that wasn't long in coming.

On August 23, 1917, during the first summer after America entered the war, a Houston policeman reportedly was arresting a black woman. A black soldier from Camp Logan interfered, and the officer, taking him into custody, struck him on the head. The soldier broke away, and the policeman fired several shots after him. A black corporal who tried to help the other two was arrested.

Although there wasn't any truth to it, word quickly spread around Camp Logan that the first soldier had been shot to death. More than a hundred men of the 24th armed themselves and set out for town to take revenge.

Before the day's mischief was done, seventeen whites and two blacks lay dead.

Sixty-three of the soldiers who had taken part in the riot were summarily court-martialed on a charge of mutiny. Thirteen were sentenced to hang. Although the National Association for the Advancement of Colored People retained a white lawyer (no less a personage than a son of Sam Houston), his efforts were unavailing. Nor were the condemned men permitted to appeal to President Wilson for clemency. In later court-martials, sixteen more were sentenced to death and more than fifty to life imprisonment.

The execution of the thirteen was carried out swiftly and in great secrecy on December 11, 1917. "In the dark of night," reported *The New York Times*, "army motor trucks conveyed the lumber for the scaffold to a little clearing in the lonely mesquite thicket. . . . There, by the light of the fires, army engineers erected the death traps. . . ."

Louis Blake Duff, in his book *The County Kerchief*, tells what happened next.

Execution was at early morning and the procession started out before daylight to reach the scene of the gallows. At length the automobile lamps trained on it. There, too, were the sentries peering out of the dark, and there thirteen ropes dangled from a great cross beam. Big Frank Johnson, he stood six foot six, when the ropes had been fastened about all the necks, broke into a hymn, "Lord, I'm Comin' Home." "Goodbye C. Company," the thirteen called. The major lowered his hand to his side with a snap. The trap was sprung and Death clasped thirteen men in one embrace.[2]

Students of capital punishment have observed that when people are executed in such large numbers in America, they are invariably members of a minority.

One Sunday morning in mid-November 1959, two young women drove up to the large, handsome house of the Clutter family on their big farm in Holcomb, Kansas. The women usually went to church with the Clutters, but today, surprisingly, the family wasn't stirring. The doors were unlocked, the cars were in the garage. Uneasily, the women entered the house and went to the room of the Clutters' teen-age daughter, Nancy.

They found Nancy in bed, shot in the back of the head, her blood splattered over the walls.

Discovered in other rooms were the bodies of Nancy's teen-age brother, her mother and father. Their wrists had been bound, and all had been killed by shotgun blasts at close range. The father's throat had also been cut.

No money could be found anywhere. No signs of a struggle. No empty shell casings (these could be evidence, and the killers had thoughtfully removed them). Some good sharp footprints, but other clues were vague.

A wealthy wheat farmer and an agricultural official in the Eisenhower administration, Herbert Wesley Clutter was widely known, and the four brutal murders shocked the state. But with almost no clues to go on, the police despaired of ever capturing the perpetrators.

Then, suddenly, prospects began to brighten. Hearing about the homicides over the radio, an inmate at the Kansas State Penitentiary thought he could identify the killers.

According to the inmate, Floyd Wells, he had once shared a cell with a petty thief named Richard Eugene Hickock. Hickock was about to be paroled, and Wells had told him he'd once worked for a well-to-do farmer named Clutter. Did Clutter have a safe in his house, Hickock wanted to know. Did he have a lot of money in it at a time? To both questions Wells answered yes.

Before Hickock dropped the subject, he had a drawing of the layout of the house. He had also told Wells he intended to rob it with the help of an old prison buddy, a half-Indian named Perry Smith, tie up the Clutters, and shoot them dead. Wells hadn't believed him then . . .

A Wanted bulletin with Hickock and Smith's mug shots and arrest records flashed out across the United States. Before long, the two ex-convicts were picked up in Las Vegas for car theft and turned over to the Kansas Bureau of Investigation.

Hickock and Smith were prepared: they had detailed, convincing alibis for the time of the killings. Little by little, however, the alibis unraveled. When Hickock, shown a photograph of the footprints found next to Clutter's body, saw they matched his boots, he broke down.

"Perry Smith killed the Clutters," he said. "I couldn't stop him. He killed them all."

Smith told a different story. He had shot the men, he said, but Hickock had shot the women. Much later he would say he had killed all four victims.

The prisoners related a tale of disappointed expectations. They'd counted on finding a safe with ten thousand dollars in it. But they'd found Clutter had no safe, and he kept very little cash in his home. All they'd gotten for their trouble was less than fifty dollars. In his confession, Smith said Clutter was "a very nice gentleman . . . I thought so right up to the moment I cut his throat." Disturbed by the gurgling noises made by the dying man, Smith had shot him.

Hickock and Smith were placed on trial in Garden City, Kansas, in March 1960. Asked to plead guilty or not guilty, they stood silent. The judge entered a plea of not guilty for them and appointed attorneys to defend them.

A well-known writer, Truman Capote, had become interested in the Clutter murders. Capote attended the trial, befriended the murderers, and interviewed many of the people involved. From his close association with the case would come a best-selling novel of crime, *In Cold Blood*, as well as a motion picture.

Of the defendants' guilt no one could have any doubt. To mitigate their offenses, their attorneys tried to introduce evidence that Smith was paranoid and Hickock had suffered a severe head injury. They were overruled.

As the trial drew to a close, the prosecutor called on the jury not to be "chicken-hearted," but to bring in a verdict of guilty of murder in the first degree. After forty minutes' deliberation, the jury did so.

"No chicken-hearted jurors, they!" exclaimed Smith, and he and Hickock, both laughing hard, were led away.

The two convicts were lodged in adjoining cells on death row in the Kansas State Penitentiary in Lansing. There they would remain for the next five years, filing appeals in the state and federal courts and missing four execution dates. Capote was a faithful visitor.

When the prisoners' last appeal was denied, the Kansas Supreme Court set a fifth date with death, April 14, 1965. Hickock and Smith invited Capote to be one of the witnesses.

"I first saw them," Capote said, "in what is called the holding room, where they were served their last meal—which needless to say, they didn't eat. [Overoptimistic, they had ordered garlic bread, shrimp, french fries, ice cream, strawberries and whipped cream.] Then they were strapped into these leather harnesses. After that I had to hold up their cigarettes for them to smoke. They were trembling violently, but not from fear but from being terribly nervous."

Smith, thirty-six, a would-be intellectual, talked about Henry David Thoreau, a nineteenth-century author. He told Capote he had willed him his personal possessions and he should make sure he received them. He gave Capote a letter of farewell he had written to him. It was one hundred pages long.

Hickock, thirty-three, talked of his mother and of some women friends. He joked to relieve the strain. When a guard commented, "This must be the longest night of your life," he chuckled. "No," he quipped, "it's the shortest." He had willed his eyes to an eye bank.

The place of execution, known as The Corner, was a huge, chilly warehouse, empty except for some timber and odds and ends. Rain pattered on the roof.

Hickock, scheduled to go first, entered, his hands manacled, his arms held tight by the leather harness. With him walked the chaplain, reciting prayers, and an escort of six guards. When they reached the corner of the warehouse where the gallows stood, the warden read the execution order.

Was any relative of the Clutters there, Hickock asked a guard. Told there wasn't, he looked disappointed.

Did he want to make a last statement, the warden inquired.

"I just want to say I hold no hard feelings. You people are sending me to a better world than this ever was."

Four agents of the Kansas Bureau of Investigation who had helped to arrest and convict him and Smith were present. "Nice to see you," he said, and they shook his hand.

Now his time had come, and he mounted the thirteen steps with the chaplain. On the scaffold the hangman was waiting. An older man, he wore a faded cowboy hat; he had been lured from Missouri by a fee of six hundred dollars for the double hanging.

The chaplain continued to pray. "May the Lord have mercy on your soul," he concluded. It was 12:19 A.M. The trapdoor fell, and twenty minutes later Hickock was pronounced dead.

A hearse pulled into the warehouse. Hickock's body, on a stretcher, was covered with a blanket and placed inside the hearse, which rolled out into the dark.

Now it was Perry Smith's turn. He was chewing gum and he winked impishly at a detective he knew. He was asked if he had any last words.

"I think it's a hell of a thing to take a life in this manner. I don't believe in capital punishment . . ." His voice drooped. "It would be meaningless to apologize for what I did. . . . But I do, I apologize."

He asked for permission to say goodbye once more to Truman Capote. When it was granted, he kissed the author and said, "*Adiós, amigo.*" At 1:02 the trap was sprung.

A strong attachment had developed between the two killers and Capote during the years he had been visiting them in prison. He said he cried for days after the execution. The prisoners were buried in a private cemetery near the penitentiary and Capote paid to have headstones put up on their graves.

On June 22, 1965, two months after the hanging of the Clutter killers, Kansas executed two of their death row friends, George Ronald York and James Douglas Latham. Their crimes had been just as senseless and brutal as Smith and Hickock's. Two soldiers in their teens, they had been confined in an army stockade for going AWOL. Breaking out, they had stolen a pickup truck and gone on a vicious rampage that left seven innocent people dead. Asked why they had done it, York replied, "We hate the world."

York and Latham were the last prisoners hanged in Kansas, which abolished capital punishment. During the following twenty-five years, no one else was executed on the gallows in the United States. Hanging was dying out.

NINE

Assassins of the President

It was March 30, 1981.

The new President, Ronald Reagan, had just delivered an address at a hotel in Washington, D.C. As he walked smiling to his limousine, the sound of shots sent people running for cover. The President, bleeding from a serious wound in the chest, was rushed to a hospital. His would-be assassin, John W. Hinckley, had just emptied a revolver full of exploding bullets at Reagan for a most peculiar reason: he wanted to demonstrate to Jodie Foster, a young actress, how much he loved her. Placed on trial the following year, Hinckley was found not guilty by reason of insanity.

Like Reagan, roughly one in ten of our Presidents has had to face an assassin's bullet. Our chief concern here, naturally, is with assassins who killed or conspired to kill a President and paid for their crime with their lives. But it is well worth our while, first, to take a look at would-be as well as actual President-killers and see what drives them to their desperate acts.

"Most assassinations in the United States," noted the National Commission on the Causes and Prevention of Violence in 1969, "have been the product of individual passion or derangement." A few assassinations, both actual or attempted, have been tied to conspiracies or political movements—notably the Lincoln assassination, about which

181

more later, and the attack on President Harry S. Truman in 1950 by the Puerto Rican nationalists Oscar Collazo and Griselio Torresala. (Truman escaped harm, but a guard was killed.)

Conspiracy has often been mentioned in connection with the most shocking of contemporary American assassinations, the murder of President John F. Kennedy on November 22, 1963. Although the killer, Lee Harvey Oswald, was a known Communist, it has never been proved that he was actually part of a conspiracy. We can only guess at his motives or whether he was mentally competent, since he was killed before he could be questioned in detail. He did, however, fit the profile of presidential assassins, as we shall see.

Another notable political assassin was Giuseppe Zangara, an Italian immigrant with anarchistic leanings. In 1933 Zangara attempted to take the life of the newly elected President, Franklin Delano Roosevelt, in Miami. No marksman, Zangara missed his intended victim; however, he did shoot four bystanders and fatally wounded Anton Cermak, mayor of Chicago, who was standing on the running board of Roosevelt's car.

Tried for murder, Zangara denied he wanted to kill Cermak, although he didn't mind having done so. Roosevelt had been his real quarry, he said, but he would just as soon have killed Herbert Hoover.[1]

"I'd kill any king or president," Zangara declared at his trial. The judge, he also proclaimed, was a crook.

Zangara was electrocuted in the state prison at Raiford, Florida, on March 20, 1933. The only time he lost his composure was when he learned no photographer was present to take his picture.

During Zangara's trial, the court heard testimony that he had a psychopathic personality. An autopsy showed his brain was physically normal. (Unless there are anatomical changes due to physical disease, the brain of even the most maniacal of murderers will appear normal, just as will the brain of a great genius—Einstein, for example.)

With few exceptions, the assassins or near-assassins of our Presidents have been eccentric, delusional or deranged. One long forgotten was Richard Lawrence, an unemployed housepainter. In 1835 Lawrence leveled a pistol at Andrew Jackson but it misfired. As Jackson raised his cane to beat him, Lawrence discharged a second pistol, but it too misfired. The would-be killer escaped punishment because he was mentally unbalanced.

A similar case was that of John Schrank, a young German immigrant who had visions. In the first of these, President William

McKinley, who had been assassinated a day earlier, rose from his coffin, pointed to Theodore Roosevelt, his successor, and said, "This is my killer. Avenge my death." Schrank woke and did nothing.

Eleven years later, in 1912, McKinley appeared to him again and asked for vengeance. Now Schrank took action. He followed Roosevelt to Milwaukee and shot him in the chest.

Luck was on Roosevelt's side. Two objects in his breast pocket—a speech fifty pages long and bent double and his metal glasses case—saved his life. Although he was bleeding, the unvanquishable Teddy delivered his speech, almost an hour long, before going to the hospital. Schrank, diagnosed as paranoid, spent the remainder of his life in mental institutions.[2]

It is hardly surprising that American assassins have traditionally been men. (Most lawbreakers are.) In 1975 the situation began to change. On September 5 of that year, Lynette (Squeaky) Fromme, a youthful follower of the psychopath Charles Manson, became the first woman to try to kill a President. Fromme pointed a .45 Colt automatic pistol at Gerald R. Ford in a park in Sacramento but was quickly disarmed by Secret Service agents. "He's not a public servant!" she cried. And: "It didn't go off. Can you believe it?"

Less than three weeks later, on September 22 (in crime, example is infectious), Sara Jane Moore, a political activist, fired at President Ford in San Francisco, missing him by just five feet. She had a long history of mental illness. Both she and Fromme were sentenced to life imprisonment.

The National Commission on the Causes and Prevention of Crime put together a list of the attributes it discerned in actual and would-be presidential assassins. Usually they are white, slight in build, foreign-born or with foreign-born parents, and come from broken homes. In addition, they are loners, can't maintain a relationship, and don't hold onto jobs long. They are passionately attached to some cause. They frequently make sure they will gain maximum public attention by attacking the President when he is before a large number of people—which incidentally assures they will be captured promptly. Typically they use a revolver.

See how many of these characteristics you can find in the assassins whose tragic stories are told in the following pages.

At first, they plotted to kidnap him at the theater. They would spirit him away to Richmond, where he would be held as a hostage and exchanged for thousands of prisoners of war. But on the night they chose for the kidnapping, the weather was foul and he didn't go out. The plan had to be abandoned.

Later, after General Lee had surrendered and the hopes of the Confederacy had gone up in smoke, the conspirators didn't want a hostage anymore. What they wanted now was revenge.

Every American knows the story. John Wilkes Booth, young, handsome, egomaniacal, was the ringleader. A star of the theater, he would be the star of the conspiracy: he would personally assassinate the President. George A. Atzerodt, a German immigrant, was to kill the Vice President, Andrew Johnson. Lewis Thornton Paine (or Powell), a Confederate veteran, was to murder Secretary of State Seward.

Only the first part of the plot succeeded:

*J. Wilkes Booth, he moves down the aisle he had measured once
  before,
He passes Lincoln's bodyguard a-nodding at the door,
He holds a dagger in his right hand, a pistol in his left,
He shoots poor Lincoln in the temple and sends his soul to rest.*

After assassinating the President on April 14, 1865, Booth fled into Virginia, where he was tracked down and killed by federal troops. Atzerodt, losing his nerve, got drunk and did nothing. Paine stabbed Seward but failed to kill him. "I'm mad! I'm mad!" he cried as he fought with Seward's son.

Paine, aged twenty; Atzerodt, aged twenty-nine; and David Herold, aged twenty-two—he had helped in Booth's escape—were speedily taken into custody. So were others who had had dealings with the conspirators. Secretary of War Stanton insisted they should be tried by a military commission—with Union officers sitting in judgment, the chances of conviction would be greater and the penalties more severe. He also had named as a co-conspirator Jefferson Davis, ex-president of the Confederacy, who would not, however, be placed on trial.

The prisoners were locked up in cells in the Old Penitentiary in Washington, D.C. Manacles connected by a fourteen-inch bar were fastened on their wrists. The shackles on each prisoner's ankles were attached by chains to a massive iron ball weighing seventy-five pounds.

Stanton himself ordered special canvas hoods made for the conspirators. Each hood was heavily padded, so the prisoner couldn't escape the consequences of his crime by beating his brains out against the wall. The hood had a small hole enabling him to breathe and eat and drink, but it had no openings for his eyes or ears and it was laced securely at the neck. The accused were obliged to wear their hoods constantly—even while sleeping—except when they were taken out to the courtroom. (The hoods are now in the Smithsonian Institution.)

Only one exception was made. This was for a woman, Mary E. Surratt, who was confined in a cell in the Washington Arsenal. Mrs. Surratt, a forty-five-year-old widow and the mother of a conspirator who had escaped, had kept the boardinghouse where Booth hatched his plans to kidnap and assassinate the President. Her ankles were bound by a light chain, and she wasn't required to wear a hood or manacles.

The case against some of the accused, especially Mrs. Surratt, wasn't strong. (It couldn't even be proved she knew about the plot.) To make its case stronger, the government suppressed evidence and ignored legal formalities, taking for granted the guilt of the accused.

Defense attorneys weren't permitted to meet with their clients anywhere but in the courtroom. Many of the government's witnesses offered no testimony related to the case, but simply fulminated against the vanquished Confederacy. Some gave their testimony in secret sessions, where they could not be cross-examined. Later, it would be revealed a number of the witnesses had assumed false identities, had criminal records, or had been threatened or bribed to give fabricated testimony.

The trial was the big event of the season in Washington. As one reporter wrote,

> Major-generals' wives in rustling silks, daughters of congressmen attired like the lilies of the milliner, little girls who hope to be young ladies have come up with "Pa" to look at the assassins; even brides are here, in the fresh blush of their nuptials. They chatter and smile and go up the three flights of stairs to the courtroom.

On June 29 the military commission brought in its verdicts. All of the accused were found guilty and given sentences ranging from six years in prison to hanging. Jefferson Davis, already in jail, was sentenced to stay there.

It had been a foregone conclusion that Paine, Atzerodt and Herold would receive the death penalty. But many were astonished when Mrs.

Surratt was sentenced to hang. Five members of the military commission appealed for mercy for her. President Johnson confirmed the sentences on July 5. Later he would claim he had never seen the commissioners' appeal for clemency for Mrs. Surratt.

The executions were set for July 7, but the prisoners learned about it only on July 6. Mrs. Surratt's lawyer and her daughter, Anna, hurried to the White House to ask the President to spare her life. They were turned away.

Anna spent the night with her mother in her cell. The following morning she went to the White House again but was denied access to the President. She threw herself on the stairs and wept.

President Johnson's daughter saw her. "My poor dear," she said, "you break my heart, but there isn't a thing I can do."

The prisoner Herold had seven sisters. Five of them, dressed in mourning costumes, sought an audience with the President. They too were turned away. All seven spent the morning of July 7 with their doomed brother, weeping their hearts out.

At 2:00 A.M., on that last day, Mrs. Surratt's lawyer woke up a federal judge and persuaded him to sign a writ of habeas corpus—an act that could have endangered the courageous judge's career if not his life. Before noon President Johnson notified General Winfield S. Hancock, commandant of the military district, to disregard the writ and carry out the execution orders.

It was a typical summer's day in Washington, blistering hot. Early in the morning the street leading to the arsenal was lined with General Hancock's troops. Soldiers surrounded the building and patrolled the arsenal yard. In their cells the condemned were saying their last farewells and receiving the ministrations of their clergymen.

The scaffold had been built on Thursday night in the yard, under the supervision of Captain Christian Rath, the hangman. It had two large traps, and over each one two ropes hung down. For Mrs. Surratt the executioner had formed the loop with just five twists, because, it was said, he didn't expect her rope would be used; like General Hancock and others, he believed she would be reprieved.

On one side of the scaffold four shallow graves had been dug. Close by were stacked four pine boxes, the coffins.

At 1:00 P.M., the soldiers in the yard were ordered to attention and the prisoners emerged into the blazing sun, walking by their open graves on the way to the scaffold. Mrs. Surratt came out first, dressed in black, wearing a black bonnet and veil. An officer supported her on each side and she was followed by two priests.

Atzerodt came next. He too was supported by soldiers and accompanied by clergymen. Herold also had to be supported. Only Paine walked by himself, bold and erect. Tall and handsome, he was dressed in a blue shirt and trousers and wore a jaunty straw hat. He was the only one to climb up the scaffold steps unaided—and, according to a clergyman, the only one who had not needed a stimulant.

Four wooden armchairs had been placed on the scaffold, and in these the prisoners were seated. Directly in front of them dangled the nooses.

Major General Hartranft, commandant of the prison, standing in the middle of the platform, read the sentences to the prisoners, some of whom were sheltered from the sun by umbrellas. Paine was looking up at the sky. Herold and Atzerodt wept. Mrs. Surratt was veiled; her expression could not be seen. The two priests fanned her assiduously. From the upper windows of a building opposite, a crowd peered out.

Mrs. Surratt was asked if she had any last words.

She had. "I am innocent."

A sudden breeze blew off the light straw hat Paine was wearing. Somebody moved to get it for him. Paine gestured to him not to bother.

The clergymen raised their eyes to heaven and prayed. The prisoners expressed their gratitude to the Army officers for the kindness that had been shown them.

All morning long General Hancock had expected Mrs. Surratt would be reprieved by the President. He had even set up a relay of cavalrymen between the arsenal and the White House so word could be brought to him without delay.

But no word had come. The general climbed up the steps to the platform and told the hangman, a conspicuous figure in his white coat and hat, to proceed.

"Her too?" the hangman asked.

The general nodded.

Soldiers pinioned the prisoners' hands and tied strips of canvas around their ankles and above their knees.

"Mrs. Surratt is innocent," Paine said. "She doesn't deserve to die with the rest of us."

The nooses were placed around the prisoners' necks. "Don't choke me!'' cried Atzerodt in agony. Rath, who admired Paine for his coolness, personally took the noose and adjusted it for him. He wanted Paine to die easily, he said.

Mrs. Surratt had remained in her chair. Finally, when the three men had been made ready, her bonnet and veil were removed and the noose was placed around her neck.

She swayed in a half-faint. "Please don't let me fall," she begged.

White canvas death hoods were drawn over the prisoners' heads.

At 1:21 P.M., Rath waved to the people on the platform to stand away from the traps. Hurriedly they stepped back. He clapped his hands three times. At the final clap, four soldiers knocked away the supports under the traps. The prisoners dropped some five feet, to the end of the ropes. "They bounded up again like a ball attached to a rubber band and then they settled down," Rath said.

After twenty minutes, Army surgeons pronounced the conspirators dead. (The Washington *Daily News Intelligencer* would report their necks hadn't been broken.)

"When Mrs. Surratt was being taken down," the newspaper said, "as the rope was cut, her head of course fell upon her breast and an individual standing by made the heartless remark, 'She makes a good bow.' He was properly rebuked by an officer standing by."

After the irons and bonds had been removed from the prisoners, the bodies, with the hoods still on, were placed inside the coffins and buried. Later the military authorities announced they would be dug up and delivered to the conspirators' friends.

In 1867 Mrs. Surratt's son, John, who had escaped, was captured in Egypt and brought back to Washington. Unlike the other conspirators, he was tried by a civilian court and the jury could not reach a verdict. A second trial was ordered, but the two-year statute of limitations on the charges of treason and conspiracy had run out, and he was released. He died in 1916.

It is a strange fact that good sometimes springs from evil. That certainly was the case with the assassination of President James A. Garfield, fatally wounded on July 2, 1881, by a disappointed office seeker, Charles Julius Guiteau. Garfield's death led directly to the founding of the United States Civil Service as we know it today.

Born in Illinois in 1841, Guiteau, as a young man, joined the Oneida Community, a communistic society of religious perfectionists in Oneida, New York. A malcontent there as elsewhere, he left to study law in

Chicago, and was admitted to the bar. His law practice was erratic: he collected small debts and swindled his clients. He gave lectures on philosophy and religion and wrote tracts on biblical subjects. He married, beat his wife, and got a divorce.

In the 1880 presidential campaign, Guiteau did some minor work for the Republican party in New York. Garfield, its candidate, won the election. Convinced Garfield owed the presidency to his efforts, Guiteau went to Washington to claim his reward.

The federal civil service, established after the Civil War, had lapsed during the corrupt administration of President Grant. Under the spoils system that prevailed, a new President would give out government jobs to his supporters. After an election people flocked to Washington in search of federal employment, besieging officials and the White House. Guiteau was only one of many.

Almost penniless, Guiteau applied for a post as a consul in France or Austria. He pressed his demands obnoxiously, making a nuisance of himself at the White House and the State Department. Rebuffed again and again, he persuaded himself the President was personally opposed to his appointment. And he had done so much to get him elected!

One night, Guiteau was in his rooming house. He fell into a trance, he would recall later, and "an impression came over my mind like a flash that if the President was out of the way, this whole thing would be solved and everything would go well." God himself, he felt, was commanding him to remove the ungrateful President.

Buying a .44 British bulldog revolver, Guiteau practiced with it in a wood near the White House. A number of times he was ready to shoot the President on the street or in church but his nerve failed him.

From a newspaper Guiteau learned that Garfield would leave Washington on July 2, 1881, for a vacation. After spending his last pennies to have his shoes shined, he hid himself in the Baltimore and Potomac railroad station. As the President passed through on the way to his private car, the deranged job seeker shot him in the back and arm.

"My God, what is this?" cried Garfield and collapsed.

Guiteau was seized a few minutes later. In his hand was a note explaining he had shot Garfield a number of times so he would die easily; it also requested troops to protect the jail where he expected to be locked up.

For more than two months Garfield fought for his life. On September 19, 1881, he died. Guiteau was now officially a murderer.

At his trial, Guiteau insisted he had only been carrying out God's will, and he mocked his lawyers; all they could do was enter a plea of insanity for him. The prosecution made a case that the accused was feigning madness, bribed experts to testify he was sane, and suppressed evidence that might prove the opposite.

On January 25, 1882, Guiteau was found guilty and sentenced to death. Chester Arthur, who had succeeded to the presidency, denied him clemency.

June 30, 1882, was the assassin's last day. After a good breakfast and a bath in his cell, he composed a poem in doggerel and a speech he planned to read on the scaffold, and autographed some pictures of himself. His sister came with flowers for his coffin but wasn't admitted. "She evidently had some excited notion," a newsman reported later, "that he would be safer and happier if she was present at the execution."

All the windows of the District of Columbia jail through which the scaffold might be visible were covered with black. A large crowd waited outside anyhow, watching as intently as if they could see what was happening within.

At 11:45 A.M., a detachment of soldiers filed into the area where the scaffold stood. At a command, their musket butts thudded on the flagstones. Overcome by the sound, Guiteau collapsed on his bed. Dr. Hicks, the clergyman with him, revived him and tried to raise his spirits.

In the jail rotunda a crowd of more than two hundred had gathered. Some had paid as much as three hundred dollars for the privilege of being present. Their eyes were fixed on the brown door through which Guiteau would enter.

Meanwhile the prisoner, still in his cell, made a last request: he wanted to have his shoes shined. The request was granted.

At about 12:30 the death procession began. Guiteau was escorted by guards, Dr. Hicks, and the warden, General Crocker. The prisoner, very pale, walked erect, a look of pride on his face. His arms were pinioned behind him. The crowd, jostling and scuffling, closed in and the police had to work hard to hold it back.

The procession mounted the scaffold. The general raised his arm to order silence and the crowd grew quiet. Crocker was standing in a corner, close to a window in the platform through which he could see the deputy who would spring the trap.

Guiteau, dressed in black, was wearing a white shirt without a collar. He looked down on the crowd with a strange expression of terror and exaltation. Dr. Hicks opened a Bible and held it in front of the prisoner.

"I read," said Guiteau in a loud, clear voice, "from Matthew, tenth chapter and twenty-eighth verse: 'And fear not them which kill the body, but are not able to kill the soul; but rather fear him who is able to destroy both body and soul in hell.' '' He read on with a singsong intonation, his body swaying from side to side, looking at his audience from time to time.

Next, Dr. Hicks unfolded a sheet of paper and held it up for him to read.

"My dying prayer on the gallows," Guiteau began. "I tremble for the fate of my murderers." His voice rose. "This nation will go down in the blood. . . . My murderers, from the Executive to the hangman, will go to hell."

If anyone present had believed Guiteau a rational being he could do so no longer.

"I am now going to read from verses which are intended to indicate my feelings at the moment of leaving this world. The idea is that of a child babbling to his mamma and papa. I wrote it this morning about 10 o'clock." He began to recite in a woeful voice.

> *I am going to the Lordy,*
> *I am so glad,*
> *I am going to the Lordy,*
> *I am so glad.*
> *I am going to the Lordy,*
> *Glory, hallelujah! Glory, hallelujah!*
> *I am going to the Lordy.*

His voice failed. He broke into sobs and his head sank on his chest. Finally, pulling himself together, he started to chant again.

> *I saved my party and my land,*
> *Glory, hallelujah,*
> *But they have murdered me for it,*
> *And that is the reason*
> *I am going to the Lordy,*
> *Glory, hallelujah! Glory, hallelujah!*
> *I am going to the Lordy.*

He broke down again and leaned his head on the clergyman's shoulder. His sobs echoed through the room. After he had read two more stanzas, Dr. Hicks laid his hand on the prisoner's forehead and whispered a blessing.

"Now began the moment which to the doomed man must have been the most terrible of all," reported the *New York Tribune* the following day.

Strong, the hangman, began to tie his legs at the ankles and knees. The work needed to be well done and it was done slowly and carefully. Guiteau was now standing on the trap and while the process of tying was going on the long rope that hung from the bar above to the floor of the scaffold rested full against his cheek. He was now deadly pale and closed his eyes as in exhaustion. The tying done, the noose was to be fitted. The rope as it hung down in a straight line almost touched the floor, so that Guiteau would fall a distance nearly equal to his own height.

Strong lifted the rope and put the noose in a calm, businesslike way about Guiteau's neck and fitted it snugly in the manner of a tailor trying a coat on a customer. He turned it a little this way and that, and looked it over with a critical eye. When the noose was finally adjusted the rope curled down like a snake from Guiteau's neck to his elbow and then up to the bar overhead. The black cap was put on and the strings drawn. The guards stepped back and Dr. Hicks turned his face away and knelt at the front rail of the scaffold. Guiteau's voice, coming with a ghostly sound through the black cap, was heard to cry almost defiantly, as if with a last effort of the will, "Glory, hallelujah! Glory!"

"Are you ready?" General Crocker asked, and waved his handkerchief at the window. In an instant the witnesses heard the sound of the bolts shooting back and the trap dropped. Guiteau's rigid body fell through. It did not sway or jerk, but the feet quivered.

Penologists have observed that most prison inmates are patriotic. The crash made by the trapdoor echoed down the corridors of the jail. At once the prisoners in their cells burst into cheers. Some were killers themselves but they didn't approve of anyone murdering their President. The cheering was so loud it reached the ears of the crowd in the street outside the jail. They joined in raucously.[3]

Five minutes later the hangman lowered the body so that doctors could listen to Guiteau's heart. Then, his hands on his knees, he bent down to watch, an expression of satisfaction on his face.

For fourteen minutes the assassin's heart continued to beat. His coffin was waiting beneath the scaffold, and after he had been pronounced dead, the body was lowered into it. The crowd of witnesses was invited to view the body. As it passed by, the assassin's brother fanned the dead man's face to keep off the flies.

That afternoon the doctors did an autopsy on Guiteau.⁴ His neck, they found, had not been broken by the fall; he had died of suffocation. Examining the brain, they said they detected signs of malaria or syphilis. In point of fact, five close relatives of the dead man—two aunts, one uncle, and two first cousins—had been certified insane.

The following year, Congress passed the Pendleton Act, reestablishing the United States Civil Service Commission.

On May 1, 1901, the Pan-American Exposition was inaugurated in Buffalo, New York, to celebrate technological progress. Before the summer was out the celebration would turn to mourning.

On September 6 President William McKinley, after touring the fairgrounds, attended a great public reception in his honor. He was guarded by about fifty men—soldiers, detectives and three members of the Secret Service. They saw no threat in the slightly built young man who stood next in the long line waiting to greet the President, his right hand bandaged with a handkerchief.

It was 4:07 P.M. A pipe organ was playing softly.

As the President reached out to take the man's left hand, two bullets blazed through the handkerchief. It began to smolder.

The President reeled. Women screamed and scurried for the exits.

The gunman made no effort to escape. "I done my duty," he said. Guards jumped on him and began to beat him.

"Don't let them hurt him," the stricken McKinley said. The man was, the President added, "some poor, misguided fellow."

At first it was reported McKinley was doing well and would recover. But gangrene set in (because, it is said, of incompetent medical care), and eight days after the shooting, he was dead. The Vice President, Theodore Roosevelt, moved into the White House.

Leon Czolgosz, the assassin, was a shy, round-faced man, the son of Polish immigrants. Born in 1873, he worked in a wire factory in Cleveland. The closing decades of the nineteenth century were marked by violent clashes between unions and factory owners. Anarchism, occasionally tinged with violence, made some headway among industrial workers. After taking part in a strike in 1893, Czolgosz went back to work under an assumed name, fearing discrimination. Although he had only five years of schooling, he immersed himself in sociological and anarchistic literature. He attended the meetings of left-wing groups.

In 1898 Czolgosz suffered a nervous breakdown. Leaving his job, he spent time on a farm owned by his family and was treated by a doctor.

In July 1900 King Humbert I of Italy was assassinated by an anarchist. Czolgosz, greatly impressed, kept a newspaper clipping of the incident.

In May 1901 Emma Goldman, a notorious Russian anarchist, gave a lecture in Cleveland. Czolgosz, who attended, was deeply stirred. Going to a local anarchist club and giving his assumed name, he asked whether they were plotting an assassination. Reportedly they wouldn't have anything to do with him. In Chicago he tried to see Goldman again but she had no time for him.

In August, Czolgosz rented a room over a saloon in Buffalo. The name he gave was John Doe. Two days later he bought a .22-caliber Iver Johnson revolver. Four days after that he took it to President McKinley's reception.

Czolgosz's trial lasted eight and a half days. He made no attempt to defend himself, but entered a plea of guilty. Complaining about McKinley's power and privileges, he declared, "I thought it would be a good thing to kill the President." He told his court-appointed lawyers, who were very reluctant to defend him, that he didn't want their help. Expert opinions were presented that he was sane and rational at the time of the shooting.

Czolgosz's counsel, in summing up, apologized for taking part in his defense and delivered a eulogy of his client's victim—a unique phenomenon in any court. The jury, after conferring for thirty minutes for the sake of appearances (their minds, they later admitted, were already made up), found him guilty.

Czolgosz faced death in the electric chair with fortitude. Born a Roman Catholic, the night before his execution he said the had lost his faith in religion after the hard times of 1893 and didn't want a priest to help him prepare for death. He added: "McKinley was going around the country shouting prosperity when there was no prosperity for the poor man. I'm not afraid to die. We all have to die sometime."

After a good night's sleep and a hearty breakfast, the prisoner entered the execution chamber at Auburn with his head held high. Some thought he looked defiant, but his chin quivered as he addressed the witnesses. "I killed the President because he was an enemy of the good people—of the working people. I'm not sorry for my crime."

The strap attaching the headpiece was drawn across his chin as he mumbled his last words: "I'm awfully sorry I couldn't see my father." (His father hadn't wanted to see him.)

The warden raised his hand in a signal. Davis, the executioner, sent 1,800 volts crashing into Czolgosz, who lurched against the straps. When Dr. Carlos MacDonald put his hand over Czolgosz's heart he felt no pulsation but requested a brief additional charge.

MacDonald, a noted specialist in mental disorders whom we met in the first chapter, performed the autopsy with other doctors. His chief interest was in Czolgosz's brain: Did it show any physical signs of abnormality? "Socially diseased and perverted" was his verdict, "but not mentally perverted." (Later medical opinion would say Czolgosz had become schizophrenic after his nervous breakdown and had developed the delusion that it was his duty to murder the President.) A death mask was made of the dead man. It shows a face both attractive and peaceful.

The unusual treatment of Czolgosz's remains deserves some mention. The law called for the destruction of the body with quicklime. To determine the effectiveness of this procedure, a few days before the execution prison officials placed twelve pounds of meat in a glass jar with a large quantity of quicklime. When the jar was opened the meat showed little evidence of disintegration. Since the main point was to destroy the assassin's remains, the officials, after lowering Czolgosz's black-stained pine coffin into the grave, poured an entire carboy of acid over the naked body inside. The dead man's clothing and personal effects were burned.

It was a sign of people's attachment to old habits (as well as of the intense hatred they felt for Czolgosz) that on the day he was electrocuted at Auburn, a crowd of a thousand hanged him in effigy at Hempstead, Long Island.

The United States Secret Service had originally been set up to be the law-enforcement arm of the Department of the Treasury and to help in its war against counterfeiters. On request, it had occasionally lent its agents to other government departments for special purposes. After the assassination of President McKinley, protecting the President full time was made its most important duty. Later, this was extended to include members of the President's immediate family, the Vice President, the

President-elect and the Vice President-elect, and former Presidents and their wives. Statutes were also enacted forbidding the immigration of anarchists into the United States.

TEN

███████████

Not Guilty (I)

In 1984 Errol Morris, a New York filmmaker, headed for Dallas to work on a new movie. His subject was a strange one: a psychiatrist called Dr. Death by the press. Dr. James Grigson had earned this name because Texas employed him to examine convicted murderers before sentencing—and he regularly testified they would kill again, thus deserving to be put to death.

In search of background material, Morris called at the Dallas County prosecutor's office. Delighted by the project, the prosecutor made available the files of murderers Dr. Death had helped him to place on death row. Among these was Randall Dale Adams, sentenced to the electric chair in 1977.

In the Adams files Morris found ample cause for astonishment, and he set about interviewing the principals in the case. He was even more astonished at the things they told him, for one after another contradicted their testimony in the trial record. Abandoning his Dr. Death project, Morris began to shoot the Adams story.

The Thin Blue Line, the docudrama Morris filmed about the Adams case, won him two major awards. Not only did it make movie history—its chilling exposé of a gross miscarriage of justice drew national attention to the plight of a man who had been condemned to death for a crime he hadn't committed.

The misfortunes of Randall Dale Adams began on November 27, 1976. Adams, twenty-seven-year-old employee of a Dallas contractor, ran out of gas, and thought himself very lucky when David Ray Harris stopped to give him a lift. He would soon learn better. Harris, sixteen, had a criminal record. He was running away from home. The car he was driving was stolen, and he had his father's .22 caliber pistol, also stolen.

After getting gas for Adams's car, the two spent the day together. They drove around in Harris's vehicle, smoked pot, drank beer, and went to a drive-in movie.

At 12:30 A.M. on November 28, a police officer, Robert Wood, saw a car driving with only its parking lights on and signaled it to stop. He walked over to the car while his partner, Teresa Turko, remained at a distance. Without warning, the driver fired five shots at him. Officer Wood fell, fatally wounded, and the car sped off.

A month later Dallas police headquarters received a call from Vidor, some three hundred miles away. The Vidor police had taken into custody a local teenager who had gone on a crime spree—and who had been boasting to his buddies that he'd "offed a pig" in Dallas.

The teenager was David Harris. Turned over to the Dallas police, he denied he had slain Officer Wood. He told about the day he had spent in Adams's company. After the movie, he said, the two had driven around, with Adams at the wheel, until the early morning. When the police officer stopped them, Adams, according to Harris, had pulled out a revolver and killed the officer. The teenager, slumped low in the passenger seat, had witnessed the killing, but no one had seen him.

The next day Adams was brought in for questioning. The shooting of the policeman was news to him, he said. He had last seen Harris when the boy dropped him off at his motel before 10:00 P.M. on November 27. Since then he had been working regularly at his job.

Harris had a police record, Adams had none. The murder weapon, like the car, had been stolen by Harris. He was not, in legal parlance, a credible witness. Still the police and the district attorney chose to believe Harris's story. Later it would be said that a cop had been killed and the authorities wanted someone to pay for it—blood for blood. Harris was a minor and therefore couldn't be executed. Adams could.

Adams was indicted and went on trial in April 1977. Harris was the prosecution's key witness. His criminal record was played down, and the judge refused to admit testimony about his crime spree in Vidor. He was questioned whether the charges against him in Vidor were being dropped in exchange for his help in convicting Adams. He denied it.

But there were other, more respectable witnesses. One was Wood's partner, Officer Turko. On the last day of testimony, three surprise witnesses also took the stand. They told of seeing Adams in the driver's seat of the car stopped by the policeman.

That weekend the defense learned one of the surprise witnesses, Emily Blocker, had been saying she couldn't identify Adams as the driver and showed interest in the $25,000 reward offered. The defense lawyers wanted to call her back to the stand. She had left town, the prosecution declared, and it didn't know where she'd gone.

Adams was quickly convicted and, with the help of Dr. Death, sentenced to the chair. In May 1979, only one week separated him from his rendezvous with death.

Then he got his first real break. Justice Lewis F. Powell of the Supreme Court ordered a stay of execution. A year later, when the full court scrutinized the record of his trial, it found a serious error in the way the jury had been selected: the prosecutors had rejected as jurors any who had reservations about capital punishment. Voting eight to one, the justices reversed the conviction and sent the case back to Texas for retrial.

The prosecutor publicly affirmed he would try Adams again and convict him again. Instead, however, he requested the governor to commute Adams's sentence to life imprisonment.

And in prison Adams would have had to remain for the rest of his life—if a filmmaker hadn't discovered the man had been framed, and made a movie about it.

The Thin Blue Line was released in August 1988. On screen, the public saw actors reenacting the murder and watched the actual witnesses in the case being interviewed. Flattered by the experience of being on camera, they relaxed and made statements that contradicted the testimony they had given on the witness stand. From these statements—and others they and other witnesses had given to the police shortly after the murder and that Morris unearthed in the district attorney's files—there emerged a pattern of prosecutorial misconduct and violation of Adams's constitutional rights that under Texas law could entitle him to a new trial.

No one's on-screen statements contradicted his courtroom testimony more than David Harris's.

Harris by now had fulfilled the promise of his early youth. He occupied a cell on death row. In 1985 he had broken into an apartment and kidnapped a woman from her bed. When her man friend attempted to rescue her, Harris shot him dead. In interviews he readily admitted he hadn't told the truth at the Adams trial: Adams wasn't in the car when the policeman was shot; he was at his motel, where Harris had dropped him off long before midnight.

"I know for a fact that he didn't do it," Harris stated. "I'm the one that was there, so I should know."

Why wouldn't he come out and say he was the one who had killed the policeman?

"Well, in that respect, I feel like I'd be putting the rope around my own neck."

Harris also admitted he had an understanding with the Dallas prosecutor that the felony charges against him in Vidor would be forgotten if he helped to convict Adams. And, in fact, no charges had been brought against him.

Late in 1988, defense attorneys appeared before a State District Court judge in an attempt to win a new trial for Adams. With the help of the movie and the documents in the files, they sought to show that Adams had been unfairly convicted.

One by one the major witnesses at the 1977 trial took the stand and recanted the testimony they had given then. Harris all but admitted his guilt. He was alone in the car at the time of the murder, he said, and the gun was in his hand when it fired the lethal shots. "I'm not a kid anymore," he added. "I realize I've been responsible for a grave injustice."

Emily Blocker, the surprise witness whose testimony had counted most heavily against Adams, now admitted she hadn't been telling the truth when she testified she had picked Adams out of a police lineup as the driver of the death car. According to her original statement to the police, the driver was a "Mexican or a very light-skinned black man." Adams was neither.

At the time of Blocker's 1977 testimony, her daughter had been facing charges of armed robbery. Soon after Adams's conviction, the charges were dismissed. Was there any link between Blocker's testimony and the dismissal? No, said Blocker. Maybe, said her daughter's attorney.

In 1977, when the defense had sought to recall Blocker and the other two surprise witnesses to the stand, the prosecutor said they had left town. Now it was established they had done nothing of the kind, but merely moved to another motel.

Another revelation: at the original trial the prosecutor had failed to inform the jury that Officer Wood's partner, Turko, had reported the driver of the murder car was wearing a jacket with a turned-up fur collar. In point of fact it was Harris—not Adams—who was wearing such a jacket.

In a serious breach of legal procedure, the prosecution had failed to provide to Adams's lawyers copies of statements made to the police that might have helped the defense. Why hadn't he given the attorneys these documents, Douglas Mulder, the former prosecutor, was asked. He couldn't remember, he answered. Perhaps he'd never seen them— or perhaps he'd simply forgotten to.

That there had been serious errors in Adams's trial few could doubt. "Applying the law which places the burden of proof on the State beyond a reasonable doubt," said Judge Baraka in his summing up, "the court would have found the applicant not guilty at a bench trial." He recommended a new trial for the prisoner.

On March 1, 1989, the Texas Court of Criminal Appeals, in a unanimous decision, set aside Adams's conviction.[1] If the prosecutors had conducted themselves properly, the court declared, Adams might have been acquitted. "The State was guilty of suppressing evidence favorable to the accused, deceiving the trial court during the applicant's trial and knowingly using perjured testimony." That didn't mean Adams was innocent—merely that he had not received a fair trial. The Dallas authorities would have to decide whether they wanted to try him again.

A few weeks later they decided not to.

Ex-prosecutor Mulder, however, stuck by his guns. "I'm convinced the death sentence was the appropriate sentence," he said. The court's ruling was "the height of stupidity."

Adams was set free. But he couldn't sue Mulder, nor could he collect a penny for his twelve years in prison. His criminal conviction remained on the record and could be brought up any time he tangled with the law—even if he was arrested, say, for the slightest traffic violation.

"Randall Adams met Errol Morris by a stroke of luck," said James McCloskey of Centurion Ministries, a church-supported group that works to win the release of people convicted of crimes they did not commit. "If he hadn't you would never have heard of him. He would have been one of those anonymous lost souls convicted and buried for life.

"The criminal justice system in the United States is the best in the world, but it's a far leakier cistern, where many people slip through a wide crack, than the public would care to believe."

"Our [legal] procedure has always been haunted by the ghost of the innocent man convicted," wrote Judge Learned Hand, a respected member of the federal bench, in 1923. "It is an unreal dream."

Judge Hand, unfortunately, was mistaken. Innocent men—and women—have indeed been convicted. "If the conviction of an innocent man were as rare as a death from bubonic plague in the United States," wrote another jurist, Jerome Frank, and his daughter, Barbara Frank, "we could afford to mourn the tragedy briefly, and turn back to everyday affairs. Unfortunately such convictions are by no means rare." The Franks' book, *Not Guilty*, published in 1956, related thirty-six cases of innocents found guilty.

In 1987, Professors Hugo Adam Bedau of Tufts University and Michael L. Radelet of the University of Florida published (in the *Stanford Law Review*) a study of 350 cases that they called "Miscarriages of Justice in Potentially Capital Cases." In these cases, tried between 1900 and 1986, 139 persons later proven to be innocent were actually sentenced to death; a number came within hours or days of being executed before a pardon or commutation of sentence saved them. The innocence of most was established by acquittal at retrial, pardons, the confession or implication of the guilty person, reversal of the conviction, other actions by the court or prosecuting attorney, or the payment of indemnification by the state.

Twenty-three of the convicts were put to death. That they were innocent is not based on any legal finding, but is solely the opinion of the authors, who lean upon the conclusions of scholars or others who were close to the prisoners or had investigated their cases. It is difficult or impossible to prove the innocence of someone who has been put to death. Usually all interest in vindicating him vanishes with his last breath, or else the heavy cost in time and money far exceeds any benefit that may result.

Still, as we shall see, in a number of cases the innocent dead have been exonerated, occasionally long after their execution, when the actual murderer confessed. In 1909, for example, Neil Shumway was hanged in Nebraska for the murder of his employer's wife. "I am an innocent victim,'' Shumway said before he plunged through the trap. Some time afterward the dead woman's husband, on his deathbed, confessed he had killed her.[2]

The execution of an innocent man had a strong influence in bringing about the abolition of the death penalty in Great Britain. The man was Timothy John Evans, hanged for the murder of his wife and child in 1950. The bodies of the victims were never found, and Evans was convicted chiefly on the testimony of one witness, John Chriswell. Four years later Chriswell confessed to the crime, and investigators, going through his house from top to bottom, found the bodies of nine other victims inside the wall. Belatedly Evans was granted a royal pardon. The execution or near-execution of an innocent person is credited with helping to end the death penalty in Maine and Rhode Island.

In 1984 Senator Howard Metzenbaum of Ohio spoke movingly in Congress of cases he knew of people who had been unjustly convicted. He also published in the *Congressional Record* a list of forty-eight such innocents. Six had been executed. In five of these cases the real murderer confessed; in the sixth, accomplices said the executed man had not been present during the crime.

How can the innocent be convicted and sentenced to death? Our legal system requires that the guilt of the accused be established beyond a reasonable doubt. Most of us are convinced, with good reason, that we have the best legal system in the world. Even so, in James McCloskey's words, ''it's a far leakier cistern . . . than the public would care to believe.''

In the pages that follow, we shall look at the biggest cracks in the cistern and some of the unfortunates who have slipped through them.

When an innocent person is convicted of murder (or any other felony) in the United States the commonest reason is that a witness has provided false information.

In more than half of the 350 cases studied by Bedau and Radelet, the erroneous conviction rested on the testimony of witnesses—witnesses who were mistaken, were unreliable, or else perjured themselves. Somehow juries usually accept the testimony of eyewitnesses over a considerable amount of credible evidence to the contrary.

In 1893 young Will Purvis was tried for the murder of Will Buckley in Louisiana. He was convicted largely on the testimony of an eyewitness, the victim's brother, Jim, and sentenced to death. Five years later

Jim decided he had been mistaken. That would have been much too late to save the condemned man's life—except that a freak accident during his hanging had saved him, and his sentence had been commuted. Of this historic case more later.

In 1927 Edward Larkman's head had been shaved and he had only ten hours to go before entering Sing Sing's death chamber. Like Purvis, he had been convicted, in good measure, because of a misidentification. A paymaster had been murdered and the authorities knew the killer had worn dark glasses. Larkman, with a record of a few petty crimes, was arrested. At police headquarters he was told to put on a pair of dark glasses and was placed not in a regulation lineup but by himself, under a strong light. A witness to the crime identified him as the killer, although she looked at him only two or three seconds. Later Larkman's sentence was commuted. In 1929 another prisoner admitted he was the killer. The law does not move fast: four more years would pass before Larkman was pardoned.

Eyewitnesses are notoriously unreliable. A man who is five feet tall and slight in build is mistaken for one six feet tall and built like a football player; a blond man with fair skin is picked out of the lineup although the actual criminal has dark hair and dark skin. Five witnesses swear the culprit was a black man when in reality he is white.

In 1932 Professor Edwin Borchard of Yale University published a landmark study of sixty-five miscarriages of justice called *Convicting the Innocent*. Misidentification helped to convict the guiltless in twenty-nine of his cases—and in *only two* of the twenty-nine was there a striking resemblance!

How can witnesses make such gross mistakes? According to Borchard, "the emotional balance of the . . . eyewitness is so disturbed by his extraordinary experience that his powers of perception become distorted . . ." Underlying the misidentification may be "the desire to requite a crime, to exact vengeance upon the person believed guilty, to find a scapegoat, to support, consciously or unconsciously, an identification already made by another."

In many miscarriages of justice, *more than a single element plays a part*. Take, for example, the tragic case of Maurice F. Mays, in which perjury and prejudice, as well as eyewitness error, helped to convict an innocent.

In 1919, Mays, a black man, was charged with the murder of a white woman in Tennessee. The keystone of the prosecution's case was the testimony of two witnesses: a police officer long hostile to

Mays and an eyewitness who hadn't seen the killer clearly. Feeling against the prisoner ran so high that the National Guard was needed to quell a lynch mob, and a number of blacks died at the hands of white rioters. In this overheated atmosphere Mays was given a death sentence. He won a second trial but was convicted and sentenced to death once more. Until the moment he was executed in 1922, he kept protesting he was innocent.

Four years later Mays was proved to be just that; a woman confessed she was the real killer. Her husband had gotten himself sexually involved with another woman, and the tormented wife murdered her—after first blackening her face so she would look like an African American.

In more than one-third of the 350 cases that Bedau and Radelet examined, the defendants were convicted on perjured testimony.

In a trial that drew worldwide attention, Tom Mooney and Warren Billings, union organizers, were found guilty of exploding a bomb that took ten lives and injured forty people during a Preparedness Day parade in San Francisco in 1916. Billings drew a life sentence, Mooney the gallows. Two weeks before Mooney was to hang in 1918, his sentence was commuted to life after a plea to the governor from President Wilson. In 1938 the two men were set free after it was established they had been convicted because of perjured testimony as well as the suppression of evidence by the district attorney.

In another case as flagrant as it is famous, nine young blacks aged thirteen to twenty—they would become known to the world as the Scottsboro Boys—were indicted for the alleged rape of two young white women on a freight train in Alabama in 1931. It was a time when many were stealing rides on the freights as they went in search of work, and the women made the accusation because they feared they would otherwise be charged with vagrancy. At the trial in Scottsboro it was proved neither woman had had sexual relations within the time frame involved. Still, after the prosecutor cried, "Guilty or not, let's get rid of these niggers!" the all-white jury found the youths guilty. Eight were sentenced to death and one to life imprisonment. After years of legal battles most were set free. (One died in prison.)

In a more recent case, Clarence Lee Brandley was found guilty of rape and murder in Texas. Brandley was a janitor in a high school near Houston, where a white girl was murdered in 1980. The principal witnesses against him were three white janitors, and he was convicted

by an all-white jury. Later the three witnesses conceded they had lied,
and another suspect was implicated. In 1989 the Texas Court of
Appeals set aside Brandley's conviction, calling it a "subversion of
justice."

Astonishingly, sometimes the actual killer is the chief accuser of an
innocent defendant. We saw that in the case of Randall Dale Adams
and we shall see it again later in the pathetic case of Leo Frank. Here
are two other remarkable examples:

In 1957 Harry Dale Bundy was sentenced to death in Ohio after a so-
called friend testified Bundy had been his accomplice in two killings.
Actually, all Bundy had done was assist the police when they were
investigating four murders the friend had committed, and he wanted
revenge. Just three days before Bundy was scheduled to be electrocuted, he was saved by an odd piece of luck: a woman happened to
recognize the friend in a picture in a crime magazine story and recalled
he had told her about four people he had killed—and a fifth he was
about to murder *with the help of the law*!

In New York in 1982 Nathaniel Carter's ex-wife was granted immunity from prosecution for murder in exchange for her testimony against
him. He was convicted and sentenced to twenty-five years. Friends
refused to give up on him, and the district attorney was finally persuaded to reopen the case. Now the ex-wife, after receiving immunity
again, this time from perjury, revealed that Carter was innocent; she
herself was the murderer. Having spent more than two years behind
bars, Carter was set free.

"If New York State had the death penalty," his counsel declared,
"God knows what would have happened to this poor man."

Circumstantial evidence is often clear-cut and convincing enough to
add up to proof of guilt. But every now and then it misleads a jury into
convicting someone completely innocent.[3]

In a striking case of misleading circumstantial evidence, Dr. Sam
Sheppard, a Cleveland osteopath, was charged with slaying his wife in
1954. Bloodstain patterns on the dead woman's pillowcase were described by the coroner as made by a "surgical instrument"; in addition, Sheppard admitted he had been having an affair with another
woman. These elements—as well as a heavily prejudiced press—
helped to convict Sheppard of second-degree murder. In 1966 he
finally won a retrial and his freedom, but his life was ruined. (Even

today people believe he was guilty because of the way the "Dr. Sam" story was distorted in the newspapers.)

In another unfortunate case, in Kentucky, Sheila Wilson was driving with her husband and a friend. The two men got into an argument and left the car, while she remained inside. There were shots, the friend returned to the car, and she drove away with him. Afterward her husband was found dead.

Fearful she might be named a codefendant, Wilson tried to hide from the police that she had been close by when the killing occurred, but they found out. In her trial in 1979 her lie counted heavily against her, and she was convicted of first-degree murder. A sworn deposition from the killer that she had no knowledge her husband was going to be killed helped her regain her freedom in 1983.

Difficult as it is to believe, in a good number of cases a defendant has been condemned to death when no crime has been committed.

In some cases of alleged rape, no rape has actually occurred. As we have already seen, neither of the two women who brought the charge against the Scottsboro Boys in 1931 had actually been raped. In another case we'll look at later, that of Willie McGee, executed in 1951, the woman who alleged he had raped her had had a long consensual relationship with him.

Innocent people can pay a heavy price when a natural death is mistaken for murder. In 1951 Emma Jo Johnson was convicted of murder in Las Vegas and received a prison sentence. She'd had a scuffle with her landlady, who died shortly afterward. An autopsy revealed the death was caused by a clot on the brain, which the coroner decided was the result of a blow received during the quarrel. After almost three years in prison Johnson was set free when the landlady's doctor testified she'd had the clot for a while and he had told her it could cause death at any time.

In another peculiar case an innocent defendant offered a false alibi that was found out and did him grievous harm. (Incidents of this kind aren't rare.) Here is the story, as set down by Chief Justice Lemuel Shaw of the Massachusetts Supreme Court in commenting on a celebrated 1850 murder case:

> . . . an innocent man, when placed by circumstances in a condition of suspicion and danger, may resort to deception in the hope of avoiding the force of . . . proofs [of his supposed guilt]. Such

was the case of a man [John Graham] convicted of the murder of his niece, who had suddenly disappeared under circumstances which created a strong suspicion that she was murdered. He attempted to impose on the court by presenting another girl as the niece. The deception was discovered and naturally operated against him, although the actual appearance of the niece alive, afterwards, proved conclusively that he was not guilty of the murder.

Unfortunately, Graham was executed before the girl—actually not his niece, but his daughter—reappeared.

It isn't unusual for a suicide to be mistaken for murder, but here is a case that fell between the two stools. In 1936, in Kentucky, Tom Jones was found guilty of the slaying of his wife. Five hours before he was to be executed, a federal court granted a reprieve; petitions for executive clemency had been filed bearing the signatures of the jurors who had convicted him as well as of two thousand others. In 1938 the state's attorney general, after investigating the case, concluded Jones had been found guilty on perjured testimony and the indictment was nolled. All along, Jones had protested his wife had been trying to shoot herself and was accidentally killed when he attempted to wrest the gun from her.

The person who has served time in prison is often liable to suspicion when a crime has been committed and the criminal hasn't been caught. The police pick him up and occasionally eyewitnesses misidentify him, and—even though he is completely without guilt—he is convicted and sentenced to death.

In at least one case a person with a criminal record was convicted *twice* through miscarriages of justice. Charles Bernstein, at the age of eighteen, was found guilty of burglary and served a prison term. After that he went straight. Years later, while he was in Minnesota on business, a bank was robbed and, because of his record, the police pulled him in. Identified by witnesses, tried, and found guilty, he got a forty-five-year prison term. Luckily the prosecutor discovered the identification was faulty and had him set free.

Four years later he was not so lucky. In Washington, D.C., a gambler was murdered and the killer escaped. His car was traced to Philadelphia, where Bernstein happened to be, and he was picked up again. Although six witnesses swore he'd been in New York at the time of the murder, Bernstein was convicted and sentenced to the chair. In 1935, only minutes before he was to die, his sentence was commuted to life by President Franklin D. Roosevelt. After eight years he was paroled. President Harry S Truman granted him an unconditional pardon in 1945.

"Expert" evidence is often a powerful factor in proving the guilt of the innocent. In the first trial of Dr. Sam Sheppard, for example, which we looked at earlier, the testimony of Coroner Gerber that the pattern of bloodstains on the slain woman's pillowcase had been made by a "surgical instrument" helped to incriminate the defendant. During the retrial, however, F. Lee Bailey, Sheppard's forceful young attorney, not only demonstrated the coroner was prejudiced against Sheppard, but obliged him to admit he knew of no surgical instrument that would have made such a pattern.

And you will remember Randall Dale Adams, who was diagnosed by "Dr. Death," Dallas's expert psychiatric witness, as a sociopath, someone who would kill again and thus deserved the death sentence— when, in fact, Adams had never killed at all.

The trouble with impartial experts, it seems, is that they are sometimes not impartial—and sometimes they are very far from expert.

The police are a popular target for the public and the newspapers when they conduct themselves improperly. People seem all too prone to forget that for every police officer who may perform an unlawful act there are a thousand who scrupulously uphold the law.

Police misconduct was found to be a factor in one out of seven miscarriages of justice in the Bedau-Radelet study. The story has another side to it, however; police officers also help to *un*convict the innocent.

In 1975 Bradford Brown, a black man, was indicted for murder in Washington, D.C. His criminal record made him a likely suspect and an eyewitness had misidentified him. (His only resemblance to the killer, actually, was in the color of his skin.) Brown was convicted and given a sentence of eighteen years to life. (The District of Columbia has no death sentence.)

Receiving a tip that Brown wasn't really the murderer, Detective Robert Kanjian made an independent investigation. "I . . . began a long and tedious struggle," he said, "to prove Bradford innocent and help prove the real murderer guilty." He succeeded, and in 1979, thanks to Kanjian's hard work, Brown was able to walk out of prison a free man. His wife and children had left him and he had wasted five years in prison—but, as Detective Kanjian remarked, "he might have lost his life." For his effort to free Brown, Kanjian won commendation in the United States Senate.

Another case: Earl Charles, black, was sentenced to death in Georgia in 1975 on two counts of murder. Charles had been identified by an eyewitness after she failed to recognize him in a photograph. He was saved from the electric chair only through the help of a police officer who remembered talking to him in Tampa on the day of the murder and had entered the conversation in his logbook.

Coerced confessions—confessions extorted by third-degree methods —are today much less common than they used to be, but they still occur. In one spectacular case, the Philadelphia police forced three false confessions out of three different men for the same crime—which none of them had committed.

In 1936 Officer James T. Morrow, who was tracking a burglar, was mortally wounded by three shots in the back. Joseph Broderick was arrested for his murder and signed a confession. Shortly afterward his attorney declared it had been coerced and Broderick was set free.

The next person arrested was George Bilger. Bilger, who was retarded, confessed to the crime and was convicted of first-degree murder in 1937 with a recommendation for execution. The judge set aside the verdict, but in a second trial Bilger pleaded guilty again. This time, he was sentenced to life.

The series of burglaries Officer Morrow had been trying to solve continued—a sure sign that the wrong man had been convicted. Two years later the right one, a suspect named Howard, was killed in a gun battle with police: his gun was proved to be the one that killed Morrow. The police, however, perhaps believing Howard had had an accomplice, found a new suspect, Rudolph Sheeler. Bilger, now vindicated, was released and placed in a mental hospital.

Sheeler was beaten and signed a confession. At his trial in 1939, when he was placed on the witness stand, his description of the officer's murder failed to match his confession; the trial was adjourned and the next day the prosecution produced another, "correct" confession. Sheeler was sentenced to life in prison.

After twelve years two law professors approached the Pennsylvania

John Wilkes Booth, Lincoln's assassin. His last words were "Tell Mother I die for my country."

Mary Surratt

Lewis Paine

George Atzerodt

David Herold

At a time of intense national hysteria over Lincoln's murder, these four were hastily tried for complicity in the plot and hanged.

The execution of the Lincoln conspirators. The hangman (in white coat) adjusts Herold's noose while another official (*right*) adjusts Atzerodt's. Paine, his arms and legs tied with white cloth strips, is being fitted with a white hood. Mary Surratt (*left*) is seated. A soldier, sickened by the heat, leans on a post supporting the trap beneath her.

A few moments later. The prisoners' bodies dangle at the ends of their ropes. "Mrs. Surratt is innocent. She doesn't deserve to die with the rest of us," Paine had said. But all four died together after General Hartranft clapped his hands three times. The ropes and the scaffold were cut up and the pieces given away as souvenirs.

Charles Guiteau, a disappointed job seeker, assassinated President James Garfield in 1881, shortly after his election.

Physicians examine Guiteau's body intently before declaring him dead. Note the weight at left which pulled down the trapdoor.

Leon Czolgosz, an anarchist, was electrocuted in 1901 for the murder of President McKinley.

John Schrank attempted to assassinate Theodore Roosevelt in 1912 but the president's life was saved by his eyeglasses case and a long speech in his pocket.

Giuseppe Zangara, electrocuted in 1933. Aiming a pistol at President Franklin D. Roosevelt, he missed and killed the mayor of Chicago instead.

A New York police lieutenant, Charles Becker, on a visit to Sing Sing, once laughingly sat in the electric chair. In 1915 he sat down in it and never got up again.

Tom Mooney as he looked in 1918, shortly before he was scheduled to hang. Pardoned in 1939, he died three years later.

The nine Scottsboro Boys meet with celebrated criminal lawyer Samuel Liebowitz shortly after eight of them were sentenced to death for rape in 1931.

Convicted of murdering his wife in 1954, Dr. Samuel Sheppard, Cleveland osteopath, won his release ten years later with the aid of attorney F. Lee Bailey.

After a fake insurance-claim plot fell through, William E. Udderzook murdered his fellow-conspirator. He was hanged on a new-style gallows that jerked him into the air.

Albert Fish, killer and eater of children, looked forward to the thrill of being electrocuted.

Two-Gun Crowley being taken to Sing Sing for execution. On death row the young gunman made architectural drawings that Warden Lawes admired greatly.

Carl Panzram, a brutal killer, confessed to twenty-one murders. On the gallows he spat at the hangman.

Supreme Court with conclusive evidence of Sheeler's innocence, including proof he was in New York when Morrow was shot in Philadelphia. The prisoner was given another trial that ended in an acquittal, and several police officials and officers were suspended for misconduct.

Far more tragic was the case of Willie McGee, a black man, in Mississippi. McGee was held incommunicado and subjected to the third degree for thirty-two days before he consented to sign a confession that he had raped a white woman. At his trial in 1945 an all-white jury deliberated just two and a half minutes before bringing in a guilty verdict, and he was sentenced to death. Twice McGee won a reversal, and twice he was reconvicted and sentenced to be executed. He was electrocuted in 1951.

The newspaperman Carl Rowan (later a deputy assistant secretary of state) in a distinguished book, *South of Freedom* (1952), revealed that the woman who charged McGee with rape had in reality had an intimate relationship with him for four years. When he told her he wanted to end it, she became furious and brought the rape charge against him. Ignored by the jury was the fact that her husband and her two children had been sleeping in the next room when the alleged rape took place, and all denied they had heard any disturbance. Members of the black community could have shed some light on the affair but had been afraid to testify.

In another case, Geither Horn, a white man, was charged with the murder of a farmhand in Washington state but denied it. To make him confess, three officers took him to an open grave and threatened to bury him alive if he refused. He gave them what they wanted. Later, he attempted to retract the confession, but the judge admitted it in evidence. (Errors or prejudice on the part of judges are sometimes a factor in miscarriages of justice.) He was sentenced to life imprisonment in 1935.

After Horn had spent twenty-four years in prison, a federal judge pronounced him innocent. The Washington legislature awarded him $6,000 for false imprisonment, and an out-of-court settlement was reached with the officers who had arrested him.

Quite a number of false confessions are completely voluntary. In one case the innocent defendant was so drunk at the time he was allegedly involved in a murder that he couldn't remember anything, and when the police questioned him he readily said he had killed the victim. In another case the accused was suffering from a mental illness. Here are some other bizarre true-life cases recorded by Bedau and Radelet:

> One defendant falsely confessed to the police as a joke; another falsely confessed to murder because she did not want to be known as a fornicator, and another falsely confessed to impress his girlfriend and then, after being convicted for that murder, falsely confessed to another murder just to prove [to the prison authorities] that a person's false confession could get him convicted— which it did for the second time!

A curious false confession was made by Eugene Padgett in 1940. While serving a twenty-year sentence for burglary in a Texas prison, Padgett admitted to killing a service-station owner; tried and convicted for this crime, he was sentenced to an additional ninety-nine years. Later he confessed the confession was false and he had made it in the hope that, while he was on trial, he would be lodged in a local jail, where it would be easy for him to break out; unfortunately for him his scheme misfired, for he was kept in Austin's high-security prison.

Because of his false confession Padgett wasn't allowed to appeal the murder conviction until he had served his full sentence for burglary, with no time off for good behavior.

Almost any particularly vicious or heavily reported crime will elicit confessions, often from notoriety-hungry people who may, incidentally, have a suicidal impulse. Perhaps the most extraordinary example of false confessions occurred after the killing of Elizabeth Short, known as the Blue Dahlia murder, in Los Angeles in 1947. Close to forty suspects provided written confessions and two hundred called the police to say they had committed the murder.

In one out of seven of the 350 miscarriages of justice studied by Bedau and Radelet, an innocent person was found guilty because of misconduct by the prosecution. The unethical prosecutor has a bottomless bag of tricks to frame a defendant. Such a prosecutor can suppress evidence that would reveal the accused is guiltless, induce witnesses to perjure themselves, fail to challenge testimony the prosecutor knows to be untrue, and falsify or misrepresent the evidence. All of these devices, we saw earlier, helped to put Randall Dale Adams in the death house at Huntsville.

Prosecutors are understandably ambitious, and a long list of successful convictions may help them move up to higher office or build a more lucrative law practice in private life. All the same, there are great numbers of prosecutors who are devoted to evenhanded justice and will not bend the law one iota.

A prosecutor of considerable stature was Homer S. Cummings, Connecticut's attorney general in the 1920s. In an extraordinary case in 1924, an itinerant named Harold Israel was accused of murder in Bridgeport. He signed a confession and the evidence gathered by the authorities, if not examined too closely, pointed to his guilt. Cummings, however, went over it with a fine-toothed comb. A ballistics expert had identified Israel's gun as the murder weapon, but in the courtroom, when the trial was about to begin, Cummings offered dramatic proof that it could not have fired the fatal shot, and the accused man was released. Up to that point Cummings had stood a good chance of becoming the state's next governor. Because Israel had already been convicted in the newspapers, however, Cummings's actions seriously damaged his political future. Fortunately President Franklin D. Roosevelt recognized his ability and named him federal attorney general.

When a police officer or a well-liked public figure is murdered, the newspapers and the public often bring so much pressure to bear on law-enforcement officials that they may find it hard to resist twisting the rules of law to obtain a conviction.

What is arguably the most flagrant example of prosecutorial misconduct in our national history occurred in the trial of the widow Mary Surratt in Washington, D.C., in 1865. As we saw in our chapter on presidential assassinations, she was charged with being a member of the Lincoln conspiracy; however, she was never proved to have taken any part in it, and scholars are generally agreed she was innocent. In order to convict her, both Secretary of War Edwin Stanton and Lafayette C. Baker, head of the secret service, suppressed evidence in her favor. The two main witnesses against her were told they would hang unless they testified for the prosecution. (One later admitted he had lied.) A "school for perjury" was conducted at the National Hotel, where perjurers were coached in fictitious testimony and promised good pay for their services.

Up to the very end, it was expected the new President would grant Surratt clemency, as the military commission that sentenced her to death had requested. But the vindictive Andrew Johnson did nothing to stop the execution (later he insisted he had never received the commission's plea), and he illegally suspended habeas corpus so she would quickly go to her death.

Careless, incompetent work by the authorities has again and again helped to convict the innocent in potentially capital cases. One example out of many:

In 1974 Sergeant Jackson was illegally arrested without a warrant in California, charged with first-degree robbery and murder, and convicted. An important piece of evidence against him was a wallet found in his possession and mistakenly identified as the victim's. Later the real murderer turned himself in and Jackson was released; luckily he had only spent seven months in prison. He sued the city of San Diego and was awarded $17,000.

Many an innocent person condemned to prison or death wins his freedom through the astute hard work of a dedicated attorney. Many others, however, owe their predicament to the incompetence of their original counsel. Such an attorney—whether appointed by the court or engaged by the defendant—may be a newcomer to the practice of law or to the criminal courts. By simply failing to ask the right questions or to challenge the prosecution's witnesses, the evidence presented, or the judge's procedures, even the best-intentioned attorney may do a client terrible harm.

When James Richardson, a poor black man, was sentenced to death in Florida for the alleged murder of his seven children, much of the blame could be laid to his counsel's inexperience. The lawyer, instead of attacking the prosecution's case (later revealed to be riddled with error), limited his defense to presenting witnesses to Richardson's good character. The sixteen years that Lloyd F. Miller, a white man, spent walking through the valley of the shadow of death might have been passed more cheerfully if his first attorney had been skilled in criminal law. Both of these unusual cases we shall discuss later in greater detail.

Study after study has shown that a disproportionate number of those who are indicted for first-degree murder and sentenced to death belong to the poorest class. Because they have no money at all, or very little, or are very ignorant, as a rule they end up with the least qualified, least dedicated attorneys. By contrast, a person of means is able to engage highly skilled and effective counsel, capable of whittling down the prosecution's case, presenting the best defense possible for their client, and using all the stratagems available under the law. "The defendant of wealth and position," said Warden Lewis E. Lawes, "never goes to the electric chair or the gallows."

Up to now we've been looking at how justice can miscarry—why the innocent have been convicted and sentenced to death, or could have been. "Human judgment," as Horace Greeley wrote more than a century ago, "is fallible; human testimony may mislead. Witnesses often lie—sometimes conspire to lie plausibly and effectively. Circumstances often strongly point to a conclusion which is after all a false one. The real murderers sometimes conspire to fasten suspicion on some innocent person, and so arrange the circumstances that he can hardly escape their toils." We have also glanced at cases of guiltless people who have been executed or spent years in prison for these reasons and others as well.

In the next chapter we'll move in for a closer look at the most remarkable of these cases and at a number of others equally noteworthy. Some, although little known to the public, have become classics of our legal history; others are almost certain to be legal classics tomorrow.

All are frightening because they show the terrible things that can happen to men and women through no fault of their own.

ELEVEN

Not Guilty (II)

In the restrictive social climate of Colonial times it wasn't uncommon for a woman to do away with a baby born out of wedlock. The punishment, of course, was death.

In 1768 a New Hampshire schoolteacher, Ruth Blay, was charged with the murder of her illegitimate child. Although there was reason to think the child had been stillborn, the community chose to believe she had murdered it, and she was indicted and convicted at Portsmouth. Her family asked the governor to grant her a reprieve.

Ruth was scheduled to be executed at noon on December 30. Wearing her future wedding gown, and seated next to her coffin, she was driven in a cart to the scene of execution. Eager to be done with the business, the sheriff hanged her early. Twenty minutes later her brother rode up, carrying a reprieve signed by the governor.

Hundreds had assembled to see the hanging. When they realized the poor woman's life could have been spared, they went to the sheriff's house and burned it down. They also strung him up in effigy. Subsequently it was established that the baby was premature and had in fact been stillborn.

Another innocent who was slaughtered in a strikingly similar incident was Elizabeth Wilson, a Pennsylvania farm girl. Elizabeth had gone to Philadelphia and found a job in a tavern. There she made the acquaintance of Joseph Deshong, who talked her into bed with promises of marriage. Going home to her family's farm in Chester County, she made preparations for her wedding but after a while learned there wouldn't be one. After giving birth to twin boys, she asked their father for help.

Deshong came to the farm and told Elizabeth he would put the infants out to nurse. Then he asked her to go for a walk with him in the woods and bring the babies along. There (in the words of Charles Biddle, vice president of the Pennsylvania Council) "he took them from her and laying them down the inhuman monster put his foot on their breasts, and crushed them to death. He then threatened to murder her if she ever mentioned a word about what he had done."

Not long after, hunters found the bodies of the twins near Elizabeth's home and she was arrested and charged with murder. At her trial she seemed to be in a state of shock and never opened her mouth. Found guilty, she was sentenced to death. Her brother, William Wilson, came to see her in jail and finally managed to pry out of her what had happened.

Wilson hurried to Philadelphia, where he went to the State House and convinced Charles Biddle that Deshong was the real killer. Biddle hastily penned a reprieve and Wilson headed for Chester as fast as he could. Unfortunately the Schuylkill was flooded with rain and it took him a long time to cross it. When he reached the place of execution, he saw his sister's body dangling on the gallows. Profoundly depressed, he withdrew from society and spent the rest of his life as a hermit.

In a case that has long been a legal classic, two brothers were sentenced to death for a murder that never took place. This strange story began in May, 1812, in Manchester, Vermont, when Russel Colvin disappeared. He and Stephen and Jesse Boorn, his brothers-in-law, had not been on the best of terms, and it was reported that all three had engaged in a bitter argument just before Colvin vanished.

Seven years later the Boorn brothers were arrested and charged with murder, after a chain of peculiar circumstances. The first was a most unusual dream, and the dreamer was Amos Boorn, an old uncle of theirs. In it Colvin appeared and said he'd been murdered; then he showed the uncle the place he'd been buried in—a hole dug in a cellar where a building had stood. Uncle Amos had this dream three times, and the story was repeated far and wide.

Next an old barn on the Boorn farm burned down. People began to say the fire was no accident—it had been set to destroy evidence of the murder of the Boorns's brother-in-law.

Some time after, a dog digging a hole near the Boorn farm unearthed some bones. They seemed to be human, and the community clamored for action. Jesse Boorn was placed under arrest.

During the following week the old cellar hole was examined and in it was found a penknife, a button with an unusual design, and a large knife. The button and the penknife were recognized as having belonged to Colvin.

The case against Jesse Boorn was firming up. But it appeared to fall apart when the bones found by the dog were studied more closely and determined not to be human. By the end of the week, however, the case had taken on new life: Jesse had charged his brother Stephen with clubbing Russel Colvin to death. Although a careful search failed to turn up any evidence to confirm Jesse's story, Stephen was arrested and locked up.

At a grand jury hearing the prosecution's lead witness against the Boorns was a forger who was in jail with them (and had been promised leniency for his testimony). He swore Jesse had confessed to him that Stephen had hit Colvin; their father had then slit his throat, and the brothers had disposed of the body. Next Stephen confessed he had murdered Colvin after a violent quarrel.[1] Although the corpse was never found, the brothers were tried, convicted and condemned to hang on January 28, 1820. On appeal, Jesse's sentence was commuted to life imprisonment but Stephen's was not.

Now Stephen began to sing a different tune: he insisted he was innocent and his brother-in-law had to be alive somewhere. With his execution just two months away, he asked his attorney to advertise for information about Colvin's whereabouts. Colvin's description was published in a New York City newspaper and, chancing to read it in a tavern, a man was reminded of someone he knew in New Jersey. An acquaintance of Colvin's was sent there and he identified that someone as Colvin.

After at first denying his identity, Colvin was at length induced to go back to Manchester. At the jail he was astonished to see Stephen in chains.

"What is that for?" he asked.

"Because they say I murdered you."

"You never hurt me," answered Colvin. "Jesse struck me with a briar once, but it didn't hurt me much.'' (Apparently he was slow witted.)

Colvin's wife, Sally, whom he had abandoned in Manchester seven years earlier, was brought in. "That is all over with," he said, and he refused to have anything to do with her.

The Boorn brothers were now allowed to plead innocent in court and the prosecution made an entry of *nolle prosequi*—that is, the state would not proceed against them. The brothers' petition for compensation was denied by the legislature.

All through his brief trial in August 1893, nineteen-year-old Will Purvis swore that he hadn't killed Will Buckley. One witness after another backed him up. They testified to his good character. They testified the boy was miles away when Buckley was shot down.

But all their testimony, honest and heartfelt as it was, blew away like dead leaves in the wind when the murdered man's brother Jim took the stand. He swore he had personally seen Purvis gun down his brother in cold blood.

That was why young Purvis stood on the scaffold now, listening to the Reverend Mr. J. Sibley beside him, praying, "God save this innocent boy."

The boy looked out at the multitude of expectant faces. Five thousand people had come to see him swing, packing the courthouse square in Columbia, Mississippi, for executions were still public there. The great throng chattered and laughed excitedly, for in a few minutes they expected to see something very special.

How very special no one standing in that square on February 7, 1894, could possibly have imagined.

Sometimes killers confessed just before being hanged. Some in the crowd thought or hoped Will Purvis would. They were to be disappointed.

"You are taking the life of an innocent man," Will said. "There are people here who know who did commit the crime, and if they will come forward and confess I will go free."

The sheriff and his three deputies went about their business. Will was trussed up, the noose pulled tight about his neck, the black cap set on his head.

Momentarily one of the deputies interrupted the proceedings. He had prepared the noose, and now he noticed he'd left the end of the rope sticking out from the hangman's knot. It just didn't look right. Coming forward, he cut the end off flush with the knot. Now all was ready.

The minister was in the midst of a prayer when the hangman raised his ax and slammed it down on the stay rope, which held the trap in place.

The trap fell. In the crowd a woman screamed.

As Will dropped through the trap a curious thing happened. The knot of the noose, instead of pulling tight as it was supposed to, came apart. Will crashed to the ground.

The crowd stood speechless.

Dazed, the boy wriggled to his feet.

"The black cap slipped from his face," the *New Orleans News Item-Tribune* would relate,[2] "and the large blue eyes of the boy blinked in the sunlight. Most of the crowd stood dumbfounded and the officials were aghast. Purvis realized the situation sooner than any of them and turning to the sheriff said, 'Let's have it over with.' At the same time, the boy, bound hand and foot as he was, began to hop toward the steps of the scaffold and had mounted the first step before the silence was broken."

A confused murmur rose from the stunned onlookers. Before, most had been convinced of Purvis's guilt. Now, somehow, they had begun to doubt it. That Will was still alive could only be an act of God. . . .

But hanging was the order of the day. One of the men on the scaffold leaned over to grasp the rope and start over again. It was just beyond his reach.

"Toss that rope up here, will you, Doctor?" he called to Dr. Ford, a local physician who was standing just below.

The doctor obediently laid hold of the rope. Then he had a second thought. All along he had been one of the small number who believed the boy was innocent. He released the rope.

"I won't do any such damn thing. That boy's been hung once too many times now."

"Don't let him hang!" voices called.

"Hang him! He's guilty!" cried others.

On the scaffold, the lawmen began to make another rope ready.

But all at once the minister, Sibley, was running up the steps. He raised his hands for silence.

"All who want to see this boy hanged a second time," he cried, "hold up their hands."

Not a single hand was raised.

"All who are opposed to hanging Will Purvis a second time," the minister shouted, "hold up your hands."

Almost every hand shot up.

Men and women were pushing forward, calling out their congratulations to the bewildered boy. His unexpected escape from death, they were sure, was a miracle.

The sheriff knit his brows. He had an order from the court to hang Will Purvis. If he didn't carry out that order because the crowd in the square was stirred up, he would be in hot water tomorrow. But if he tried to execute the boy against the will of thousands of people, he and not Purvis might die.

He called on a young attorney for advice. They conferred at the foot of the scaffold. Purvis had to hang, the lawyer said. The court's sentence had to be carried out.

By now a slip-proof noose had been prepared, and the hangman was ready.

Dr. Ford had been listening to the attorney's colloquy with the sheriff. "I don't agree with you," he said. "Now, if I go up on that scaffold and ask three hundred men to stand by me and prevent the hanging, what are you going to do about it?"

The sheriff hesitated.

"I'm ready to do it too," Ford added emphatically.

The sheriff nodded. Going up to the prisoner, he untied his bonds. The crowd broke into cheers. It was calling for the sheriff to release Will as the boy was led back to jail.

Now a legal struggle was begun to free Purvis. His case was carried to the Supreme Court of Mississippi on the ground of double jeopardy. The court held the prisoner had been tried and found guilty; just because lawmen had been slipshod in making the noose was no reason to free the prisoner or commute his sentence. He was resentenced to hang.

Purvis's new date with death was July 31, 1895.

The tribulations of young Will Purvis were rooted deep in the passions of the Old South.

After the Civil War, the Ku Klux Klan and kindred organizations had come into being with the mission of keeping the newly freed black man in his place. One of these organizations in Mississippi, toward the end of the century, was called the White Caps.

A tightly knit group, the White Caps used to ride about the country-side at night dressed in white costumes. Often these were smeared with paint the color of blood. Although, like the klan, their aim was to terrify the black inhabitants, only occasionally did they practice violence. Members took an oath in blood to keep the group's secrets secret.

In 1893, in Marion County, Mississippi, a band of White Caps decided a black hired hand of Will Buckley, one of its members, was in need of a flogging. Buckley was never informed of this, and he was away at the time the beating took place. When he found out what had happened he was furious.

With his brother Jim and the beaten man, Will Buckley presented himself at the next meeting of the grand jury at the county seat. He gave evidence about the flogging and, breaking his oath, revealed the group's innermost secrets. Three White Caps who had taken part in the beating were indicted. Aware of Buckley's actions, the White Caps resolved to take immediate revenge.

For what happened next, we turn to Professor Edwin Borchard's classic account in his book *Convicting the Innocent*:

> On his way home, accompanied by his brother Jim, and by the flogged negro, all on horseback, Will Buckley traveled a forest road which was hardly more than a lane beaten through the heavy underbrush by woodsmen. As the three horsemen, Buckley in the lead, came through a ravine, in which the underbrush was unusually dense, to a small stream over which they had to pass, a shot pierced the stillness. Buckley with a moan swayed in his saddle, then fell to the ground, dead. The assassin, who had been concealed in a blind, jumped out into the road, reloaded his gun, and fired at the others, but they instantly spurred their horses and escaped unscathed.
>
> The road on which Buckley was killed led by the home of the Purvis family. It was generally believed that young Purvis, although but a mere lad of nineteen, was a member of the White Caps. *Two days after* the tragedy, bloodhounds were taken to the place of the murder and after much coaxing, picked up a cold scent which led them in the direction of the Purvis home. A neighbor of the Purvis family, who owned land on both sides of their small farm, and who had repeatedly attempted to gain their

holdings, was one of the first to throw suspicion on the boy. Purvis was placed under arrest. . . .

Questioned, Will Purvis admitted he'd joined the White Caps a few months earlier but insisted he was innocent. As we have seen, he produced witnesses who swore he was far away when the murder took place. But this evidence counted for nothing when the state's chief witness, Jim Buckley, pointed his finger directly at the boy and declared, "Will Purvis, there, killed the man." The prisoner was found guilty as charged.

It was the night before Will was to go to the gallows a second time. People in the county were stirred up because the Supreme Court had rejected his appeal, but no one more than the boy's friends. Under cover of darkness, a group of them snatched him from the jail and took him to a farm in an out-of-the-way place. Their plan was to hide him until the authorities could be persuaded to commute his sentence.

A new election for governor was coming up. The Purvis case was an important issue, and the two candidates took differing positions on it. One favored hanging Will if he was caught, the other opposed it.

The pro-Purvis candidate won. Soon after his inauguration, Will came out of hiding and gave himself up. On March 12, 1896, the governor commuted his sentence to life imprisonment.

In 1898 Jim Buckley, the state's chief witness against the boy, was assailed by doubts. He approached state officials and said he was no longer certain the man who killed his brother was Purvis.

With Buckley's accusation withdrawn, the case against Will crumbled. After four years in prison, three of them at hard labor, he was granted a full pardon in 1898. Soon afterward he married. With the years he made good as a farmer and became the father of seven children.

Purvis had every reason to be happy now but one. Nobody had ever discovered the real murderer of Will Buckley. Until that happened, how could he feel completely exonerated?

In 1917 an elderly man named Joe Beard joined the Holy Rollers. His new faith required him to make a clean breast of his sins. Soon after, on his deathbed, he revealed that in 1893, when the White Caps voted to kill Buckley, he and another member, Louis Thornhill, had been selected by lot to do the killing. Thornhill was the one who actually slew Buckley, he said; Purvis hadn't even been present.

The district attorney wanted to present Beard's confession to the grand jury. Before it met, however, the old man died. He had never signed a written confession before witnesses, as Mississippi law required, so the real killer couldn't be prosecuted.

With Beard's confession Will Purvis was vindicated at last. In 1920, more than twenty-five years after it convicted him, the state officially acknowledged his innocence and made a kind of restitution: it voted him five thousand dollars "for services done and performed . . . in the State penitentiary under the provision of an erroneous judgment."

But it could never compensate him for the terrible agony he had suffered while waiting to die on the gallows.

> *Little Mary Phagan,*
> *She went to town one day.*
> *She went to the pencil factory*
> *To get her little pay.*
>
> *She left her home at seven.*
> *She kissed her mother goodbye,*
> *Not one time did that poor child think*
> *That she was going to die . . .*

A ballad that commemorates the rape and murder of thirteen-year-old Mary Phagan in Atlanta on April 26, 1913, is still sung in the countryside of Georgia. Unfortunately it identifies the killer as Leo Frank—although serious students of the case (including the judge who sentenced him to death) have generally agreed he didn't commit the crime.

Leo Frank has been described as "sensitive" and "intelligent." A Cornell University graduate, he settled in Atlanta, where he managed a pencil factory he owned in partnership with his uncle. He married an Atlanta girl and was the president of the Atlanta chapter of B'nai B'rith.

April 26 was Confederate Memorial Day and the pencil factory was closed. At noon, before going to see the parade, Mary Phagan came to Frank's office to collect her wages. According to Frank, she left immediately afterward. Later her dead body was discovered in the basement. She had been raped and strangled and beaten to death.

Soon afterward Frank was arrested and charged with the girl's murder. A black named Jim Conley, the factory janitor, had told a strange story: Frank had shown him the girl's dead body in the office and ordered him to take it down to the basement in the elevator. Somehow the police believed the janitor rather than Frank.

At the trial Conley was the chief prosecution witness. Besides implicating Frank in the murder, he said he had repeatedly seen him forcing girls in the factory to perform abnormal sex acts with him. Atlanta was in an uproar. "If the Jew doesn't hang, we'll hang you," people told the defense attorneys. Both the judge and the jury were threatened. Outside the courthouse, as the jurors weighed their verdict, a crowd kept chanting, "Hang the Jew!" Frank was sentenced to death.

Defense committees were organized to save the prisoner. William J. Burns, head of a celebrated detective agency and a former Secret Service agent, was hired to find new evidence. Not only did he uncover proof of a police frameup, but he also found a black woman who had been Conley's lover and swore he'd told her he had murdered Mary Phagan. She also had a pile of notes from Conley in which he admitted he practiced the same sexual perversions he had attributed to Frank. While pursuing his investigations, Burns came close to being lynched by a mob.

On the basis of the detective's discoveries, in 1915 John Slaton, governor of Georgia, commuted Frank's sentence to life imprisonment. This act not only destroyed Slaton's career; it unleashed an outbreak of violence. A mob attacked the governor's mansion. Armed mobs roamed through the streets, assaulting Jews and forcing Jewish businesses to close. Reportedly, about half of Georgia's Jewish population of three thousand left the state.

Two months after Slaton's action, on August 17, 1915, a vigilante group calling itself the Knights of Mary Phagan invaded the prison farm where Frank was working. Without opposition from the guards, Frank was abducted, taken to the dead girl's neighborhood, and lynched while a mob roared approval. Then, with happy faces, they posed for photographs next to the dangling body.

This incident, according to *The New York Times* "one of the nation's worst outbursts of anti-Semitism," contributed to the resurgence of the Ku Klux Klan. It also was a catalyst in the organization of the Anti-Defamation League of B'nai B'rith.

In 1982 a man in his eighties, Alonzo Mann, came forward to tell newsmen he had been a fourteen-year-old office boy in the pencil factory managed by Frank in 1913 and had seen Conley carrying Mary Phagan, unconscious, down the stairs, but Conley had threatened to kill him if he mentioned it. Mann's mother had also told him he must remain silent.

An appeal was made by Jewish organizations to exonerate Frank. Although it won the backing of the governor, the State Board of Pardons and Paroles turned it down. "I did the best I know how, and that's all I can do," said Mann. "The pardoning board is wrong."

In 1986, more than seventy years after his death, Leo Frank was granted his pardon by the same pardon board. The board had unanimously reversed itself, "in recognition of the state's failure to protect the person of Leo Frank and thereby preserve his opportunity for continued legal appeal of his conviction, and in recognition of the state's failure to bring his killer to justice, and as an effort to heal old wounds."

On January 26, 1939, Isidore Zimmerman, twenty, was sitting in a holding cell in Sing Sing. He had been a dweller in the death house for nine months, and each day he had died a little.

Now, in a few hours, he would die altogether.

During his time on death row thirteen men had gone to the chair, some screaming wildly. As for Isidore, he had resolved he would die like a man.

What do you want for your dinner tonight, the guard asked.

If he was going like a man he would eat like a man. He said he wanted a salad, a good-sized steak, cheese blintzes a double dessert (jello and ice cream), a pack of cigarettes, some expensive cigars. The kitchen couldn't supply the blintzes, he was told; he'd have to be satisfied with potato pancakes.

The barber, another convict, came in and, working his clippers, cut away the hair on the crown of Isidore's head. The tailor cut an opening in his trouser leg to admit the electrode. He prayed with the rabbi and asked him to visit his family; they would need to be comforted. The rabbi promised he'd do everything he could, and Isidore felt better.

His father and two of his brothers were admitted. His mother couldn't come, they said; she didn't have the strength. He pictured her in her kitchen, her lips moving in a silent prayer, one hand over each eye, the two candles flickering.

For three hours they stayed with him, talking, discussing arrangements for his funeral, listening to what he wanted them to tell his five brothers and sisters at home.

He wasn't afraid to go, he said. "Tell them I died a good death, with expectations of a better world." They hugged and kissed him and said goodbye.

The condemned were allowed to have their favorite records played on a phonograph in the corridor until their time was up. "Who's Sorry Now?" "Ah, Sweet Mystery of Life," and "I Wonder Who's Kissing Her Now" (he had received a "Dear John" letter from his sweetheart) were three Isidore had chosen. He listened to these and to the records selected by the others scheduled to die with him.

During the unending days and nights on death row, the prisoner had burnished in his mind what he would say in the execution chamber when they asked if he had any last words.

"A terrible mistake has been made somewhere along the line," he would begin. "I'm going to my death as an innocent man. I know my conscience is clear; I hope others can say the same tonight." He prayed he wouldn't forget the words and would have the self-possession to speak them.

They were going to make a big splash in the death house that night, he and his companions. The biggest mass execution in eighteen years, people were saying. For Robert Elliott, the executioner, it would mean big bucks. He would collect $750 for just the brief time it took him to shoot 2,000 volts of electricity into the five prisoners.

The execution would have its special note of irony, at least for one of them. In the crime for which all five were to die, Isidore Zimmerman had played no part at all.

In the early morning hours of April 10, 1937, on Manhattan's Lower East Side, a crowd of fifty or so were carousing and playing cards at an all-night restaurant. It had been robbed just a month earlier and now the police checked on it regularly.

At 3:20 A.M., two detectives were sitting with the proprietor when the door swung open and four young men entered. Three of them brandished pistols.

"This is a stickup!" one of them shrilled. "Everybody up!"

Gunfire began to explode. When the smoke cleared, Detective Michael J. Foley could be seen sitting in a chair, blood seeping from a fatal wound in his side as he covered two of the robbers with his pistol.

The pair was seized by the crowd and beaten severely. The other two had escaped, but they were soon in the hands of the police.

None of these was Isidore Zimmerman. Isidore would be arrested later. About to enter Columbia University on a football scholarship, he intended to study law. Instead, he would face the charge that he had been the armorer—the one who had supplied the weapons carried by the holdup men. He hadn't held the gun that killed Foley, hadn't even set foot inside the restaurant or helped plan the robbery. But under New York State law he would be as guilty as if he had fired the fatal shot.

At the trial of the East Side boys, as the press called the defendants, two unindicted co-conspirators were key prosecution witnesses. Turning state's evidence, they attributed to Isidore the part they themselves had performed: providing the guns for the holdup. When Isidore's lawyer challenged their veracity, the judge sustained the prosecution's right to use their testimony.

In April 1938, all five defendants were convicted of murder in the first degree and sentenced to death. It was another feather in the cap of New York County's crusading district attorney, Thomas Dewey, who had his eye on the governor's seat in Albany.

Now, nine months later, young Isidore Zimmerman was about to settle his account with society. How many hours he had left he wasn't sure, but, whatever the number, he was ready.

Abruptly, the door to his small cell was opened and the head keeper was smiling at him and telling him that Governor Lehman had granted him executive clemency and his sentence had been commuted to life imprisonment.

He was too keyed up to grasp it. "I don't want executive clemency."

Then it sank in and he was glad. The rest of his days he might have to pass in a living tomb of steel and concrete, but where there was life . . . There was no hope at all for three of the men who had been sentenced with him: Elliott "fried" them in the chair that night. The fourth, like Zimmerman, was reprieved.

Watching the years inch past within the grim gray walls was often painful for a prisoner who knew he didn't deserve to be there. It was painful also to think of the two who had perjured themselves to put him there and who were on the outside, enjoying the full, free life that should have been his. Where he was, even when you didn't look for trouble, trouble came looking for you. Isidore had four teeth knocked out and his ribs cracked in fights. He spent eight months in solitary. He was assaulted by guards and his skull was fractured. He was blinded in his right eye.

Because he refused to eat one meal, he was denied food for a whole year and told to get his friends to feed him. (They did.) Twice, deep in despair, he tried to kill himself. The first time he rammed his head against a concrete wall; the second time he attempted to hang himself. Nothing worked.

In twenty-four years and eight months, he saw the insides of five prisons: Sing Sing, Auburn, Attica, Green Haven, Dannemora.

His hard-pressed family put up money for a long string of appeals and hearings. Then, in 1962, when he had all but given up hope, the New York Court of Appeals ruled that one of the witnesses who had testified against him had made repeated false statements—and the prosecutor had not only failed to correct the falsehoods, but had committed other acts that denied Isidore a fair trial. He was set free.

In prison, lifers hadn't been given vocational training. Without a trade it was hard for Isidore to find work. Sympathetic employers were willing to hire him, but he didn't last long; fellow employees objected to working next to an ex-convict. Finally he found a job as a warehouseman. He married. He helped to found the Fortune Society, devoted to helping ex-convicts, and he served as its president. With Francis Bond, a writer, he told his story in a book, *Punishment Without Crime*, published in 1964. "The most amazing prison-life true story ever published," *Life* magazine called it.

In 1967 the indictment originally drawn up against him thirty years before was finally dismissed. He was exonerated.

"You can give a prisoner a pardon; but you cannot give him back a moment of his imprisonment," wrote George Bernard Shaw. If Isidore couldn't retrieve his lost years, perhaps he could win monetary compensation. Under the doctrine of sovereign immunity the state couldn't be sued unless it was willing. With a lawyer's help Isidore applied to the New York State Legislature. Three times the legislature passed a bill granting him the right to seek compensation—and three times Governor Nelson A. Rockefeller vetoed it.

At last, in 1981, Governor Hugh Carey approved a bill enabling Isidore to bring suit. He sued for $10 million. In 1983 a judge reviewed his claim and reduced it to $1 million. After paying lawyer's fees and expenses he would have $300,000 left. He told reporters he would move to a better apartment and continue the fight he had been waging against capital punishment.

"There is a message in my story," he said. "It could happen to anybody."

Four months later, Isidore Zimmerman died of a heart attack. He had spent one thousand dollars of the award.

On the night of August 1, 1963, Fred Pitts, twenty-eight, a pulp cutter, and Wilbert Lee, twenty, an Army private on leave, drove into a service station in Port St. Joe, Florida. With them was a woman, Willie Mae Lee, and several other people. Pitts and Lee got into an argument with the two white attendants because the restrooms were marked WHITES ONLY.

A few days later the bodies of the two gas station attendants were discovered. Both men had been shot to death. According to the police, Willie Mae Lee told them that Pitts and a different soldier had slain the two attendants. After Army authorities stated that the soldier in question had a watertight alibi, the woman changed her story. Lee was the soldier involved, she now said.

Pitts and Lee were placed under arrest. They signed confessions for the police—but later said they had done so only because the police were beating them. They were tried and sentenced to death.

In 1972 the case of the two condemned men was still under appeal when the Supreme Court threw out the death penalty. Meanwhile, the woman whose accusation had landed them on death row was telling a different story. Pitts and Lee hadn't killed the two attendants, she said, the police had forced her to name them. State officials, however, ignored her new statement.

Somehow Pitts and Lee had the good fortune to attract the attention of Gene Miller, a reporter, and he wrote a book about their case. While still in manuscript the book (later published as *Invitation to a Lynching*) was read by Arthur Kennedy, legal adviser to Florida's governor, Reuben Askew. Convinced that the two were innocent, Kennedy discussed the case with the governor, who ordered it to be thoroughly investigated. After reviewing the findings, Askew declared, "The evidence . . . is conclusive. These men are not guilty." He granted them a pardon.

After twelve years in prison, Pitts and Lee were released. In the crowd of newsmen covering the event was Gene Miller. He was blinking away tears as the two men walked to the car that would carry them away. "God, that's a beautiful, beautiful sight," he said.

On August 22, 1963, Lloyd E. Miller, Jr., sat in his cell in Statesville Prison counting the hours to midnight. At 12:00, he was to go for a walk—his last. It was his seventh date with death in seven years.

But Miller's lawyers still hadn't given up. At 2:00 P.M. that day, in the United States Court of Appeals in Chicago, they began to present new evidence—evidence they hoped would cast enough doubt on Miller's guilt to save him from the chair.

By 4:30 P.M., the federal judge had heard enough to know he needed to hear more. Just seven and one-half hours before Miller was scheduled to die, the judge granted him a reprieve.

Before the year was out, Miller's conviction was set aside. But the State of Illinois wasn't nearly ready to throw in the towel. Years of appeals, hearings and legal hassles lay ahead.

Finally, in 1967, the Supreme Court, in a stunning 9–0 decision, reversed Miller's conviction. After more than eleven years behind bars he was set free. But he could still feel the tug of the leash of the law; at any time, he could be rearrested and charged again. It was 1971 before the state's prosecutors decided they couldn't win. For the first time in sixteen years the electric chair no longer cast its shadow over him.

It was a brutal child murder—one Lloyd Miller swore he hadn't committed—that brought him to a cell in death row.

In Canton, Illinois, on November 26, 1955, shortly after 4:00 P.M., the brother of an eight-year-old girl named Janice May wondered where she had gone and went looking for her. He found her near the railroad tracks, covered with blood and close to death. The child had been raped and severely beaten. Taken to the hospital, she was pronounced dead at 5:47 P.M.

Two days later Miller, a twenty-nine-year-old Canton taxi driver with a history of emotional instability, was arrested in Danville, Illinois. The morning after the murder of Janice May he had begun to behave peculiarly. Without saying a word, he had illegally taken his cab and driven it out of town. He had abandoned it. Then he had continued to travel by bus. When the taxi was reported missing, the police put two and two together and concluded he was fleeing after assaulting the girl.

Taken into custody, Miller said he'd had nothing to do with the crime. He had left town, he said, because his ex-wife was threatening to put him in jail for failure to pay child support.

Miller was booked on a larceny charge and grilled relentlessly by relays of policemen. He was denied permission to have a counsel present. He asked to see his parents, but was told they didn't want to see him. He was informed by the police that they had a sworn statement from a woman acquaintance of his, June Lang, that he had confessed to her he had killed the child. He denied he had made any such confession.

The police also told Miller they had physical evidence pointing to his guilt. For example, a pubic hair taken from his body had been compared with a pubic hair found in the dead girl's vagina. The two hairs were identical.

Miller agreed to take a lie-detector test. The results were inconclusive, but he was told they showed he had lied. He denied it.

For fifty-two hours he was held incommunicado.

"Lloyd, why don't you admit this," a police officer said, "so we can get you to a mental institution for mental care?" If he refused to confess, he was told, the authorities would see to it that he went to the chair; if he confessed, he would be "all right."

Worn out by the continuous grilling, Lloyd finally gave in. A confession was quickly prepared. (It was, incidentally, inconsistent with the known facts of the case.) He signed it, he said, without even reading it.

Only after the confession was in the hands of the authorities was Lloyd permitted to see his parents. They quickly engaged a counsel and paid him a thousand-dollar retainer. (Later they would mortgage their home to pay for their son's defense.) Lloyd promptly recanted his confession.

Lloyd was indicted for rape and murder. The judge refused to allow his attorney to have a scientific examination made of the physical evidence against him. With little experience (he had never handled a criminal case before), the attorney lost round after round to the prosecution. In part this was due to the judge's attitude. For example, when the defense moved to have Lloyd's confession thrown out because it was obtained under duress, the judge denied the motion. "I have never known of a case," he said, "when I felt that any officer was trying to railroad or pin something on a defendant against his will."

A strong piece of evidence in the prosecution's case was a pair of shorts with dark stains, found a mile from the scene of the crime. Holding up the shorts, the prosecutor said they belonged to Miller and were stained with Janice May's blood. The two pubic hairs that had been made so much of were never introduced as evidence. (Later we shall see why not.)

The trial went on for eighteen hopeless days. At the end Lloyd was convicted and sentenced to die in the electric chair.

Now the frantic fight to save the condemned man's life began. One team of defense lawyers replaced another as appeal after appeal was filed.

In 1963, as we saw earlier, Lloyd was just seven and one-half hours away from death when the United States Court of Appeals in Chicago granted him a reprieve and a habeas corpus hearing. At last the defense was permitted to have a scientific examination made of the exhibits against him. The results were startling. The stains on the "bloody" shorts turned out to be paint. (The state conceded it had known this during the 1956 trial.) Not only that: they were too small to fit the defendant. The two pubic hairs (one taken from Lloyd) were found not to be from the same person.

But that wasn't all the evidence that had been withheld in the 1956 trial. Lloyd's landlady testified he'd been asleep in his room at the time the prosecution contended he had assaulted the girl. His woman acquaintance, who had testified he'd confessed the crime to her, now said he hadn't. It was made clear she was emotionally unstable, and the prosecution had been well aware of that when it originally put her on the witness stand.

At the end of the hearing the Chicago judge ordered Lloyd's conviction set aside.

But a year later the Federal Court of Appeals, responding to a plea from the state, reversed the judge's decision. Lloyd was back under sentence of death once more.

Finally, on February 13, 1967, the Supreme Court upheld the 1963 decision that Lloyd had been improperly convicted. According to the court, "the prosecution deliberately misrepresented the truth." The justices singled out for particular censure the prosecutor's failure to declare the stains on the shorts were made by paint, not blood. The prosecutor, the court pointed out, had even waved them in front of the jury. "In the context of the revolting crime," declared Justice Potter Stewart, the shorts' "gruesomely emotional impact upon the jury was incalculable."

The court's sharp criticism of the prosecution's tactics stirred up the Illinois State Bar Association. For nine months it conducted an inquiry into the conduct of the state's attorneys. In 1968 it gave the results: it exonerated the prosecution completely and charged the Supreme Court with "misapprehending the facts."

Many were surprised, including *Time* magazine. The bar association, *Time* commented, seemed to be saying that, "while a witness is required to tell 'the truth, the whole truth and nothing but the truth,' no such restrictions apply to prosecutors bent on winning a conviction."

Perhaps we should leave the last word on this unusual case to Willard J. Lassers, one of the thirteen attorneys who helped save Lloyd Miller's life. In his notable book *Scapegoat Justice*, about the Miller case, Lassers observed, "When a crime outrages society, it pushes the authorities to lash out and to make a sacrifice of someone. They do so, not usually through vindictiveness, but because of the unremitting public pressures which warp their judgment."

Jerry Banks, twenty-three years old, black, and largely unemployed, went hunting on November 7, 1974, near Stockbridge, Georgia. He had three children and a wife at home, and he hoped his old 12-gauge shotgun would enable him to bring them back some venison.

In the woods Banks's yapping dog led him not to a deer but to two silent forms on the ground. Bending over, he saw they were a dead man and woman, each with two bullet wounds in the back. Excited, he made his way to the nearest road, stopped an automobile, and asked the driver to inform the sheriff. Then he stayed with the bodies until the police arrived. The dead man and woman turned out to be a local band director and a nineteen-year-old ex-pupil of his.

On December 5 the police took Banks's single-barreled shotgun and did some test firings. They had found three spent shotgun shells near the scene of the shootings, and the tests convinced them the shells had been fired by Banks's gun—despite the fact that shotguns don't make bore markings.

Six days later Banks was charged with murder. He had an alibi—a neighbor testified he'd been at her home helping her husband at the time established for the shootings. On January 31, however, Banks was tried and found guilty. On the following day he was sentenced to die in the electric chair.

Soon the driver Banks had stopped on the woodland road came forward, complaining he should have been called as a witness in the trial but hadn't. In September the Georgia Supreme Court ruled the prosecution had knowingly withheld significant evidence and it reversed the conviction. A new trial was ordered.

At Banks's second trial his attorney put only one witness on the stand. He failed to have Banks himself testify or to call the couple who could vouch for his alibi. Banks was found guilty and sentenced to death once more.

The next six years Banks spent on death row. In that time other serious questions surfaced about the way the state had handled its case against him. Seven people who had been close to the scene of the crime on November 7, 1974 (two were actually police officers), swore they had heard several shots fired in rapid succession and had reported them to the sheriff. One of these witnesses said that, a few minutes after hearing the shots, he'd seen a man with an automatic shotgun near the place. But none of the seven had ever been called to testify at Banks's trials.

Neither had another person who had notified the sheriff that two hours before the killings he'd seen two men and a woman sitting in a station wagon that looked like the band director's. They were arguing.

Moreover, ballistics experts declared Banks's single-barreled shotgun couldn't possibly have fired four shots as rapidly as the seven witnesses had reported. Only an automatic weapon could do that.

Banks's attorney by now had been disbarred for misconduct in other cases. The new evidence was presented by Banks's new attorneys to the same judge who'd tried him twice before. A new trial wasn't justified, the judge ruled.

The attorneys appealed to the Georgia Supreme Court. The court again ordered Banks retried.

While the prisoner was sitting on death row, he was interviewed by Tom Wicker, a *New York Times* columnist and opponent of the death penalty.

"I just don't believe God'll let 'em kill me for something I didn't do," Banks told him.

"Knowing the fallibilities of law enforcement as he does," commented Wicker, "he added what ought to be the final verdict on capital punishment.

" 'Suppose they did kill somebody. Two or three years later they found out he was innocent. What they gonna do, say we made a mistake?' "

At Banks's third trial, in 1980, a significant piece of new evidence was introduced. A witness who hadn't been heard from before revealed that

Banks's shotgun couldn't have fired the fatal shots. Later in the year a circuit court judge dismissed the charges against Banks and ordered him set free.

But a stranger fate than the state had originally decreed for Jerry Banks was in store for him. Banks had been away from his family for six years. Three months after he came back home, his wife told him she was going to get a divorce.

The shock turned Banks from a falsely accused double murderer into a real one. He took his wife's life and his own.

In 1983 Banks's three orphaned children brought a suit against the county, charging it with mishandling their father's case. The county agreed to settle for $150,000.

At 6:50 A.M. on October 25, 1967, James Richardson, a poor, illiterate black laborer, and his wife went off to pick fruit in Arcadia, Florida. They left at home their seven children—six daughters and a son, ranging in age from two to eight. Betsy Reese, a middle-aged neighbor, would look after them.

At noon Reese gave the children a lunch of beans, rice and cheese. A short while later they began to shriek with pain and foam at the mouth. They went into convulsions.

By morning all seven children were dead.

An autopsy showed the children had literally drowned when their lungs filled with liquid. Found in their bodies were substantial amounts of parathion—deadly to insects and deadly to human beings.

Someone had mixed the pesticide into their food. To the sheriff the father seemed the most likely suspect. He was arrested and charged with the murder of the oldest child. (If he was acquitted he could then be charged with the murders of the other six, one by one, until he was found guilty.)

Richardson was tried in May, 1968. The district attorney presented evidence that on the night before the children ate the poisoned food, Richardson was visited by an insurance salesman and he made a payment on policies amounting to $3,500 on the children's lives. The following morning, the prosecution maintained, after the parathion had been mixed into the food the neighbor was to give them, he had gone coolly off to work.

As if the case against Richardson wasn't convincing enough, the district attorney placed on the witness stand two prisoners who had shared a cell with the accused. They testified Richardson had admitted to them he had poisoned the children.

"It's one of the strongest cases I've ever presented to a jury," the district attorney would say later.

Richardson's lawyer was a volunteer. Inexperienced in criminal cases, he did little more than present witnesses who testified to his client's good character. Richardson was found guilty and sentenced to die in the electric chair.

The condemned man was locked up on death row. "I could taste the scent of death in my nostrils," he said.

In 1972 he was still sitting on death row, his case under appeal. That was the year the United States Supreme Court rendered its historic ruling in *Furman* v. *Georgia*. The death-penalty statutes in all the states were struck down because they gave juries too much leeway in deciding who should live and who should die. Rather than try Richardson again, Florida commuted his sentence to twenty-five years' imprisonment.

The inmate was transferred to a medium-security prison. "It's a terrible feeling knowing that I may have died for something I didn't do," he said. "But I tell myself that if I did die, I would be going home to my children."

His wife visited him whenever she could raise the fare. He was made a trusty. He learned to read and write. He earned a high school diploma. He became an ordained Southern Baptist minister.

Not everyone believed Richardson had murdered his children. One person who was sure he hadn't was noted Washington lawyer and author Mark Lane, who wrote a book, *Arcadia*, about the case. Another was an Arcadia resident who daringly stole from the office of the former prosecutor a box file on the case that yielded documents showing Richardson was innocent. Because of fear of prosecution, however, they were kept hidden. Only in 1989, through Lane's intervention, were these papers turned over to the authorities. The state appointed a judge to hear claims that the prisoner had been railroaded, and a special prosecutor to investigate them.

The evidence laid before the judge by Richardson's lawyers and the special prosecutor exposed a shocking miscarriage of justice.

In the 1968 trial, it was shown, the district attorney had failed to reveal that Richardson hadn't actually purchased insurance on the lives of his children—the cornerstone of the case against him. The salesman had called on him uninvited, and had merely left with him a business card outlining policies for the entire Richardson family. According to the sheriff's original testimony, however, Richardson had shown him an insurance receipt—and the district attorney had failed to challenge the lie.

In 1989 the neighbor, Betsy Reese, who had given the children the fatal meal and who had testified against Richardson in 1968, was in a nursing home, under treatment for Alzheimer's disease. Two of her nurses deposed that when she was still lucid she had told them *more than a hundred times* that it was she who had put the poison in the children's food!

Moreover, the district attorney had concealed significant information that should have disqualified Reese as a witness in 1968. The woman had been married three times. Her first husband had died under suspicious circumstances, after eating a meal she had prepared for him. Her second husband she had shot to death, for which she served four years in prison, and she was on parole at the time the children were poisoned. She was also said to bear a bitter grudge against Richardson because he'd introduced her third husband to his cousin—and the husband had gone off with her.

Another clincher: A woman who as a child used to share meals with the Richardson children testified that when she came in to eat lunch with them on the day they were poisoned, Reese shoved her away. But that same morning, for breakfast, she had eaten—with no untoward effect—grits from a pot in which parathion was later found. Since Richardson had gone to work at 6:50 A.M., the parathion must have been added after his departure.

But still that wasn't all. A man who had testified at the first trial that Richardson, while sharing a cell with him, had confessed to the killings, now retracted his earlier statement. Richardson, he said, had made no confession. Instead, the man now testified he had perjured himself because a deputy sheriff had threatened to beat him if he refused.

On April 25, 1989, the judge overturned Richardson's murder conviction and set him free. He had gone into prison at the age of thirty-two. He was fifty-three when he walked out. He had narrowly escaped execution for a crime someone else had committed.

"I never had no doubt he was innocent," his wife said. "He loved his family."

TWELVE

Last Words,
Last Wishes,
Last Laughs

In 1989 three-hundred-pound William Paul Thompson was helped onto a gurney in the execution chamber at Nevada State Prison in Carson City. The chamber, formerly the scene of lethal gas executions, had recently been converted for use in lethal injections.

Thompson had been sentenced to death for the murder of a drifter who "just got in my way"; at the time, he was fleeing after killing two drug informers. He claimed he had also murdered three others.

The condemned man found consolation in religion. He told reporters he was paying society back with "the only thing I have to offer it." His last words, spoken from the gurney, were, "Thank you for letting me die with dignity."

"At last I'll get some high-class education," said John W. Deering, a murderer, when he willed his body to the University of Utah.

Deering, who had spent more than half of his life within prison walls, died before a firing squad in 1938.

George Appel, who murdered a New York policeman, had a lively sense of humor that didn't fail even when he was being strapped into the electric chair in Ossining in 1928.

"Well, folks," said Appel, grinning as he looked at the tense faces of the witnesses, "pretty soon you're going to see a baked Appel."

Stephen T. Judy was sentenced to die for the murder of a young woman and her three children. Saying he preferred death to life in prison, he refused to make any final appeals. Twenty-four years old, he was electrocuted in Indiana State Prison in 1981.

Of Judy's last requests one was granted and one denied. After his head had been shaved for contact with the electrode, he asked for photographs of his new haircut, and these were taken. With his last meal he asked for four bottles of cold beer. These were refused. As he walked to the chair he pointed to the slit made in his trousers leg to admit the electrode. "I'm going to send the State of Indiana a bill for fifteen dollars," he joked.

"I don't hold no grudges. This is my doing. Sorry it happened," were his last words.

Nineteen-year-old murderer James Bolger sat grinning nervously in the electric chair at Sing Sing in 1930 and with the bravado of a teenager told the witnesses, "I die as I lived—with a smile."

Mike Kosmowski, who wore a wooden leg, had been convicted of murder with the help of evidence provided by a newspaper reporter. Before he was executed in Sing Sing in 1927, he wrote a will leaving the wooden leg to the newsman.

"I hope you have to use it before you die," Kosmowski said.

Ward McConkey was hanged in Pittsburgh in 1882. On the scaffold he protested his innocence.

"Goodbye, all you murderers," he said as the death cap came down over his head.

August 24, 1933, was a cloudy day. For Frank Negron and Alex Carrion in Sing Sing, it was also the last.

"Just our luck," growled Negron to his fellow murderer. "We haven't even got a decent day for it."

San Quentin's warden, Clinton T. Duffy, when he saw a depressed-looking convict on death row, would sometimes read him the following poem, given to him by one of the row's former tenants:

> *"If I could have my last wish,"*
> *Said the prisoner one day,*
> *As they led him from the death cell*
> *To the chair not far away,*
>
> *"Please grant me this request, sir,*
> *Ere you tighten up the strap,*
> *Just tell the Warden I would love*
> *To hold him on my lap."*

The ambition of Kenneth Neu, a young Louisiana man with a history of mental problems, was to become a famous nightclub singer. That dream ended when he murdered two men. In court, where he entered a plea of insanity, he was wearing the shoes of one of his victims, the suit of the other. The jury wouldn't buy his plea, and he was sentenced to death. That didn't stop Neu from singing until his execution in 1935. His favorite piece was a one-line parody of a famous old song: "I'm fit as a fiddle and ready to hang."

Albert Fish, a benevolent-looking old house painter, was a ghoul and a serial killer. He practiced a wide variety of perversions, taking particular pleasure in having children beat him with a nail-studded paddle until he bled. Reportedly he also stuck four hundred needles into his body. But his most special perversion was cannibalism. He murdered at least fifteen children and ate them. (Curiously, he had six children of his own whom he was very fond of.)

Fish was found sane enough to be executed. He expressed great pleasure at the prospect. "What a thrill it will be if I have to die in the electric chair," he said, beaming. "It will be the supreme thrill. The only one I haven't tried." When he was executed in 1936, he walked eagerly to the chair and helped the executioner attach the electrode to his leg.

In 1967 Aaron Mitchell, who'd shot a policeman to death during a robbery, sat strapped inside San Quentin's green execution chamber. A moment before the room was sealed he twisted his head around so he could see the witnesses and cried out to them, "I am Jesus Christ!"

According to Warden Lewis E. Lawes, Prisoner Number 77681 ordered for his last meal "one Long Island duck, one can of peas, one pint of olives, mixed and cooked into a brown stew and served with dumplings, four slices of bread, boiled rice, tomato salad, strawberry shortcake, a pint of vanilla ice cream, and some good cigars." After consuming nearly all of it, he announced, "I'm ready to ride that thunderbolt, boys."[1]

Although Lawes believed in capital punishment when he was appointed warden of Sing Sing, he later became its outspoken opponent. Not all of his prisoners agreed with him. One, Number 76800, expressed the feelings of many residents of death row when he said, just before going to the chair, "Warden, I hope you don't succeed in your effort to abolish capital punishment. It is better to burn in the chair and have it over than to rot in prison with a life sentence."

Number 69711, a former amateur boxer, requested permission to walk to the chair on his hands and then worried that the newspapers wouldn't tell how game he'd been. His last words were, "Goodbye, Warden, old-timer!" and, to the executioner, "Step on the gas!"

Irene Schroeder went on a crime spree with W. Glenn Dague, a former salesman who had deserted his family for her. After the pair had robbed a grocery store, she shot a state policeman to death. Her little boy had been in the car with her at the time, and his telling a policeman, "My mother killed a cop like you," helped to convict her.

Although Schroeder tried to save her lover by taking complete responsibility for the crime, both were condemned to death. On the morning of their execution in 1931, when the prison matron awakened her and asked if she could do anything for her, the twenty-two-year-old Schroeder said, "Please tell them in the kitchen to fry Glenn's eggs on both sides. He likes them that way."

She was the first woman put to death in Pennsylvania's electric chair.

Guy Clark, who had murdered his wife, was hanged in 1832. While being escorted to the gallows through the slushy streets of Ithaca, New York, he took pleasure in splashing the onlookers on the sidewalks. The sheriff told him to hurry up or they would be late.

Clark advised the sheriff not to worry about it. "Nothing will happen until we get there," he said.

The night before Pat Harnett was to be hanged in the Ohio State Prison in 1885 an official suggested he might wish to mount the prison wall to see his last sunset. Harnett agreed. As Andrew Palm relates, Harnett "gazed at it intently for some time, and a halo lit the sky; the attendants expected to hear some expression of regret or sentiment; but they were shocked to hear him say: 'When that sun goes down again I shall be flying about among the little angels.' "

Frank Plaia and Mike Sclafonia were scheduled to be executed in 1930 for the murder of a married couple. Formerly friends, they had turned into enemies, each charging the other with the killings.

Plaia was executed first. A few minutes afterward Sclafonia walked into the death room. He examined the chair and, reaching into a pocket, took out a handkerchief and wiped the seat vigorously.

"After that rat sat in it," he said, "I want it clean."

"It is my desire," wrote William E. Udderzook, three weeks before his hanging, "that my remains will rest in Baltimore, if not in the same lot, at least in the same cemetery with those of Mr. W. S. Goss, a friend ever dear to me, that our bodies may return to the mother dust, and our spirits may mingle together on the bright sunny banks of deliverance, where pleasures never end. . . ."

What is curious about these florid sentiments is that Udderzook had beaten the aforementioned W. S. Goss, his brother-in-law, to death after a fake insurance-claim plot to collect money on Goss's life had misfired, and Udderzook had decided to make the false claim true. The murderer died on the gallows—which jerked him upward instead of dropping him—in the West Chester, Pennsylvania, county jail in 1874.

Leslie Lowenfield was about to die in the electric chair at the Louisiana State Prison in Angola in 1989. He had burst in on his former mistress and five of her relatives as they sat around a kitchen table eating boiled crabs and shot the entire family dead in a jealous fury. A paranoid schizophrenic according to his lawyer, he had never accepted his guilt.

"Don't give up on me, although my life will be over tonight," he urged the witnesses with his last breath, "because the one responsible is still out there."

Although many of the condemned die protesting their innocence, many others do just the opposite. Such a one was William W. Hoyer, a young man who had murdered his wife and little daughter. In his last days religion had reconciled him to his death. Seated in the electric chair in 1926, he said, "I wouldn't take ten years, let alone life, to escape this chair. I deserve to go. I ought to go. I want to go."

William E. Cook, a criminal from the age of twelve, had been labeled incurably insane by a federal judge, but a judge in California decided he was sane enough to go to the gas chamber in 1952. As Cook sat down in the chair, he shook his fist at the witnesses. His last words were written on his knuckles: "Hard Luck."

A crowd of five thousand had gathered at Fort Smith, Arkansas, on September 3, 1875, to see the first six-man hanging ordered by the Hanging Judge, Isaac C. Parker. One of the six was Dan Evans, who had murdered a man for his boots.

Looking down at the upturned faces of the multitude, Evans observed, "There are worse men here than me."

Twenty-one-year-old George Swan had been sentenced to death for two murders during a restaurant holdup in New York. In 1933 he entered the execution chamber puffing on a cigar, a pink flower stuck in a shirt buttonhole.

"It's about time this thing happened," he said, exhaling smoke. "It's been a long time coming. Goodbye, everybody!"

In 1967 Luis José Monge was about to be executed at the Colorado State Prison for the murder of his wife and three of his ten children. A worried look came over his face as a physician fastened electrodes to his body to monitor his heart action.

"Doctor," Monge asked innocently, "will that gas in there bother my asthma?"

"Not for long," replied the physician.[2]

One of the most unusual orders for a last meal was recorded by Dr. Amos O. Squire, official physician at Sing Sing. The prisoner requested bread and water.

"That's the only grub for a bum like me," he said.

The authorities supposed the prisoner wanted to show his repentance, but they soon learned better. When the time came to take the condemned man to the electric chair, the guards found they couldn't open the lock to his cell. He had dipped the bread in the water, kneaded it, and stuffed it into the keyhole. As the guards laboriously extracted the bread, the convict jeered at them and joked. He was having his last laugh at the system and at the same time delaying his execution thirty minutes.

After the execution all the locks on death row were replaced so the keyholes wouldn't be accessible on the inside.

Leo Jankowski had murdered a guard at Clinton Prison in Dannemora, New York, during an attempted jailbreak. When he was being taken to the death chamber, in 1920, he broke away from his escort, rushed up to the electric chair, and planted a kiss on it.

"I was never so happy to see anything!" he cried out, tears running down his cheeks.

Tormented by severe tuberculosis, Jankowski had been looking forward eagerly to his execution.

Alan J. Adams was standing on the scaffold in Northhampton, Massachusetts, in 1881, about to pay the price for murder. The sheriff's voice must have quavered as he informed the prisoner he was going to read him the execution warrant.

"Damned if I care what you read," was Adams's reply. "You'd better get yourself a drink to steady your nerves."

In 1859 Thomas N. Ferguson, aged twenty-seven, was executed in Salt Lake City for murdering his employer while drunk. Asked if he had any last words, he delivered a harangue that went on, according to various reports, from four to eight hours—no doubt one of the longest "last words" ever heard.

In his speech Ferguson lambasted the judge who had sentenced him. The judge "had too much whiskey in his head to know the day he sentenced me to be executed on,'' he said. That day was a Sunday, hardly the time for an execution in devout old Utah.

On appeal the date had been changed to a Friday.

Not quite a runner-up for the longest address by a condemned man was one by Preston Turley, who spoke about the evils of drink for forty-five minutes on the scaffold. He would have spoken longer, but the hangman (not to mention the spectators) had lost patience. Turley, a former Baptist minister, had been fired for drunkenness, and later murdered his wife in a drunken fury as his three children looked on. Their testimony helped to convict him.

"Don't you want to go and see Pa hung?" he repeatedly asked his children before his hanging in Charleston, Virginia (today West Virginia), in 1858. He expressed great disappointment when he couldn't spot them in the crowd in front of the gallows.

At Sing Sing a Jewish convict waiting to be executed requested a full-course kosher dinner for his last meal. After he had finished it, to his keeper's surprise he asked for a ham sandwich, and it was brought to him.

"I never tasted ham before," the prisoner commented, "It isn't bad at all.''

Juanita Spinelli's last request was to die with the pictures of her three children and one grandchild fastened over her heart. There was a brief delay as she was about to step inside San Quentin's gas chamber. She waited outside calmly, discussing the weather, until she was told to enter.

Spinelli, known as the Duchess, was the first woman legally executed in California. Ugly and nasty tempered, she was the mastermind of a gang responsible for many stickups, burglaries and auto thefts in California in the 1930s. She was sentenced to death for ordering the murder of one of her henchmen.

The Duchess held up her execution for a year and a half with appeals. When they were turned down, she laid a curse on those who had condemned her, declaring, "My blood will burn holes in their bodies.'' However, shortly before her execution in 1941, she graciously relented, saying, "I have asked God to forgive them.''

Leong Fook, a Chinese, had been sentenced to death in California for the murder of his landlady. The day before his execution, in 1929, he became very upset on hearing he'd have to leave his false teeth and eyeglasses behind when he went into the death chamber.

"I need them where I'm going," he almost screamed. "They must go in my coffin with me!"

Assured his request would be granted, Leong bowed and went blissfully to sleep.

A convict who was to be executed the following day asked Warden Lawes if he could be given a stiff drink of whiskey before going to his death. The rules forbade it, the warden told him, but the man continued to plead, and the warden finally gave in.

Half an hour before the prisoner was to take his last walk, the warden entered the holding cell with a small bottle he had filled with whiskey. As the procession prepared to leave the cell, Warden Lawes came up close and passed the tiny bottle to him.

The prisoner looked at the warden and gave the bottle back. "You need this more than I do," he said.

The doomed man grinned as the warden emptied the bottle.

Joshua Jones told his neighbors his wife had killed herself, but he couldn't convince them. Neither could he convince the jury, which sentenced him to hang for her murder. Making the best of a bad situation, he sold his body to two doctors for ten dollars and their promise to educate his son. Jones spent the money for delicacies to vary his prison diet. When the day came for him to be hanged, in 1839, at Coudersport, Pennsylvania, he found he still had a dollar left.

Sandwiching the bill between two slices of bread, he ate it.

"Give my apologies to the families of my victims," said Arthur Gary Bishop before he lost consciousness on the gurney at Utah State Prison in 1988. The ghoulish Bishop, an excommunicated Mormon missionary and onetime Eagle Scout, confessed he had shot, bludgeoned, strangled or drowned five young boys so he could enjoy sexual pleasure by viewing their nude bodies afterward. To re-experience his first murder, he said, he had bought and killed twenty puppies.

"I allowed myself to be misled by Satan," he wrote in a final statement.

Leslie B. Gireth welcomed his execution at San Quentin in 1943 because he was eager to carry out his part in an unfulfilled contract with a dead woman. Gireth was a married man and the woman was his sweetheart, Dorena Hammer. They had wanted desperately to marry, but his wife had refused to divorce him, and he and Dorena had made a suicide pact. After shooting her, however, he'd lost his nerve.

For his last meal Gireth ordered two hamburgers and Cokes— exactly what he and Dorena had before she died. As he walked into the execution chamber, in his cell he could hear his portable phonograph playing *Clair de Lune*—Dorena's favorite piece, which they had listened to together the night he shot her.

After attacking and killing a fellow inmate, Charles de la Roi was sentenced to die in California. The day before he went to the gas chamber in 1946, he was asked if he had any last request.

"Warden," the convict replied, "I'd like a little bicarb because I'm afraid I'm going to get gas on my stomach tomorrow."

Sitting down in the electric chair in 1931 in New Jersey, Charles Fithian, a young murderer, said, "I want to make a complaint. That soup I had for supper tonight was too hot."

On the gallows at Leavenworth Prison in 1930, the mass murderer Carl Panzram was asked if he had any last words.

"Yes, hurry it up, you Hoosier bastard. I could hang a dozen men while you're fooling around!"

Panzram, one of the most vicious felons in the annals of American crime, was first arrested when he was eight years old on a drunk and disorderly charge. A burglar and a killer, he confessed to twenty-one murders; for the last one, the slaying of a fellow inmate, he was sentenced to death.

When an anti-capital-punishment organization tried to win a commutation for him, Panzram wrote to President Herbert Hoover, declaring he had a constitutional right to be hanged. "I believe the only way to reform people," he said, "is to kill them."

Francis "Two-Gun" Crowley has been called the twentieth century's Billy the Kid. Perhaps patterning himself after movie gangsters, he took part in one savage crime after another. At length the police trapped him in one of the greatest gun battles in Manhattan's history.

Crowley held three hundred officers at bay outside his hideout until, wounded by four bullets and overcome by tear gas, he was taken prisoner.

During his stay on death row the unruly convict assaulted a guard, set fire to his cell, and raised all kinds of hell. But gradually he calmed down. A starling became a regular visitor to his cell and he fed it and tamed it.

On the night of his execution, in 1932 (he was nineteen years old), he pointed to a big water bug running around his cell. "See that? I was about to kill it. Several times I wanted to crush it. It's a dirty-looking thing. But then I decided to give it a chance and let it live."

He went calmly to his death. His last words were: "Give my love to mother."

The doomed man came walking down the hallway that led to the death chamber. Dr. George Beto, Texas corrections department chief, heard him singing. The song was "Swing Low, Sweet Chariot." The convict moved slowly and carefully, his eyes shut.

The singing didn't stop while guards strapped him in the chair.

Perhaps the man had some last words, an assistant said. Shouldn't he be interrupted?

Beto was against it. "He was entrancing himself," he said later.

The prisoner went on singing till death stopped his song.

The night before his execution in Utah in 1912, J. J. Morris entertained his guards with jokes. One concerned two criminals who were to be hanged from a bridge. Beneath it rushed a raging river.

"The first man," said Morris, according to the *Salt Lake Tribune*, "slipped from the noose when he was swung off the bridge, and he fell into the water. He swam to the shore and escaped.

"When they started to swing the other fellow, he said, 'Now be sure to tie the knot tight, for I can't swim.' "

William Force sat in the electric chair in 1930, about to be put to death for a prison murder.

"What are you so nervous about, boy?" he said to the executioner, who was busily making last-minute adjustments. "Take it easy. I'm in no hurry."

It was June 1930, and Robert H. White, condemned to death by the

State of Nevada, would shortly, very shortly, be breathing gas instead of air.

He was consulted about his last wishes. Did he want anything else? He reflected. "Yes. A gas mask."

Joseph L. Tice, sixty-three, murdered his wife. She had left him because he drank too much, and he went to her place of work in a drunken rage and stabbed her to death. His last words before he died in the electric chair in 1892 were: "Oh, if I didn't drink that whisky!"

Tice was the second man electrocuted at Auburn. He had promised the prison doctor that if he was conscious after the bolt struck, he would close his right hand. He didn't.

Another unfortunate whose end was hastened by an addiction was John E. Pryde, hanged in Minnesota in 1896. Pryde, a lumber-camp cook, lost all his money gambling, and then robbed and murdered a logger.

"Nothing but gambling brought me to this," he said before his execution. "I hope every gambling hell in this city may be closed by law and kept closed."

Charles Starkweather was nineteen years old when he was strapped into Nebraska's electric chair in 1959. A year and a half earlier he had started on a murder spree with his fourteen-year-old girlfriend that ended only after he had stabbed, shot or strangled her family and eight others. His crimes, he insisted, were all committed in self-defense.

Before his execution the local Lions Club asked him to donate his eyes to an eye bank.

"Hell, no," was his amiable reply. "Nobody ever did anything for me. Why in hell should I do anything for anyone else?"

Before being strung up in Minnesota in 1891, William Rose consumed an abundant breakfast of oysters and eggs. Climbing up on the scaffold, he calmly uttered his last words in classic Midwestern style: "Goodbye, all!" As he dropped through the trap, the rope broke and the unconscious Rose had to be suspended from another.

Rose was executed for the murder of a neighbor, Charles Cheline. Cheline's last words are also remembered. "Help, quick!" he cried. "I am shot through the body deader than hay!"

"God, in permitting me to die, must have some wise design," said Police Lieutenant Charles Becker to his priests shortly before his execution in Sing Sing. He was innocent, he swore. And then, mysteriously: "I am sacrificed for my friends."

Becker, described as the "crookedest cop who ever stood behind a shield," was charged with arranging the murder of a big-time bookie. Later it would be said that the prosecutor, Charles Seymour Whitman, had put Becker on trial to appease public fury over police corruption. Elected governor of New York with the help of Becker's conviction, Whitman refused to grant him clemency.

Becker's widow, Helen, had a silver plate attached to his coffin saying:

> CHARLES BECKER
> MURDERED JULY 30, 1915
> BY GOVERNOR WHITMAN

The police promptly removed the plate.

"I shall meet death like a man, and I hope those who see me hanged will live to see the day when it is proved that I am innocent—and it will someday."

Jack O'Neill finished speaking and the death hood was pulled down over his face, as he stood on the scaffold in 1898 in Massachusetts. Convicted of the rape-murder of Hattie McCloud, O'Neill, an Irishman, had been sentenced to death at a time when a wave of hatred for Irish immigrants was sweeping the state.

Only a short while afterward, the dead man's words were proved true. A newsman in Cuba, interviewing a soldier dying of wounds in the Spanish-American War, heard his confession that he had murdered McCloud, together with details no one but the real killer could know.

"I love you."

Those were the last words spoken by twenty-eight-year-old Sean Patrick Flanagan, lying on the gurney in Nevada's state penitentiary in 1989. Oddly, the person he was addressing was the prosecutor, Dan Seaton, who had obtained his conviction.

"He means it in terms of Christian love and forgiveness," said Seaton. "I'm sure he'd kill again."

A man who hated his own homosexuality, Flanagan was eager to be punished for the murder of two other homosexuals. He had confessed to the killings when he was arrested for an entirely different offense: jaywalking.

Epilogue

On August 6, 1890, the murderer William Kemmler coolly settled down in New York State's brand-new electric chair, proud to be the first to die in it. Since his day, we in America have legally executed more than 8,000—by the chair, the noose, the firing squad, and lethal gas and injection. (Illegal executions, by lynching, accounted for at least another 3,498 deaths in the same period.)

Capital punishment is alive in the United States, but no one can say it is well. Today thirteen states no longer have a death-penalty statute. Vermont, which lacks a valid statute, is classed as a fourteenth. The District of Columbia doesn't sanction capital punishment, nor do Puerto Rico, Samoa, or other American territories.

The remaining thirty-six states all have the death penalty, but that doesn't mean all apply it. *Since 1976, condemned criminals have been executed in only thirteen states.* Of these, four lead all the rest: Texas, with thirty-four executions as of June 1, 1990; Florida, with twenty-one; Louisiana, with eighteen; Georgia, with fourteen. (Within this time frame these four states have accounted for seventy-one percent of all executions.)

Styles in executions have changed. Lethal injection, used first in Texas in 1982 to kill Charles Brooks, is our dominant technique today; twenty states practice it. Electrocution comes next, but the twenty-five states that once used it have dwindled to fourteen. The gallows, once

253

universal, has become an anachronism; it remains on the statute books in Washington and Montana and nowhere else, with lethal injection available as an alternative—but neither state has put anyone to death in more than twenty years.

Of the eleven states that originally made use of the gas chamber, just four retain it: California, Maryland, Mississippi and North Carolina. The last offers the needle as an alternative, and it is gladly accepted.

In 1935 (peak year for executions in America) we put one person to death every forty-four hours—199 executions in all. After that the numbers began to fall. The most executed in any one of the last fourteen years was twenty-five (1987). Yet today more than 2,000 are sitting in cells on death row.

America's murder rate is one of the highest in the modern industrial world. Every year close to 20,000 people come to a violent end, thanks to their fellow human beings. In the past fourteen years, more than a quarter million of us have died in this way. Yet from 1976 to June 1, 1990, only 123 murderers were executed.

It is a curious fact that although executions have fallen off spectacularly, more people support the death penalty today than at any time in the past fifty years. In poll after poll, four out of five Americans have affirmed their belief that killers should be killed. (African Americans are an exception; as a group, most oppose the death penalty.)

It's easy to see why so many of us favor capital punishment. We feel—we *know*—our lives and those of our loved ones are in greater danger than ever before. In 1988 the number of violent crimes, including murders, showed a rise. Every day, television and the newspapers unnerve us with their vivid stories of the violence around us. At the same time we learn about homicidal felons who are allowed to plea-bargain for lighter sentences, only to return to the streets and again stalk the innocent.

Politicians running for office fan the flames of our anxiety, playing up the menace of crime and the unbending stand they will take against it. George Bush, campaigning for the presidency in 1988, provided a notable example. Another was Florida's Bob Martinez, who, seeking reelection as governor, reminded the public, "I now have signed some ninety death warrants in the State of Florida." Virtually the entire nation applauded when he signed Ted Bundy's.

Why, then, are executions at such a low ebb?

There are many reasons.

One is that educated people are no longer entirely convinced that capital punishment is a deterrent to murder. Certainly it deters the murderer who is executed, but we can hardly be certain it deters anyone else. Studies have shown again and again that a well-publicized execution (Caryl Chessman's, in 1960, is a case in point) is followed by a jump in the murder rate. Even staunch adherents of capital punishment like Ernest van den Haag have reservations about the deterrence argument.

What about states that have abolished the death penalty? Do they have a higher murder rate than those that retain it? Numerous studies have proved they do not.

What about countries that have given up capital punishment? The highly conservative British Royal Commission on Capital Punishment looked into this matter exhaustively. In 1953, it declared that "there is no clear evidence in any of the figures we have examined that the abolition of capital punishment has led to an increase in the homicide rate, or that its reintroduction has led to a fall."

The fact is that virtually all the Western democracies have abolished capital punishment. The only Western industrial nation that still keeps it is the United States. And even here (as in the rest of the world) it is apparently dying out.

In the 1960s there were so many legal challenges to the death penalty that executions were unofficially suspended. In 1972 an appeal in the case of *Furman v. Georgia* led to a landmark Supreme Court decision that the death penalty, as handed out under the various state statutes, was "cruel and unusual" because it was so unevenly applied. The court prohibited all executions until more equitable statutes could be passed.

The states passed their new statutes. In 1976, in *Gregg v. Georgia*, the court restored capital punishment—but it ruled there must be separate trials to determine the guilt of the accused and the penalty. Sentencing guidelines restricted execution to only the most heinous murders. Appellate court reviews were made automatic.

More and more, today's juries show an unwillingness to shoulder the responsibility for taking a life. Federal judges have been increasingly responsive to appeals from convicts facing death. Governors seem more loath to authorize executions. In recent years the sentences of more than half of those condemned to death have been commuted on appeal, and we have been made aware of innocents sentenced to death for crimes they never committed.

As if in response to this growing anti-capital punishment trend, the Supreme Court, under Chief Justice William H. Rehnquist, has been seeking ways and means to reduce appeals and increase executions. In 1989, for example, the court ruled no state is required to provide counsel for impoverished death row inmates to make more than a single direct appeal to a state court. It has ruled too that nothing in the Constitution bars the execution of convicts as young as sixteen or of the mentally retarded. It has placed severe limitations on habeas corpus—the right of prisoners to challenge the constitutionality of their conviction or sentence.

Meanwhile, as shown in a recent study in the *Vanderbilt Law Review*, a "majority of states are quietly shaping a new ultimate punishment, life without parole," *The New York Times* reported not long ago. "Thirty-one states have adopted a life prison term with no chance of parole for certain offenses." According to Edward Carnes, Alabama assistant attorney general, this form of punishment means "no parole, no commutation, no way out until the day you die—period." It is favored by juries because it protects society while avoiding worries about taking a life. Nor is it more expensive, reportedly, than a protracted legal appeal, which may cost $3 million or more in legal, court and prison fees per capital case.

Supporters of the penalty call it "death by incarceration."

In many of the countries that ultimately abolished capital punishment, for a long period no one suffered the death penalty, until finally the government decided to abandon it altogether. To judge by the trend we have been witnessing at home since 1967, the same pattern may be emerging in the United States.

But given our high murder rate, the vengeful mood of the public, and the hardening line of the Rehnquist Supreme Court, all it may take to reverse the present trend is some spectacular, horrendous crime— the killing of the Lindbergh baby and the assassinations of Presidents Lincoln and Kennedy come to mind—and the long lines may start moving again in double quick time into the chamber of death.

Notes

ONE

1. Warden Durston, in his report of the execution (made available to the author by Commissioner Thomas A. Coughlin III of the New York Department of Correctional Services), commented, "The people in the locality took no extraordinary interest in the matter." According to *The New York Times* of August 7, 1890, however, "Just before 7:00 it seemed as if all Auburn had congregated in the immediate neighborhood of the prison."
2. Virtually all the dialogue in this book is quoted directly from actual witnesses, newspaper reporters, historians, or others closely associated with the participants in the events. In a few instances, the author gives dialogue without quotation marks. This dialogue represents remarks reported at the time in indirect discourse.
3. According to Dr. MacDonald, Kemmler's "manner and appearance indicated a state of subdued elation, as if gratified at being the central figure of the occasion, his low order of intelligence evidently rendering him unable to fully appreciate the gravity of his situation."
4. Before the bill was passed "two men, who had apparently been killed by coming in contact with wires carrying alternating current, were revived after several hours' work by doctors. . . . Westinghouse officials were jubilant . . . and for a while it appeared as if the proposed new law would fail. Brown explained . . . that while a shock which merely stunned the heart might not kill, one that passed through the nervous system would invariably prove fatal, but this was not fully convincing. Finally, a compromise clause was inserted in the bill which provided for an autopsy immediately following the execution to 'prevent any possible chances of the subject ever returning to life,' and the bill with this provision was quickly passed." (Lewis E. Lawes, *Life and Death in Sing Sing*, pp. 185–6.)
   The bill also provided for the solitary confinement of the condemned while awaiting electrocution and for the disposal of the body by burial in quicklime, and forbade newspapers to publish any details of the execution. The state prisons were

designated as the place of execution, instead of the counties where the criminal was convicted, and the warden was to replace the sheriff in carrying out the law.
5. Cockran was one of the most successful and affluent lawyers of his time. He later defended Tom Mooney, the labor organizer, and Lieutenant Charles Becker, a New York policeman, both free of charge, so it is possible he defended Kemmler without compensation also. Winston Churchill, who in his youth was well acquainted with Cockran, said he modeled his oratorical style on Cockran's.

TWO

1. The masculine pronoun is used throughout this book to refer to a condemned prisoner, as less than one percent of all those executed are women.
2. The electrocution in 1915 of Lieutenant Charles Becker has been described as the clumsiest in Sing Sing's history. Becker was given a 1,850-volt jolt. "As the big body heaved upward," relates Andy Logan in his fine book *Against the Evidence*, "the loose strap gave way, the body lunged forward, the head twisted about, and from the left temple an unexpected flame spurted and blazed steadily through the long full minute of the first jolt of current. When the lever was pulled back, the two prison doctors found that Becker's heart was not only still beating but pounding strongly. Becker was said to be the largest man who had been brought into the execution chamber, and the experts had misjudged the amount of current. . . . Now the loose strap was buckled . . . and . . . another jolt was applied. When the doctors moved forward, they found the heart was still pounding. It was only after a third jolt that Becker . . . was finally pronounced dead." Many people, including Warden Thomas Mott Osborne, have argued that Becker was innocent.

THREE

1. Naturally there are exceptions. When James Wells, a murderer, went to the chair in Little Rock, Arkansas, in 1922, the executioner was completely inexperienced. Wells sat in the chair singing until the executioner managed to make the first contact. It silenced Wells—but eleven shocks were needed to kill him. In 1989, Horace Dunkins, Jr., was being executed in Georgia, but the cable was misconnected. The shock knocked Dunkins senseless but left him alive. The cable was reconnected, to the satisfaction of everyone but the condemned man.
2. On July 19, 1977, Governor Michael S. Dukakis of Massachusetts vindicated Sacco and Vanzetti, proclaiming that "any stigma and disgrace should be forever removed from their names." August 23, 1977, the fiftieth anniversary of their execution, was named Sacco and Vanzetti Day. Books continue to be published arguing for and against their innocence.
3. Convinced her husband was innocent, Hauptmann's widow, Anna, made repeated efforts to have him exonerated, suing the state in 1981 without success. Several middle-aged men have claimed the Lindbergh baby never died, and that they were he; one even sued Colonel Lindbergh's estate for a share after the colonel's death in 1974.

   A number of books try to prove or disprove Hauptmann's guilt. In one of the latest, *The Lindbergh Case* (Rutgers University Press, 1987), Jim Fisher, associate professor of criminal justice at Edinboro University, Pennsylvania, concludes Hauptmann was guilty, after an examination of all the evidence in New Jersey's files. Fisher includes a statement from an FBI agent that Hauptmann attempted to trade a confession for leniency.

4. The federal government maintains no execution facilities of its own. Persons condemned to death under federal law are executed in a prison of the state where their crime was committed.
5. The Rosenberg children always believed their parents were innocent. As Robert and Michael Meeropol (they took the name of their step-parents), they made repeated efforts to exonerate the Rosenbergs, including the writing of the book *We Are Your Sons: The Legacy of Julius and Ethel Rosenberg* (Houghton Mifflin, 1975). There is also a National Committee to Reopen the Rosenberg Case, affiliated with the National Coalition to Abolish the Death Penalty (see Note 7). According to Stephen H. Gettinger, the documents the Rosenbergs were accused of transmitting were worthless (*Sentenced to Die*, Macmillan, 1979).
6. Why did Bundy kill? Shortly before his execution he attributed his urge to murder women to the influence of hardcore pornography, which became an obsession with him. Dr. David Abrahamsen, a psychiatrist and author who has studied serial killers, says that a man who commits a violent sexual crime against a woman he does not know is acting out "strong and repeated fantasies of revenge and power" that are unconsciously aimed at his mother.

   According to law-enforcement authorities, at any given time there are thirty-five or more serial killers roaming the country and killing at random.
7. Opponents of the death penalty are organized under the banner of the National Coalition to Abolish the Death Penalty, with headquarters in Washington, D.C. The coalition was founded in 1976, when the United States Supreme Court ruled that states could resume executions, after a hiatus of ten years. Also active in the movement to abolish the death penalty is Amnesty International USA of New York City, the Legal Defense and Educational Fund, as well as the NAACP and the Capital Punishment Project of the American Civil Liberties Union.
8. Bundy, the Florida Department of Corrections informed the author (letters, November 1 and 20, 1989), "declined the prison's offer to allow him to request a special last meal, so the standard fare [steak and eggs] was prepared and offered. He refused it." His last words were "Give my love to my family and friends."

   Florida's executioner is "an anonymous, private citizen, and is paid $150 for an execution."

FOUR

1. Tongs were originally mutual-aid associations brought over from China. Some engaged in criminal activities such as trafficking in drugs and prostitution. Feuds between them were known as tong wars, and murders of members of the competing tongs were not uncommon. The last of these "old style" killings occurred in 1927, but in recent times the feuds and killings have resumed.
2. This was not the prison's first test. In an earlier one, the gas had been tried on bedbugs and found effective, according to *Las Vegas Age*, February 2, 1924.
3. But apparently they do. Reports continue to appear that suggest lethal gas has not removed all the pain from an execution. United Press International reporter Dan Lohwasser was a witness to the execution of Jimmy Lee Gray in 1984. "I thought I had some pretty hard bark on me from being in Vietnam, but I was pretty shook up," he said afterward. "There was a steel pole running from the floor to the ceiling behind Gray's chair, and I watched him slam his head into this pole for eight minutes as hard as he could."
4. Dead in the sense that they gave no signs of life. With today's medical equipment, presumably such signs could have been detected.

5. Former Governor Edmund G. Brown, in his book *Public Justice, Private Mercy: A Governor's Education on Death Row* (Weidenfeld and Nicolson, 1989), spoke out about Chessman, whose plea for clemency he turned down in 1959: "Twenty-eight years after his death, what can I say that I learned? Chessman was a nasty, arrogant, unrepentant man, almost certainly guilty of the crimes he was convicted of. But I don't think those crimes deserved the death penalty then, and I certainly don't think so now. His sentence should have been commuted . . . such action was virtually impossible, especially for an elected official with programs he hoped to implement for the common good. . . . I also believe that I should have found a way to spare Chessman's life."

FIVE

1. "It wouldn't do to give him hepatitis!" was the wry comment of Henry Schwarz-schild of the American Civil Liberties Union (*The New York Times*, December 23, 1982).
2. Actually, New York's Death Commission had considered execution by lethal injection as far back as the 1880s before deciding in favor of electrocution, as explained in Chapter 1.
3. "Two years ago," commented a lawyer for the convicts, "the government took legal action against a manufacturer who sold euthanasia drugs for animals, and they stopped sales because the drugs hadn't been tested. It seems to me that if the Food and Drug Administration requires that drugs used on dogs and horses be shown to be quick and painless, they ought to do at least as much for drugs used on people."
4. What measures could be taken to revive a prisoner if a reprieve were granted after an execution had actually begun? The author put this question to the corrections authorities in two states.

   According to James A. Lynaugh, director of the Texas Department of Corrections, "We have never experienced the scenario that you described in your letter, nor do we anticipate it since we do not proceed with an execution until we are certain that all appeals have been rejected." (Letter to the author, June 15, 1989.)

   David W. Guth, a spokesman for the North Carolina Department of Corrections, wrote that if a stay of execution is forthcoming, the procedure would be held up. "Once the process of lethal injection begins, it is, for all intents and purposes, irreversible. . . . since the reinstatement of the death penalty in 1977, we have not been faced with such a 'last-second' scenario." (Letter to the author, August 7, 1989.)
5. Jim Mattox, Texas attorney general, favored televising the execution. "If executions serve as a deterrent," he said, "then there's a very logical argument they should be done publicly." But Robert Gunn, chairman of the Texas Board of Corrections, was of a very different opinion. He declared that telecasting Autry's execution "could have an effect on the death penalty itself." No execution at an American prison has been shown on television.

   Another case involving a request by a condemned prisoner may be of interest here. Roger DeGarmo, a death-row inmate, proposed to sell seats to his execution (the state permits condemned prisoners to invite five personal witnesses) to the highest bidders. Corrections officials rejected his idea, but the publicity it received led to a reprieve.
6. "The fact that we were willing to take her organs and scatter them out across the world," wrote Dr. Jesse H. Meredith, head of the medical team and professor of surgery at the Bowman Gray School of Medicine, Wake Forest University, in Winston-Salem, "did not convince them that would be the best way to make sure

she wasn't resuscitated, and they never relented in that fear. They even said they knew of a person who had been executed by lethal injection, was delivered to the family at the back door of the prison and was now alive in Mexico. This fear results from the fact that after the person is killed, the State has no control over what happens.'' (Letter to the author, July 8, 1989.)

SIX

1. Written in 1925 by Alfred Hayes and later set to music by Earl Robinson.
2. Slovik's story of his "first desertion" at Elboeuf appears intentionally inaccurate. His fellow replacement, Tankey, was with him, and Tankey too remained behind. Later, he said he never heard the order to move out, and no charge was ever brought against him. Slovik's confession makes no mention of Tankey.
3. Slovik's widow, mistakenly believing herself eligible to receive his GI life insurance, applied for it and was denied payment. In 1978, President Jimmy Carter sponsored a bill for $70,000 to be paid to her, but she died before Congress voted on it. In 1987, Slovik's remains were removed from France and reburied in his hometown.
4. Both a best-selling novel by Norman Mailer, *The Executioner's Song*, and a motion picture were based on Gilmore's life.
5. References to the punishment of animals that have been used in acts of sodomy are scarce in America, less so in Europe. According to a German study (Johann Glenzdorf and Fritz Treichel, *Henker, Schinder und Arme Sünder*, vol. 1, p. 10), the rule was that the animal was tried and executed with the sodomite. Sometimes animals responsible for human deaths, after being condemned, were dressed in human garments for execution.

SEVEN

1. For an account of body snatching in America and elsewhere the reader is invited to consult the author's book *Body Snatchers, Stiffs and Other Ghoulish Delights*, Fawcett Gold Medal, 1987.
2. Burning at the stake was a common punishment for slaves in earlier days. The last case on record, for rape and murder, took place in 1828. Rebellious blacks, after being hanged, might have their heads fastened to posts at crossroads. Sometimes the body would be quartered and the quarters set up in various sections of the county.

EIGHT

1. Judge Parker's courtroom and the gallows have been reconstructed and may be seen at Fort Smith National Historic Site.
2. According to United States Army records, thirty-five soldiers were executed for murder, mutiny, and rape in World War I. During the period 1942–48, the Army put 146 servicemen to death (including Private Eddie Slovik, who was shot for desertion "with intent to avoid hazardous duty"). The United States Navy has not executed anyone since 1849.

NINE

1. Assassins hardly ever exhibit remorse. Usually they insist they have played a historic role and take pains to explain why they did what they did. They sometimes

seem to want to take some of their victims' fame for themselves. "They can gas me but I am famous," declared Robert Kennedy's murderer, Sirhan Sirhan.

2. Like Schrank and Lawrence, many have used the insanity plea to escape punishment. Under the M'Naghten rule, inherited from British law, a person who kills while not in his right mind may not be found guilty of murder. This rule takes its name from Daniel M'Naghten, a schizophrenic Irishman who believed that various persons were conspiring against him. He attempted to assassinate Robert Peel, the British prime minister, in 1843, but shot Peel's secretary by mistake.

The M'Naghten rule holds that a defendant is not culpable if he was "laboring under such a defect of reason, from disease of the mind, as not to know the nature and quality of the act he was doing; or, if he did know it, that he did not know he was doing what was wrong." To prove insanity, many states require that a defendant must have been "substantially confused" or unable to control himself. A few have abolished insanity pleas altogether.

Sometimes the prosecution successfully counters an insanity plea by arguing that the defendant is feigning madness.

3. Children as well as adults celebrated Guiteau's execution. Andrew J. Palm, in his book *The Death Penalty* (1891), provided two interesting examples of their behavior. In the first, some boys in Norwich, Connecticut, procured a rope and hanged another boy. After they had left, the half-dead child was rescued by his friends. In the second, which occurred in a nearby state, "some little girls had caught the spirit of the situation from hearing so much said about the Guiteau case. . . . Having no boy to hang, they took a large doll, which answered the purpose very well, only they were not satisfied because it did not kick and struggle."

4. Guiteau's remains, unlike those of the Lincoln conspirators, were never turned over to his family. Instead, Army doctors removed the flesh, producing a bleached skeleton, apparently with the intention of displaying it to the public, to satisfy its hunger for revenge. This was never done; reportedly the bones ended up in the Army Medical Museum's storage vaults.

TEN

1. In recent years, the appeals process has grown longer and longer in capital cases and many, including Chief Justice William H. Rehnquist of the United States Supreme Court, want to expedite it. The Adams case provoked comment that opposed Rehnquist's position, pointing out that capital punishment is "the only criminal penalty that cannot be reversed."
Robert Seelenfreund, a lawyer with the New Jersey Public Defender's Office, in a letter to *The New York Times* (March 25, 1989), wrote of Adams,

Of the more than 2,000 people on death row throughout the country, few will similarly inspire movies. Even fewer are, like Mr. Adams, demonstrably innocent. But it would be a mockery of our system of due process to afford capital defendants fewer rights than noncapital defendants. The appellate process in death penalty litigation is so lengthy not because clever lawyers subvert the system, but rather because of the grave consequences in every capital case.

I do not recall many voices protesting the length of the American Telephone and Telegraph Company divestiture case; Chief Justice William H. Rehnquist has certainly not issued a statement expressing outrage over the legal bills generated by the buyout of Nabisco. Our legal system is arguably too complex; it is a rather crude wish, however, to expect that prisoners facing execution should be singled out to be exempt from the ordinary litigation process.

2. A case even more tragic involved a Methodist minister in Georgia, executed for the rape and murder of his sister-in-law. A few years later, Judge Lucius Quintus Cincinnatus Lamar, who had sentenced the minister, was sitting in his office when he received word that a man about to be hanged in Mississippi for an entirely different crime had confessed on the scaffold that he was the sister-in law's killer. Shutting his office, Judge Lamar went home, embraced his wife and children (one son would grow up to become a justice of the United States Supreme Court), and then shot himself dead.

3. "Aware of this danger, Colorado, when it restored the death penalty in 1901, provided that it should never be used where the accused is convicted on purely circumstantial evidence." (Raymond T. Bye, *Capital Punishment in the United States*.)

ELEVEN

1. Why did Stephen Boorn confess to a murder he hadn't committed? The quarrel that led to the killing, he said, had been started by Colvin. Apparently, Boorn hoped to be tried for manslaughter rather than first-degree murder.

Some readers may wonder how the Boorns came to be convicted without a corpus delicti. This term literally means "the body of the offense"—not the body of the victim. In law, it means the fact or facts that indicate a crime has been committed.

In a murder, the corpus delicti is the fact that a death has occurred and that a criminal act was responsible for it. Often the corpus delicti is the dead body itself, but for murder to be proved it isn't necessary for a body to be found. It is sufficient if witnesses swear they saw the body, and so provide evidence that a crime has taken place. Circumstantial evidence, such as an identifiable tooth or bone fragments, may provide a corpus delicti.

2. This account of Purvis's near-execution is based in good part on "The Story of Will Purvis," by John A. Yeager and Henry C. Yawn, published in Sunday editions of the *New Orleans Item-Tribune* from May 31 to June 27, 1920. The authors were Mississippi legislators instrumental in the passage of the bill to pay compensation to Purvis.

TWELVE

1. Newspapers and the public always display interest in the last meal eaten by a condemned man. Following an old tradition, he is usually allowed to order anything that the prison commissary can supply or the warden is willing to. In Sing Sing, it was the custom for the prisoner to place an extravagant order, in which he considered the tastes of his neighbors on death row, and then he had the dishes distributed to them. He himself had little or no appetite in his final hours, but smoked incessantly. Prisoner 77681 was an exception.

2. Monge was the last person executed in the United States before the ten-year hiatus in capital punishment that ended with the voluntary execution of Gary Gilmore in 1977. Like Gilmore, he donated his eyes to an eyebank and the corneas were successfully transplanted.

Selected Bibliography

This bibliography is suggestive rather than complete. The author has consulted other books, pamphlets and periodicals too numerous to list. The most important newspaper articles used are mentioned in the text.

Abels, Jules. *Man on Fire: John Brown and the Cause of Liberty*. New York: Macmillan, 1971.

Andrews, William. *Bygone Punishments*. London: W. Andrews, 1899.

Asbury, Herbert. *Gem of the Prairie: An Informal History of the Chicago Underworld*. New York: Alfred A. Knopf, 1940.

Atholl, Justin. *The Reluctant Hangman*. London: John Long, 1956.

————. *Shadow of the Gallows*. London: John Long, 1954.

Bacon, Margaret Hope. *The Quiet Rebels: The Story of the Quakers in America*. Philadelphia: New Society Publishers, 1985.

Bakeless, John. *Turncoats, Traitors and Heroes*. Philadelphia, J. B. Lippincott, 1959.

Barfield, Velma. *Woman on Death Row*. Nashville: Oliver Nelson Books, 1985.

Barnes, H. E. and Teeters, Negley K. *New Horizons in Criminology*. Englewood Cliffs: Prentice Hall, 1959.

Bedau, Hugo Adam. *The Death Penalty in America*. New York: Oxford University Press, 1982.

———— and Radelet, Michael L. "Miscarriages of Justice in Potentially Capital Cases." *Stanford Law Review*, November 1987.

Beichman, A. "First Electrocution." *Commentary*, May 1963.

Bell, Clark. "Electricity and the Death Penalty." *Journal of the American Medical Association*, March 9, 1889.

Bender, David L. and Leone, Bruno, series editors. *The Death Penalty: Opposing Viewpoints*. St. Paul: Greenhaven Press, 1986.

Berriault, G. "Last Firing Squad: Executioners of Utah." *Esquire*, June 1966.

Berry James. *My Experiences As an Executioner*. Detroit: Gale Research Company, 1972.

Bishop, George V. *Executions*. Los Angeles: Sherbourne Press, 1965.

Bishop, Jim. *The Day Lincoln Was Shot*. New York: Harper & Brothers, 1955.

Bleackley, Horace W. *The Hangmen of England*. London: Chapman & Hall, 1929.

Block, Eugene B. *When Men Play God*. San Francisco: Cragmont Publications, 1983.

Boatner, Mark M. III. *Civil War Dictionary*. New York: David McKay, 1988.

Borchard, Edwin. *Convicting the Innocent*. New Haven: Yale University Press, 1932.

Bowers, William J. with Pierce, Glenn L. and McDevitt, John F. *Legal Homicide: Death as Punishment in America, 1864–1982*. Boston: Northeastern University Press, 1984.

Brooks, Juanita. *The Mountain Meadows Massacre*. Norman: University of Oklahoma Press, 1962.

Brown, Wenzell. *Women Who Died in the Chair*. New York: Collier Books, 1963.

Burt, Olive Woolley. *American Murder Ballads and Their Stories*. New York: Oxford University Press, 1958.

Bye, Raymond T. *Capital Punishment in the United States*. Philadelphia: Committee on Philanthropic Labor of Philadelphia, 1919.

Camus, Albert. *Réflexions sur la peine capitale*. Paris: Calmann-Lévy, Editeurs, 1957.

Capote, Truman. *In Cold Blood*. New York: Random House, 1965.

Carter, Dan T. *Scottsboro*. Baton Rouge: Louisiana State University Press, 1969.

Caughey, John W. *Their Majesties the Mob*. Chicago: University of Chicago Press, 1960.

Chan, Loren B. "Example for the Nation: Nevada's Execution of Gee Jon." Nevada Historical Society Quarterly, Summer 1975.

Chen, Jack. *The Chinese of America*. San Francisco: Harper & Row, 1980.

Chessman, Caryl. *Trial by Ordeal*. Englewood Cliffs: Prentice Hall, 1955.

Clark, Champ and the Editors of Time-Life Books. *The Assassination*. Alexandria: Time-Life Books, 1987.

Clarke, James W. *American Assassins*. Princeton: Princeton University Press, 1982.

Commager, Henry Steele and Morris, Richard B. *The Spirit of Seventy-Six: The Story of the American Revolution as Told by Participants*. New York: Harper & Row, 1975.

Cooper, David D. *The Lesson of the Scaffold*. Athens, Ohio: Ohio University Press, 1974.

Davis, William T., ed. *Bradford's History of Plymouth Plantation 1606–1646*. New York: Charles Scribner's Sons, 1908.

Dinnerstein, Leonard. *The Leo Frank Case*. Athens, Georgia: University of Georgia Press, 1987.

DiSalle, Michael. *The Power of Life or Death*. New York: Random House, 1965.

Draper, Thomas, ed. *Capital Punishment*. New York: H. W. Wilson, 1985.

Drimmer, Frederick. *Body Snatchers, Stiffs and Other Ghoulish Delights*. New York: Fawcett Gold Medal, 1981.

————. *Captured by the Indians: 15 Firsthand Accounts, 1750–1870*. New York: Dover, 1985.

Duff, Charles A. *A Handbook on Hanging*. Totowa, New Jersey: Rowman and Littlefield, 1974

Duff, Louis Blake. *The County Kerchief*. Toronto: Ryerson Press, 1949.

Duffy, Clinton T., as told to Dean Jennings. *The San Quentin Story*. Garden City: Doubleday, 1950.

———— with Hirschberg, Al. *88 Men and 2 Women*. Garden City: Doubleday, 1962.

Earl, Phillip I. "By the Knife; Tonopah's Gregovich-Mircovich Murder Case." In Hartigan, Francis X., ed. *Essays in Honor of Wilbur S. Shepperson*. Reno: University of Nevada Press, 1989.

Eshelman, Byron. *Death Row Chaplain*. Englewood Cliffs: Prentice Hall, 1962.

Fisher, Jim. *The Lindbergh Case*. New Brunswick, New Jersey: Rutgers University Press, 1987.

Flexner, James Thomas. *The Traitor and the Spy: Benedict Arnold and John André*. Boston: Little, Brown, 1953.

Frank, Judge Jerome and Frank, Barbara. *Not Guilty*. Garden City: Doubleday, 1957.

Gardner, Earle Stanley. *The Court of Last Resort*. New York: William Sloane Associates, 1952.

Gardner, Martin R. "Executions and Indignities: An Eighth Amendment Assessment of Methods of Inflicting Capital Punishment." *Ohio State Law Journal*, Vol. 39, No. 1 (1978).

Gaute, J. H. H. and Odell, Robin. *The Murderers' Who's Who*. Montreal: Optimum Publishing Company Ltd., 1979.

Gettinger, Stephen H. *Sentenced to Die* New York: Macmillan, 1979.

Gillespie, L. Kay, Ph. D. "Utah's Executed Men." (Work in progress, 1990.)

Glenzdorf, Johann and Treichel, Fritz. *Henker, Schinder und Arme Sünder*. Bad Münder am Deister: Wilhelm Rost Verlag, 1970.

Goins, Craddock. "The Traveling Executioner." *American Mercury*, 1942.

Gould, Lewis L. *The Presidency of William McKinley*. Lawrence, Kansas: Regents Press of Kansas, 1980.

Hale, Leslie. *Hanged in Error*. Baltimore: Penguin Books, 1961.

Hampton, Wayne. *Guerrilla Minstrels*. Knoxville: University of Tennessee Press, 1986.

Hanchett, William. *The Lincoln Murder Conspiracies*. Urbana and Chicago: University of Illinois Press, 1983.

Hatch, Robert McConnell. *Major John André*. Boston: Houghton Mifflin, 1986.

Hearn, Lafcadio. *Gibbeted*. Los Angeles: John Murray, 1933.

Hentig, Hans von. *Vom Ursprung des Henkersmahlzeit*. Tübingen: J. C. B. Mohr (Paul Siebeck), 1958.

Hertzog, Peter. *Legal Hangings*. Santa Fe: Press of the Territorian, 1966.

Holmes, E. W. "The Anatomy of Hanging." *Pennsylvania Medical Journal*, July, 1901.

"Horror Spawns a Masterpiece." *Life*, January 7, 1966.

Horwitz, Elinor Lander. *Capital Punishment, U. S. A.* Philadelphia: J. B. Lippincott, 1973.

Huie, William Bradford. *The Execution of Private Slovik*. New York: Little, Brown, 1954.

Isenberg, Irwin, ed. *The Death Penalty*. New York: H. W. Wilson, 1977.

Joll, James. *The Anarchists*. New York: Little, Brown, 1964.

Jones, Ann. *Women Who Kill*. New York: Holt, Rinehart and Winston, 1980.

Joyce, James Avery. *Capital Punishment*. London: T. Nelson and Sons, 1961.

Karlsen, Carol F. *The Devil in the Shape of a Woman*. New York: W. W. Norton, 1987.

Kennedy, Ludovic. *The Airman and the Carpenter*. New York: Viking, 1985.

Kershaw, Alister. *A History of the Guillotine*. London: John Calder, 1958.

Kimmelman, Benedict B. "The Example of Private Slovik." *American Heritage*, September/December, 1987.

Lassers, William J. *Scapegoat Justice: Lloyd Miller and the Failure of the American Legal Systen*. Bloomington: Indiana University Press, 1973.

Lawes, Lewis E. *Life and Death in Sing Sing*. New York: Garden City Publishing Company, 1928.

————. *Meet the Murderer*. New York: Harper, 1940.

————. *Twenty Thousand Years in Sing Sing*. New York: Ray Long & Richard R. Smith, 1932.

Lawrence, John. *A History of Capital Punishment*. New York: Citadel Press, 1960.

Lee, John Doyle. *Mormonism Unveiled: or the Confessions of the Late Mormon Bishop, John D. Lee*. St. Louis: Bryan, Brand & Company, 1877

LeNotre, G. *The Guillotine and Its Servants*. London: Hutchinson, 1929.

Lens, Sidney. *The Labor Wars*. Garden City: Doubleday, 1973.

Levin, Eric. "Cunning Poisoner—or Redeemed Christian—Velma Barfield Draws Nearer to Her Day of Execution." *People*, October 29, 1984.

Logan, Andy. *Against the Evidence: The Becker-Rosenthal Affair*. New York: Avon, 1970.

McClellan, Grant S. *Capital Punishment*. New York: H. W. Wilson, 1961.

McComas, J. Francis. *Graveside Companion*. New York: Obolensky, 1962.

MacDonald, Carlos F. "Death Penalty by Electrocution." *New York Medical Journal*, May 7 and May 14, 1892.

————. Infliction of the Death Penalty by Means of Electricity. New York: D. Appleton, 1892.

———— and Spitzka, Edward Anthony. "The Trial, Execution, Autopsy and Mental Status of Leon F. Czolgosz." *The Medical News*, January 4, 1902.

McKinley, James. *Assassination in America*. New York: Harper & Row, 1977.

Magee, Doug. *Slow Coming Dark: Interviews on Death Row*. New York: Pilgrim Press, 1980.

Mannix, Daniel P. in collaboration with Cowley, Malcolm. *Black Cargoes*. New York: Viking Press, 1962.

Mencken, August. *By the Neck*. New York: Hastings House, 1942.

Meredith, J. H. "Organ Procurement from the Executed." *Transplantation Proceedings*, June, 1986.

Morgan, H. Wayne. *William McKinley and His America*. Syracuse: Syracuse University Press, 1963.

Mosley, Leonard. *Lindbergh: A Biography*. New York: Doubleday, 1976.

Mullen, Robert. *The Latter-Day Saints*. New York: Doubleday, 1966.

Nash, Jay Robert. *Murder in America*. New York: Simon and Schuster, 1980.

Nathanson, Stephen. *An Eye for an Eye?* Totowa, New Jersey: Rowman & Littlefield, 1987.

Nelson, Truman. *John Brown at Harper's Ferry*. New York: Holt, Rinehart and Winston, 1973.

Nizer, Louis. *The Implosion Conspiracy*. New York: Doubleday, 1973.

Oehler, C. M. *The Great Sioux Uprising*. New York: Oxford University Press, 1959.

Palm, Andrew J. *The Death Penalty*. New York: G. P. Putnam's Sons, 1891.

Panati, Charles. *Panati's Extraordinary Endings of Practically Everything and Everybody*. New York: Harper & Row, 1989.

Parry, L. A. *History of Torture in England*. Montclair, New Jersey: Patterson Smith, 1975.

Potter, John. *The Fatal Gallows Tree*. London: Elek Books, 1965.

Prettyman, Barrett, Jr. *Death and the Supreme Court*. New York: Harcourt, Brace & World, 1961.

Radin, Edward D. *The Innocents*. New York: William Morrow, 1964.

Radzinowicz, Leon. *A History of English Criminal Law*. New York: Macmillan, 1948.

Rawson, Tabor. *I Want to Live*. New York: Signet Books, 1958.

Reid, Don. *Eyewitness*. Houston: Cordovan Press, 1973.

Renshaw, Patrick. *The Wobblies*. New York: Doubleday, 1967.

Reston, James, Jr. "Invitation to a Poisoning." *Vanity Fair*, February, 1985.

Royal Commission on Capital Punishment. *Minutes of Evidence Taken Before the Royal Commission on Capital Punishment (1949–50)*. London: H. M. S. O., 1949.

Rule, Ann. *The Stranger Beside Me*. New York: W. W. Norton, 1980.

Sawyer, Joseph Dillaway and Griffis, William Elliot, ed. *History of the Pilgrims and Puritans*. New York: Century History Company, 1922.

Schmidt, Franz. *A Hangman's Diary*. Montclair, New Jersey: Patterson Smith, 1973.

Scott, George Ryley. *The History of Capital Punishment*. London: Torchstream Books, 1950.

Sellin, Thorsten, ed. *Capital Punishment*. New York: Harper & Row, 1967.

Sheridan, Lee W. *I Killed for the Law*. Harrisburg: Stackpole, 1938.

Sifakis, Carl. *Encyclopedia of American Crime*. New York: Facts on File, 1982.

Simon, Rita James. *Women and Crime*. Lexington, Massachusetts: D. C. Heath, 1975.

Smith, Gibbs M. *Joe Hill*. Salt Lake City: University of Utah Press, 1969.

Snow, Edward Rowe. *Piracy, Mutiny and Murder*. New York: Dodd, Mead, 1959.

Squire, Amos D. *Sing Sing Doctor*. Garden City: Garden City Publishing Company, 1937.

Staris, Barrie. *John Brown: The Sword and the Word*. New York: A. S. Barnes, 1970.

Starkey, Marion L. *The Devil in Massachusetts*. New York: Time, 1963.

Stevens, Leonard A. *Death Penalty*. New York: Coward, McCann & Geoghegan, 1978.

Strauss, Frances. *"Where Did the Justice Go?" The Story of the Giles: Johnson Case*. Boston: Gambit, 1969.

Teeters, Negley K. *Scaffold and Chair*. Philadelphia: Pennsylvania Prison Society, 1963.

———— and Hedblom, Jack H. "*. . . Hang by the Neck . . .* " Springfield, Illinois: Charles C. Thomas, 1967.

Tomlinson, R. G. *Witchcraft Trials of Connecticut*. Hartford: Bond Press, 1978.

Upham, Charles W. *Salem Witchcraft*. Williamstown, Massachusetts: Corner House Publishers, 1971.

Usher, Roland G. *The Pilgrims and Their History*. Williamstown, Massachusetts: Corner House Publishers, 1984.

Van Doren, Carl. *Secret History of the American Revolution*. New York: Viking, 1941.

Walker, Gerald. "Young Man, Be an Executioner." *Esquire*, August, 1963.

Waller, George. *Kidnap: The Story of the Lindbergh Case*. New York: Dial Press, 1961.

Wallis, Charles L. *American Epitaphs*. New York: Dover, 1973.

Walters, Jean Ann. *A Study of Executions in Utah*. Orem, Utah: Psychological Research Associates, 1973.

Ward, Estolv E. *The Gentle Dynamiter: A Biography of Tom Mooney*. Palo Alto: Ramparts Press, 1983.

Weisman, Richard. *Witchcraft, Magic, and Religion in 17th-Century Massachusetts*. Amherst: University of Massachusetts Press, 1984.

Wellman, Paul I. *A Dynasty of Western Outlaws*. Garden City: Doubleday, 1961.

Wertenbaker, Thomas Jefferson. *The Puritan Oligarchy*. New York: Charles Scribner's Sons, 1947.

West, Ray B., Jr. *Kingdom of the Saints*. New York: Viking Press, 1957.

Willison, George F. *Saints and Strangers*. New York: Reynal & Hitchcock, 1945.

Wolfe, Burton H. *Pileup on Death Row*. New York: Doubleday, 1973.

Wood, James Horace. As told to John M. Ross. *Nothing But the Truth*. Garden City: Doubleday, 1960.

Young, William and Kaiser, David E. *Sacco and Vanzetti*. Amherst: University of Massachusetts Press, 1985.

Zangrando, Robert L. *The NAACP Crusade Against Lynching, 1909–1950*. Philadelphia: Temple University Press, 1980.

Zimmerman, Isidore. *Punishment Without Crime*. New York: Manor Books, 1973.

Zimring, Franklin E. and Hawkins, Gordon. *Capital Punishment and the American Agenda*. New York: Cambridge University Press, 1986.

INDEX

271